Enigma Books

Also published by Enigma Books

Dennis D. Wainstock

The Decision to Drop the Atomic Bomb

Published in the United States by
Enigma Books
New York, NY
www.enigmabooks.com

The Decision to Drop the Atomic Bomb by Dennis D. Wainstock was originally
published in hardcover by Praeger Publishers, http://www.greenwood.com/
praeger, an imprint of Greenwood Publishing Group, Inc., Westport, CT.
Copyright © 1996 by Dennis D. Wainstock.

First Paperback Edition 2011

ISBN: 978-1-936274-00-0
eISBN: 978-1-936274-01-7

Printed in the United States of America

Cataloguing-in-Publication Data Available

To the students at Fairmont State University's
Gaston Caperton Center in Clarksburg, West Virginia

Contents

Preface

This book is a general history of Japan's attempts to surrender and the United States' decision to drop the atomic bombs on Hiroshima and Nagasaki. It concentrates on the last five months of World War II, April to August 1945. Although the study touches on the military, economic, and cultural aspects of the period, it focuses primarily on the political.

The sheer quantity of material was daunting, but the research was rewarding. It was filled with a rich mix of colorful and outstanding personalities, dramatic action, and momentous decisions that would influence the world to the present day.

The study raised a number of questions. How wise were President Harry S. Truman and Secretary of State James F. Byrnes in not including the retention of Emperor Hirohito in the Potsdam Declaration? Should they have relied more on the advice of State Department experts? Were military reasons the primary motive for President Truman's decision to drop the atomic bombs? Despite evidence to the contrary, why did Japan's leaders continue to place their faith in the Soviet Union to mediate an end to the war? Who was right among the American generals in their disputes over whether an invasion of the Japanese home islands was necessary? Why did Truman rely more on the advice of General George C. Marshall and not on Admiral William D. Leahy, the top presidential military adviser? And as important, what role did the Soviet Union play in Truman's decision to drop the atomic bombs?

The author's research owes much to the trail-breaking contributions by scholars who have written monographs and biographies in the field. I am also grateful to Salem-Teikyo University in Salem, West Virginia for providing me the financial opportunity to travel to Tokyo. There were many people who proved helpful to my project, but I am most grateful to my father, Louis Wainstock, a World War II veteran; Professor Wesley Bagby of West Virginia University; Lieutenant Colonel Sugimoto Mikio of the National Institute for Defense Studies in Tokyo; archivist John Taylor of the National Archives in Washington D.C.; and Debbi Dyer and Brenda Eddy of AccuWrite, who cheerfully typed up my numerous manuscripts.

The Decision to Drop the Atomic Bomb

Introduction

Japan's Desperate Military Situation, April to July 1945

In 1853 the United States opened up Japan to the modern world when it sent a naval expedition, under diplomatic relations. Japan's leaders learned that this was a prelude to being colonized by the Western powers.

They knew that industry, the main determining factor in a nation's strength, made the Western nations powerful. Very quickly, the Japanese adopted a policy of industrialization in order to acquire the strength to preserve Japan's independence. Japan's growing industrial might enabled it to defeat China in 1895 and Russia in 1905, and to occupy Korea in 1910.

But industrialization brought new problems. As Japan industrialized, it began to trade its industrial products for food and raw materials. Since population follows food supply, more food meant more people. If an enemy nation cut off Japan's trade or blockaded the island, many of its people would starve, and its rising industries would come to a halt. Japan built a navy to keep its trade lanes open, but it was still insecure. Rival nations could simply stop trading with Japan or conquer areas with which it needed to trade. To prevent this, the Japanese military seized Manchuria, China's northern province, in 1931 and in 1937 invaded the heart of China.

America's major enemy in Asia has always been the strongest industrial power. In 1941 Japan was the strongest Asian power, with the largest industry and thus the greatest capability of any nation in that region to threaten America's trade and security. When Japan invaded China, it upset the balance of power. The United States learned that if Japan conquered China, it would become an even greater threat. The United States immediately sided with the weaker power China and gave it economic and military aid.

In July 1941 the United States, England, and the Dutch cut off trade with Japan. This was a crippling blow to Japan's economy. Most of Japan's oil came from these three countries. Before lifting the embargo, the United States demanded that Japan withdraw from China and Vietnam. The Japanese military rejected this as unreasonable and attacked the U.S. naval base at Pearl Harbor in Hawaii. They also overran most of Southeast Asia, including the Dutch East Indies, to secure oil.

The bombing of Pearl Harbor united Americans in a rage against Japan. The war was now on in earnest.

The Pacific

During the first six months after Pearl Harbor, between December 1941 and June 1942, the Japanese drove the Americans out of the West Pacific and the British and Dutch out of Asia. Japan had conquered Hong Kong, Singapore, the Dutch East Indies, Malaya, Burma, Indochina, Guam, Wake Island, and the Philippines. Japan extended its power to the tip of Australia in the south and to the Aleutians in the north. It got as far east as India and as far west as Midway Island, only 1,500 miles from Hawaii.

But Japan had overexpanded. Its industrial resources, only 10 percent of those of the United States, could not hold this vast area indefinitely. Some of its troops were tied down in Manchuria, and the Chinese, from their fortress capital of Chungking, still managed to hold off a million Japanese troops. Japan's battle lines, said Admiral Teijiro Toyoda, were "all out of proportion to our strength in men."[1]

In May and June 1942 the U.S. navy halted further Japanese expansion in the Pacific. In the Coral Sea in May, the Americans sank more than 100,000 tons of Japanese shipping and stopped the Japanese advance toward Australia. In June, the Japanese lost four aircraft carriers and a navy cruiser at the Battle of Midway. This devastated the Japanese carrier force, and the cream of Japan's naval aviators had been lost. After Midway, said Admiral Yonai Mitsumasa, "there was no further chance of success."[2]

The defeat was kept secret; only the top leaders of Japan knew the truth. To the people, they presented it as an "outstanding victory."[3] Even the Japanese army knew nothing about it.

"The army and navy were always on a competitive basis," said Prince Higashikuni, "always fighting against each other and keeping secrets from each other."[4]

After Midway, U.S. Marines drove the Japanese back island by island. They took Guadalcanal, New Georgia, Choiseul, Bougainville, Tarawa, Kwajalein, Eniwetok, New Britain, Kavieng, Rabaul, Truk, and the Marianas Islands in the southwestern Pacific. The most important of the Marianas was Saipan, only 1,500 miles from Tokyo. "If the Japs had a goose left," said air force general Curtis LeMay, "it cooked the day of the first mission from the Marianas."[5]

In late 1944 and early 1945 the United States took back the Philippines. Under General Douglas MacArthur, the U.S. army liberated Manila, Bataan, and Corregidor, and the navy defeated the Japanese at the Battle of Leyte.

By 1945, U.S. Marines were ready to land at Iwo Jima, 760 miles south of Tokyo. It was only four and a half miles long and two and a half miles wide. "It was a loathsome little cinder clog," said a Japanese soldier, "only an island of sulfur, no water, no sparrow, and no swallow."[6] But it was strategically important. It would give B-29s a shorter flight to Japan than the long 1,500-mile flights from Saipan and help in the invasion of Okinawa to follow.

The Japanese were ready, under General Tadamichi Kuribayashi, with 21,000 troops dug in. They had 1,500 caves, scores of block houses, pillboxes of ferro concrete with walls five feet thick and ceilings ten feet high that were sandbagged, humped around with fifty feet of sand and piggybacked with machine-gun turrets, all of which were invisible. A Japanese poem described the coming battle:

> Where dark tides billow in the ocean
> A wink-shaped isle of mighty game
> Guards the gateway to our empire:
> Iwo Jima is its name.
>
> We brave men who have been chosen
> To defend this island strand
> Filled with Faith in certain triumph
> Yearn to strike for Fatherland.
> Oh, for Emperor and homeland
> There's no burden we won't bear.
> Sickness, hardship, filthy water
> These are less to us than air.
>
> Officers and men together
> Work and struggle, strive and trust,
> Till the hated Anglo-Saxons
> Lie before us in the dust.[7]

The battle of Iwo Jima was a death struggle. On February 19, 1945, 80,000 Marines stormed ashore on the eastern half of the island. On the first day, they suffered 2,420 casualties to secure a beachhead 4,000 yards wide and 1,000 yards deep. After five weeks of battle, the Americans had suffered 6,281 dead and 19,000 wounded. Nearly the entire Japanese garrison of 21,000 fought to the death.[8]

The Battle of Okinawa

From April 1 to June 21, 1945, Okinawa, the largest of the Ryukyu Islands chain, was the biggest single battle of the Pacific. A stepping stone to Japan, it would provide the United States with an excellent staging area of airfields and anchorages less than 400 miles of Kyushu, Japan's southern island.

Under Lieutenant General Mitsuru Ushijima and Rear Admiral Minoru Ota, the Japanese mobilized 77,000 troops and 25,000 Okinawan civilians. In addition, the Japanese navy organized special attack suicide bombers named kamikazes, after a terrible typhoon that destroyed a Mongol fleet in 1281 that was trying to invade Japan.

The Japanese hoped that kamikaze pilots would cause damage to the U.S. navy beyond what it was willing to endure. A kamikaze pilot would aim his explosive-filled plane straight at American ships. If a number of Japanese planes attacked simultaneously, a certain proportion would get through U.S. anti-aircraft fire.[9] The pilots were young men, mostly volunteers just out of school who were willing to sacrifice their lives for their country.[10]

The kamikaze was an expression of Japan's desperate military situation. By early 1945, under Vice Admiral Matome Ugaki, it had become the dominant part of Japan's air strategy. "We had to do it that way," said General Kawabe, commander of the Japanese army air force. "We had no other way to use our pilots."[11] The Imperial navy agreed. Its admirals argued that if they could force an American naval retreat at Okinawa, they could turn the tide of war just enough to secure favorable terms "from the clearly victorious enemy."[12]

The Japanese strategy was twofold. The kamikazes would damage and cut off the enemy fleet at sea. This would isolate the invading army, which would be destroyed piecemeal. "The prospect cannot be said to be good by any means," said army chief of staff General Yoshijiro Umezu, but the Japanese must "fight to the bitter end" and the morale of the people will be enhanced "so as to give full play to their strength."[13]

On April 1, 1945, the United States launched a massive amphibious assault force. Under General Simon Bolivar Buckner, Jr., a force of 180,000 men landed under the protection of a heavy barrage of naval gunfire. At the same time, 1,727 carrier-based aircraft bombed Okinawa. "The ferocity of the bombing is terrific," wrote a Japanese private in his diary. "Bomb from six to six."[14]

Like Iwo Jima, the Battle of Okinawa was a death struggle. At sea, the kamikazes struck hard. They disabled more than half of the aircraft carriers, scores of destroyers, ammunition ships, and mine sweepers.[15] Five thousand sailors died at sea; the worst loss suffered by the U.S. navy in any naval campaign.[16] On the island, the Japanese had entrenched themselves in the southern hilly region and bitterly contested every inch of that terrain. They would not surrender. When cornered, they would charge suicidally into the U.S. lines. "This gave us some idea of what we had to do to defeat them," said President Harry Truman.[17] But, although not official policy, "American Marines seldom took prisoners in the Pacific."[18]

In Okinawa, the casualties were enormous. The United States lost 12,613 dead and about 40,000 wounded. "One out of every three Americans," said Truman, "ended up dead, wounded, or missing."[19] Perhaps as many as 110,000 Japanese and Okinawa residents were killed.[20] This was a prelude to the proposed invasion of the Japanese homeland, the island of Kyushu. "Now there was no thinking in the General Staff that the Allies could be stopped," said Admiral Tomioka. "The only hope was to discourage them by inflicting very heavy losses on the invading forces, losses up to 30 or 40 percent of the first waves."[21]

General Curtis Lemay

On January 20, 1945, Major General Curtis LeMay took charge of the Twenty-First Bomber Command, with its headquarters on Guam. When he joined the army air force in 1928, LeMay, a big, husky, full-faced man, was only thirty-nine. An inveterate smoker, he had a cigar or pipe clenched between his teeth and an exasperating habit of speaking in low, indistinct, and sometimes garbled tones. Before being assigned to the Pacific, he had commanded B-17s in Europe and had numerous encounters with the Luftwaffe.

Before LeMay's arrival and during his first six weeks at Guam, B-29 daylight precision-bombing raids were not very successful, often because of treacherous, unpredictable weather. But even with good weather, the B-29 crews were fatigued from long overseas flights. They often missed their targets by considerable distances. Also, high wind velocity at high altitudes over Japan strained both men and equipment. Other problems included a low fuel reserve on high altitude missions, and errors in navigation forced some aircraft to return early or bomb a target of opportunity. Not one of the eleven priority targets was destroyed in the first 2,000 sorties.[22]

To offset the difficulties of precision bombing, LeMay decided to depart radically from the traditional doctrine of strategic bombardment. He knew that Japanese war production depended heavily on home industries that operated close to major factory areas. Incendiary bombing of Japanese cities would destroy the home industries and reduce the people who lived there to "a state of chaos, despair, and submission."[23] "These operations were not conceived as terror raids against the civilian population of Japan," said LeMay. "But by destroying these feeder industries the flow of vital parts could be curtailed and production disorganized."[24] Although Secretary of War Henry Stimson did not want the United States to get "the reputation of outdoing Hitler in atrocities," he agreed that "it was rather difficult to prevent area bombing."[25]

LeMay's tactics were innovative. The B-29s would attack major Japanese industrial cities at night and drop M-69 incendiary cluster bombs. Bombing altitudes would be under 10,000 feet to avoid the strong gas-consuming winds of high altitudes. To allow for greater bombload, LeMay reduced crew members and got rid of armament and ammunition. "We justified our elimination of guns," said LeMay, "on the grounds of expected weakness of Japanese night fighters and the speed of our own B-29s."[26] In addition, he ordered aircraft to attack individually. This would forgo formation over the base at the start of the mission and save a tremendous amount of gasoline. The B-29s were to fly directly from base to target and return. LeMay's imagination and flexibility of mind, said air force general Carl Spaatz, "contributed beyond measure to our victory, and were indeed our secret weapon."[27]

Japanese cities were vulnerable to incendiary bombing. Most of Japan's buildings were solid masses of flimsy homes and workshops made of wood, plaster, and paper frame. Only 10 percent were made of stone, brick, metal or reinforced concrete. Moreover, Japan's fire fighting equipment was antiquated, its firebreaks were pitiful, and water supplies, never adequate, were dangerously low.[28] "No definite policy of air raid shelter protection for the public was established," said Japan's minister of home affairs Genki Abe, "because the government feared public reaction would interfere with normal routine life."[29] But Home Defense Commander Prince Higashikuni said that "there was noting that could be done anyway."[30] "Once the heart of the Empire had been gouged out," Japanese air force leaders added, "Japan was licked."[31]

The Tokyo Raid

At 1 p.m., November 1, 1944, Tokyo residents saw their first B-29s. Dropping no bombs, they flew over the capital on a reconnaissance mission. This was repeated twice before the first bombing raid on November 24, 1944. During this raid and the one following it on November 27, seventy B-29s dropped bombs principally on military targets in outlying areas on the Kwanto plain near Nagoya and in the Kinki district near Wara. "When the raids first began," said Higashikuni, "there was little damage, and a strong determination to repulse the enemy."[32]

Despite the people's determination to resist the intruders, Tokyo, like the rest of Japan, was not prepared for a massive bombing raid. Equipment for fighting fires was primitive. It was mainly each family for itself. Many homes kept a grappling hook, a broom, a bucket of sand, a shovel, and a barrel of water. Each home also had some type of dugout in its yard made of timber construction, but often no more than a front line foxhole. Although there were anti-aircraft defenses, fighter planes, and searchlight batteries, all were inadequate.[33]

On March 9, 1945, the sky was clear over Tokyo. A thirty-mile-an-hour wind was blowing from the north. Because of the wind, Japan's air raid detection apparatus was not functioning normally. Earlier, 302 B-29s, consisting of three wings, had taken off from bases in the Marianas. They were flying low at 4,900 feet. The first planes over Tokyo acted as trail blazers, dropping incendiary bombs to mark a fiery cross. The rest were guided by it.

At 12:08 a.m. the bombing began in earnest. Within half an hour, fires on the ground were out of control. Flames shot hundreds of miles into the air, so high that pilots had difficulty keeping their aircraft under control, and some crews had to use oxygen masks.[34] "Tokyo," said one pilot, "caught fire like a forest of pine trees."[35] There was little resistance. "To our great surprise," said LeMay, "enemy air opposition was meager and anti-aircraft fire was no worse than that encountered at high altitudes."[36]

On the ground, it was an inferno. Those who did not die in the flames choked to death or were trampled to death by escaping mobs. The winds whipped the fires into tornados of flames, racing from district to district, "leaping streets, firebreaks, and canals at dazzling speed."[37] Panic-stricken crowds tried to cross the bridges over the Sumida River; many fell into the river and drowned, or were crushed to death. "Our system of fire prevention was utterly useless," said a Tokyo fire marshal.[38] "Fanned by a gale then prevailing," said Marquis Kido, lord privy to the seal, "the air bombings developed to an unexpected disaster."[39] "I came to the conclusion," said Masatoshi Nomuna, a member of the Ministry of Railroads, "that the war was lost."[40]

The March 9 bombing was devastating. In two hours, with a loss of only fourteen U.S. planes, the B-29s dropped 1,783 tons of incendiaries, destroying sixteen and one-half square miles of Tokyo. Eyewitnesses reported "bodies in school yards, in parks, in public shelters, in vacant lots, and huddled under railroad viaducts."[41] The official death toll fixed the number at 88,793 dead and 130,000 injured, but unofficial estimates placed it at 100,000 or more dead. Over 250,000 homes were destroyed and a million residents left homeless. "The weight and intensity of this attack caught the Japanese by surprise," said the U.S. Bombing Survey. "No subsequent urban area attack was equally destructive."[42]

There were seven major raids on Tokyo, with the last one on May 25. In all, the B-29s dropped 13,244 tons of incendiaries, burning out 56.3 square miles or 51 percent of the city. In these seven raids, the B-29s burned everything important enough to burn. The U.S. Air Force reported that "further bombing would only have wasted bombs to no purpose."[43] Air force reports of damage are not exaggerated, said one newspaperman. "If anything, they constitute the most shocking understatement in the history of aerial warfare."[44]

Primary and Secondary Bombing Targets

There were five primary targets: Tokyo, Nagoya, Osaka, Kobe, and Yokohama. Much of Japan's war industries were crammed into them.

Less than thirty-six hours after the Tokyo raid on March 11, the B-29s hit Nagoya, the third-largest city, with a population of 1,500,000. The results proved disappointing, with only 2.05 square miles destroyed. On March 19, a return engagement destroyed another five square miles. "Each flight had left an alley of flames," said one crew.[45] In these two raids, the B-29s dropped a total of 370 tons of incendiaries.[46] On both occasions, enemy opposition was slight.

Osaka was next on the schedule. With a population of 3,250,000, it was Japan's second largest city, the size of Chicago, and ranked with Tokyo in importance to Japan's industrial economy. In a concentrated attack, the bombing generated a terrible firestorm that gutted 8.1 square miles. To the pilots, the greatest source of alarm was the hot air currents rising from the fires. "We headed into a great mushroom of boiling, oily smoke, and in a few seconds were tossed 5,000 feet into the air," said one B-29 pilot. "We dropped down again with a terrible jolt, and pulled out in the clear."[47] This was the air force's third successive maximum effort in ninety-six hours.

On March 17 the B-29s struck Kobe, a transportation center and Japan's sixth largest city, with nearly a million people. In two hours and ten minutes, 306 B-29s, more than were used in the Tokyo raid, dropped 2,328 tons of incendiaries on Kobe. Fire destroyed one-fifth of the city, including 11,000,000 square feet of dock area. In three major raids up to June 5, a total of 843 aircraft dropped 5,876 tons of fire bombs, destroying 8.8 square miles or 56 percent of the city.[48]

In eight days, from March 9 to 17, the air force dropped 11,000 tons of incendiary bombs on Tokyo, Wagoya, Osaka and Kobe. It burned out more than twenty-nine miles of Japan's chief industrial centers. By comparison, in Germany's greatest fire raid on London, it dropped only 200 tons of bombs, and the 8th Air Force's record strike at Berlin on February 3, 1945, dropped only 2,250 tons.[49]

A seaport city, Yokohama, with a population of 1,250,000 was wiped out in one major raid. On May 29, 454 bombers dropped 2,569 tons of incendiaries destroying nearly nine square miles of the city. After looking at Yokohama, one bomb analyst said, "The parts left over were not worth bombs."[50]

By late June, the U.S. air force had dropped 42,237 tons of fire-bombs on Tokyo, Nagoya, Osaka, Kobe, and Yokohama. American bombers had gutted a total of 102 square miles of Japan's metro-politan areas.[51] These cities were no longer considered essential targets. This was only a sample, said army air force general Henry H. Arnold, "of what the Jap can expect in the future."[52]

With the primary cities down, the B-29s went to work on the smaller towns. The air force drew up a list of 182 Japanese cities of more than 25,000 and assigned priority numbers. The days of the all-out raids were gone. Instead, the air force, still based in the Marianas, split up into smaller fleets against several targets, with up to 150 planes bombing about five cities in a single day. The pilots would "cross them off the list in batches of half a dozen at a crack."[53]

The smaller attacks began in June. Among them were Kago-shima, Omuta, Hamamatsu, and Yokkaichi (on June 18); Shizuok and Fuknoka (on June 20); Kune (on June 22); and Moji, Okayama, and Sasebo (on June 29). These cities, composed largely of wood, bam-boo, and paper, "had gone up in flames." By this time, air resistance and anti-aircraft fire were insignificant. In June, B-29 loss rates were 0.08 percent; in July, loss rates dropped to 0.03 percent; and in August to 0.02 percent. The bombing of Japan became so safe that the air force would drop leaflets beforehand warning the residents of an upcoming bombing raid. To the pilots, a bombing raid on Japan "was considered to be about the safest pastime a man could enjoy."[54]

By the war's end, the air force had heavily bombed almost every city of consequence. Of these 120 Japanese cities and towns; eighty-one were destroyed. In the six largest cities, the air force gutted 49 percent of the homes in Tokyo, Kawasaki, and Yokohama. It destroyed 32.6 percent of the homes in Osaha and Kobe and 31 percent in Nagoya.[55] Of the smaller cities, Aomori, in northern Honshu, was the hardest hit: 90 percent of it was destroyed. Other cities included Hamamatsu at 80 percent; Shizuoka, 70 percent; Toyohashi, 60 percent; Yokkaichi, 60 percent; Kawasaki, 50 percent; and Kagoshima, 80 percent.[56] In total, air attacks destroyed 2,502,000 houses, and another 614,000 were torn down to clear firebreaks, leaving 22,000,000 persons homeless.[57] "Shortly," reported the U.S. air force's Combined Intelligence Committee, "Japan will become a nation without cities, with her transportation disrupted, and will have tremendous difficulty in holding her people together."[58]

Bombing Analysis

Some Japanese leaders agreed that the bombing greatly helped destroy Japan's power to continue the war. As a result of the fire raids, said Marquis Kido, "Japan will virtually lose her fighting power in the latter half of the year."[59]

The B-29s, said Rear Admiral Tocshitane Takata, "were the greatest single factor in forcing Japan's surrender."[60]

"Japan had been so wrecked by bombardment," said manufacturer Chickuhei Nakajima, "that it would take from two to five years for her to get back on her feet."[61]

"It is my opinion," said Lieutenant General Kawabe, "our loss in the air lost us the war."[62] In the long run, said Prime Minister Baron Suzuki, "Japan would be almost destroyed by air attack."[63]

"Fundamentally," added Prince Konoye, "the thing that brought about the determination to make peace was the prolonged bombing by the B-29s."[64]

The U.S. Strategic Bombing Survey said that the air attacks were "definitive" in Japan's decision to surrender. These attacks, said the survey, "broadened the realization of defeat," brought it home to the people, and added "a tremendous quantitative weight" to Japan's peace forces.[65] "Why did Japan lose the war?" asked General LeMay. "Because in the final analysis her military leaders did not understand the potentialities of air power."[66]

Undoubtedly, the bombing of Japan's cities helped contribute to its decision to surrender. But it was only part of a broader strategy that included the blockade, mining, and destruction of Japan's air and sea arm. In addition, its troops were bogged down and isolated in China and Southeast Asia; Germany and Italy, its allies, had surrendered. The United States had defeated its marines in the Pacific; and Japan's lack of industrial might, only 10 percent that of the United States, prevented it from holding back a concentrated American counterattack.

Economic Strangulation

Japan could not survive a naval and air blockade of its islands. Surrounded by water, it was economically dependent on foreign sources for food and raw materials. At least 20 percent of its food and most of its raw materials came from overseas. This included 90 percent of Japan's oil, 88 percent of all iron, and 24 percent of all coal.[67]

Consequently, a blockade of Japan was one of the main objectives of U.S. air and sea power.

By the spring of 1945, U.S. air bases were within striking range of Japan to begin a successful mining operation. The mines were of two sizes: 1,000 pounds for water up to fifteen fathoms, and 2,000 pounds for water up to twenty-five fathoms. After falling to the sea bottom, they could function properly in ten feet of mud. Some mines were equipped with a "ship count" device, which permitted a certain number of ships to pass before detonation. Others had a "delayed arming device" that allowed a mine to come alive only after a specified amount of time had elapsed. These devices effectively foiled Japanese mine sweepers.[68]

In Operation Starvation, the U.S. air force mined the Japanese home islands in four stages. Stage I took place from March 27 to May 2, when the B-29s mined the Shimonoseki Strait, which handled 40 percent of all merchant marine traffic and the great shipping ports of Kure, Hiroshima, Tokayama, and Sasebo. In Stage II, May 3 to May 12, the B-29s mined all major shipping lanes between the great industrial cities, which depended on water transportation for 75 percent of their goods. The Industrial Center Blockade, extended from the Shimonoseki Straits east to Tokyo Bay on the vital Kobe-Osaka port system. In Stage III, from May 13 to June 6, the "minelayers" sowed the ports in northwestern Honshu and continued repeated drops over the Shimonoseki Straits, the important bottleneck area. By this time, direct ship routes to the Asiatic mainland "thinned away to almost nothing."[69] In Stage IV, from June 7 to July 8, the B-29s intensified the mining of northwestern Honshu and Kyushu ports; and in Stage V, from July 9 to August 15, the B-29s mined Pusan, on Korea's southern tip, and other Korean ports.

In four months, with the loss of only fifteen U.S. planes, over 1,500 B-29s laid 12,053 mines, to bring almost all Japanese shipping to a standstill. They approached at low altitude, mined by instrument, and disappeared into the night before the Japanese could effectively intercept.[70] By July, the air force reported that shipment of almost all raw materials had ceased, and "the shipment of food was only a fraction of that required."[71] At this time, Japan's desperation was evident when the government issued a degree urging the people to collect acorns, "perhaps the only food that still existed in abundance."[72]

"The blockade," said the Strategic Bombing Survey, "favored the growing conviction that defeat was inevitable."[73]

Destruction of Japan's Merchant Fleet, Navy, and Air Force

Because of Japan's dependence on foreign sources for food and raw materials, it needed a large merchant fleet. In 1942, Japan's merchant fleet reached its maximum size of 5,000 vessels with a total gross weight of 7,500,000 tons. By the spring of 1945, Japan's fleet was down to 2,500,000 tons; and by the war's end, it was virtually destroyed.[74]

U.S. submarines played a crucial role in sinking Japan's merchant fleet. They sank 63 percent of Japan's merchant fleet, or over 1,500 ships.[75] This was one of the most decisive factors in helping to restrict needed food and raw materials to Japan. "We suffered heavy damage from your submarines," said Admiral Teijiro Toyoda, and the greatest effect was felt "by the lack of ships and consequent inability to bring material from the south."[76] "Your submarines," added Admiral Nagano, "constituted the main difficulty in getting oil north on our ships."[77]

By the first half of 1945, the U.S. submarines and air attacks had severely curtailed Japan's coal and oil imports. By March, coal imports had virtually ceased, and iron ore was entirely cut off.[78] "The oil in stock will last six months more," said Kido in April, after which "the home front may crumble."[79] By June, oil imports into Japan were completely cut off. Japan's situation was desperate.

By the summer of 1945, Japan's once mighty navy had almost ceased to exist. In 1942, at the Battle of Midway, Japan lost four carriers and a heavy cruiser. At the bitter struggle for the Solomons in October and November 1942, it lost two battleships, three cruisers, and twelve destroyers. In the four-day sea battle of the Philippines in October 1944, Japan lost three battleships, four carriers, ten cruisers, and eight destroyers. On April 7, 1945, the United States sunk the remnants of Japan's Imperial navy off the coast of Bonomisaki in southern Kyushu, including the giant battleship *Yamato*, the chief glory of the fleet. In public discussions, the Japanese navy said "nothing about its fleet." It spoke only of air squadrons, but many guessed the truth.[80]

Because Japan is surrounded by sea, the war would go to whoever controlled the sea, and that meant control of the air. Control of the air would enable vessels to travel as far as that control extended. It permitted amphibious landings, close air support to ground forces, and successful bombing of Japanese cities and industries.

By the summer of 1945, the U.S. air force had dropped 15,000 tons of bombs on Japan's aircraft industry, and Japan's air force was so damaged that it no longer provided a menace to any of America's Pacific operations. Japan's monthly aircraft production had dropped from 1,000 a month in 1944 to 600 by July 1945. "What is left will continue to be troublesome," said Admiral Leahy, "but there is no longer any reasonable probability of their being able to stop our forward movement."[81]

"Air supremacy," said the U.S. Strategic Bombing Survey, "was the major factor which determined the timing of Japan's surrender and obviated any need for invasion."[82]

Disintegration of Japan's Economic Structure

Japan's industrial might was only 10 percent that of the United States. Its ability to develop reliable operating equipment in research and technical design work was low; its radar and communications equipment was weak; it could not build sufficient ships or escort vessels; it lacked construction equipment to build adequate airfields; its anti-aircraft was outmoded; it always lacked oil; it could not afford to build adequate shelters for the population; it could not both disperse industry and repair damaged plants.[83] "The country's production dwindled to such a point," said Prince Higashikuni, "that any swift restoration of it came to be considered beyond hope."[84]

On the material side, said Admiral Teijiro Toyoda, "our country was woefully weak."[85] Even before the war began, said General Kawabe Torashiro, many people "had considerable anxiety as to whether the national potential could maintain such a war."[86]

Other problems contributed to the worsening situation. Although the main railroad lines continued to operate until the end, the transportation system was near collapse. Frequent bombing destroyed rails, highways, and bridges. Huge losses in rolling stock and in motor transport caused overcrowding of passenger trains and irregular movement of freight.[87] The nation suffered from runaway inflation. Sugar and soap were rare. Consumer goods vanished from the market. To some, it looked like "the life of the people was reaching the limits of endurance."[88]

Most crucial, the food situation was worsening. Before Pearl Harbor, the average caloric intake of the Japanese people was about 2,000 calories per day, as against 3,400 in the United States. By the summer of 1945, it was about 1,680. It is estimated that 2,000 calories a day is a minimum requirement. In reality, on the average, the Japanese consumed 10 percent less than the Germans ate during the worst period of World War I under the British blockade.[89] The average Japanese had one small bowl of watered soup for breakfast and some pickles, and a piece of fish and a few vegetables for lunch. Supper was mostly a repetition of breakfast.[90] "The number of emaciated men and women in the country is conspicuous," said the *Yomiuri-Hochi* newspaper. "No one can work properly, and production will inevitably decline."[91]

Public Opinion

The military dreaded public opinion. It controlled speech, press, and thought by various legislation. The military also had civilian spies, known as neighborhood associations, who publically denounced "traitors" and threatened to haul those who criticized the war "before a military tribunal."[92] "There are elements," said a Japanese army circular, "which we will have to watch carefully lest they endanger the conduct of the war."[93] "The military's oppression of public opinion," said Kido, "grew more and more vigorous with the passage of every year."[94]

Where the air attacks began in the spring of 1945, the military could not as effectively control public opinion. The fall of the Pacific Islands meant little to the ordinary person, but when the B-29s came to the home islands, public morale suffered greatly, and a feeling of defeat set in. The incendiary bombing, said Rear Admiral Keizo Komura, led "to a decline in the will of the people to continue the war."[95]

When the air raids became frequent, said Prince Higashikuni, the people felt the government should end the war, but they "could not make their feeling public."[96] The reality of defeat came to many when the United States dropped leaflets naming the places to be bombed and then bombed them.

"When the U.S. did that," said Dr. Kawai, chief editorial writer of the *Nippon Times*, "then there was real terror."[97]

Preparation for Invasion

By the summer of 1945, many of Japan's best troops had already been killed. Of the 668,000 deployed in the Pacific, U.S. armed services had killed 316,000. In China, the Japanese lost 103,000 troops of the 1,100,000 deployed; the rest were still tied down there.

In Burma, it lost 40,000 of its 220,000 troops.[98] Since the United States commanded the sea and air around Japan, its overseas troops were pinned down in Asia and "useless to the homeland."[99]

In June, after the fall of Okinawa, the Japanese began preparing in earnest for the coming invasion of their home islands. The army established its western headquarters at Hiroshima and eastern headquarters at Tokyo. Although the army had two million troops in Japan proper, only half of them were adequately armed. The army "busied itself laying in stocks of bamboo spears and wooden guns."[100] It was inducting maimed men and feeding its troops only one meal a day, "a bowl of rice mixed with bean cake, and all of them were suffering from malnutrition and its consequent effects: general debility, stomach disorders, and the like."[101]

The air force had more than 9,000 planes in the home islands. About 5,000 had been fitted for kamikaze attack.[102] Although the government and imperial household felt concern for the "destruction of the Japanese people," they "were already being shattered by direct air attacks, and the expected invasion raised few fears."[103]

Conclusion

By the end of July 1945, if not before, Japan was militarily defeated. Fire raids had ravaged its major cities; its best troops were killed or missing in East Asia and the South Pacific, and many were still fighting in China. Twenty-two million Japanese were homeless, and the U.S. naval and air blockade had cut off imports of fuel, food and raw materials from Japan's conquests in China, Korea, and Manchuria. U.S. submarines roamed Japanese waters, sinking tankers and freighters that tried to run the blockade. Japan's navy had ceased to exist, and its air force was severely diminished. U.S. battleships and cruisers were shelling port installations and military compounds within gun range of the Japanese shores. At the same time, carrier-based fighters and bombers flew with near–impunity over the islands, bombing targets of opportunity—railway tracks and trains, motorized troop convoys, factories, and air fields.[104]

After April 1945, Japan's leaders sought a diplomatic solution to end the war. The problem was America's insistence on unconditional surrender. To a proud people, acceptance of unconditional surrender would not allow the Japanese to "save face" or honor. At the very least, Japan's civilian and military leaders agreed, the United States must allow them to retain Emperor Hirohito, but the military wanted additional conditions. All agreed, however, to seek Soviet mediation to persuade the United States to abandon its demand for unconditional surrender and negotiate with Japan an end to the war. Chapter 1 will discuss and analyze these events.

1.

Japan's Peace Moves: Tojo and Koiso Cabinets

On October 20, 1941, General Hideki Tojo became prime minister of Japan. At age fifty-seven he was not a military figure. He stood 5 feet 2 inches tall and weighed only 115 pounds. He earned the nickname "Razor Tojo" because of his slashing tongue. Of average intelligence, he studied and worked hard, excelling above more gifted colleagues. "I am just an ordinary man possessing no shining talents," he said. "Anything I have achieved I owe to my capacity for hard work and never giving up."[1]

Tojo took over from Prince Fumimaro Konoye, whose regime fell after he failed to obtain a summit conference with President Franklin Roosevelt in Hawaii. Konoye hoped he would persuade Roosevelt to lift the oil embargo against Japan, applied on July 25, 1941, after Japan's occupation of South Vietnam. But for reasons still unclear, Roosevelt did not agree to the summit.

Although Tojo did not think the United States was interested in peace with Japan, he continued to rely on negotiations to lift the oil embargo. But when the United States demanded that Japan disengage from China before lifting the oil embargo, Tojo gave the order to attack Pearl Harbor on December 7, 1941. At the same time, Japanese forces overran the South Pacific, Southeast Asia, and the Dutch East Indies to obtain needed oil.

Tojo had no clear plan for victory against the United States. The Japanese considered Americans "soft" and unwilling to fight a long, tough war in the Pacific. The Japanese put great confidence in the superiority of their "fighting spirit" over the industrial superiority of the United States. They hoped that their conquests in Southeast Asia and the crippling defeats of U.S. forces at Pearl Harbor and in the Philippines would lead the United States to negotiate a peace more favorable to Japan than it was previously willing to do.[2]

But the bombing of Pearl Harbor proved to be Japan's fatal mistake. It united Americans against it, and America's industrial strength was 90 percent greater than Japan's.

In the period between December 1941 and June 1944, Japan's defeats at Midway, the Solomon and Marshall Islands, and New Guinea brought about frequent cabinet shuffles and weakened Tojo's hold on the government. The loss of Saipan in July 1944 finally brought down Tojo's cabinet.

After the loss of Saipan, many Japanese agreed that the war was lost. Japanese leaders, including Admirals Keisuke Okada and Mitsumasa Yonai, Prince Konoye, and the Lord Keeper of the Privy Seal Marquis Koichi Kido, the Emperor's closest political adviser, agreed that the war should be brought to an end. In fact, they brought sufficient pressure to force Tojo's resignation.[3] Fearing that the result would be "general upheaval and revolution," most of the business world was against continuing the war.[4] The general public was in shock. Government reports said Saipan was "heavily fortified and defended," but this proved false.[5] "Now," said Major General Sadanori Harada, "the entire mainland of Japan was exposed to strategical bombardment."

Prince Higashikuni concluded, "The war was lost."[6]

After Tojo's resignation on July 18, General Kuniaki Koiso, known as the "Tiger of Korea," formed a new Cabinet. Despite his nickname and fierce appearance—"catlike eyes, a flat nose and thin lips," he lacked the courage to stand up to the Japanese army and find a way out of the war,"[7] said Konoye, but "the situation was such that they couldn't do it."[8] Japan's original war-making coalition had great strength within the top army command and still constituted "a distinct threat of revolt or coup."[9]

Koiso's one accomplishment in the direction of peace was the creation of the Supreme Council for the Direction of the War. Originally formed as a liaison between the military and the Cabinet, it became a separate, more powerful inner group with the power to decide the issue of war and peace. Although its decisions had to be ratified by the Cabinet, it had direct access to the emperor. Known as the Supreme Council or Big six, it comprised six regular members: the prime minister, foreign minister, army and navy ministers, and the army and navy chief of staff. Like the Cabinet, the Supreme Council did not operate by majority votes, but on general agreement or unity. When unity on important issues was lacking, they were presented to the emperor. If those seeking peace could gain control of the Supreme Council, they could, working in the greatest secrecy and with direct access to the emperor, unlock the door to peace.[10]

Hirohito Turns to Suzuki

To the Japanese, Emperor Hirohito was sacred and inviolable. The emperor was Japan, and Japan was the emperor. The Japanese did not separate the two. The equation of the emperor and the homeland was mystical, emotional, and viewed within "a reverent haze."[11] Because the United States insisted on unconditional surrender, Japan's leaders feared the worst for Hirohito should the country surrender. The United States might try him as a war criminal, imprison or execute him. It might abolish the entire imperial dynasty and institute another government by force.

Born in Tokyo on April 29, 1901, Emperor Hirohito succeeded to the throne in 1926. Married in 1924 to Princess Nagako, Hirohito and his wife had two sons and five daughters. In his youth, Hirohito had developed an interest in marine biology, and it became his burning passion throughout life. He spent much time classifying sea animals and plants at the Biological Institute in the Imperial Palace and published numerous scholarly works on his scientific research.

Never an enthusiastic supporter of the war, by 1945, Hirohito was an unhappy deity. Most of the time he spent in his underground bunker, forty-five feet beneath the long, one-story Imperial Library. He had to move through dark passages from room to room away from the imperial gardens and the wild flowers that delighted him. He was not unattractive, even if his glasses were thick and his sight was myopic, but his solid though slightly stooped five feet six inch frame had diminished from 140 to 123 pounds. At forty-four years, gray streaked his thinning black hair, his right cheek twitched persistently, his "high-pitched voice more shrill, his oval face puffier, and his narrow eyes pouchier" as he suffered the "ravages of insomnia."[12]

On February 14, 1945, Prince Konoye met with Emperor Hirohito at the Imperial Household. Konoye expressed the view that "defeat was certain," but if Japan surrendered immediately, America would probably leave the imperial system alone.[13] Konoye feared most a Communist revolution following defeat. Under such circumstances, he continued, "the longer we continue the war, the greater will be the danger of revolution."[14]

The emperor appeared not to be convinced. He referred to the views of General Yoshijiro Umezu, chief of the Imperial General staff, that the United States' goal was to destroy the imperial system and reduce the country to a "heap of ruins," and that "it was prudent to continue the war" and seek the friendly cooperation of the Soviet Union.[15] This view was the opposite of the one Konoye had expressed. In reply, Konoye repeated his view that a continuation of the war would make the Allies more "intolerant of the Emperor system," and the "excesses of the Army should be checked," to which end "decisive action on the part of the Emperor was needed more than anything else."[16]

Konoye went away from the meeting bitterly disappointed. He told Shigeru Yoshida, a leading pacifist and friend, that the emperor "did not seem to be as well informed as he might be on the actual course of the war," and he blamed the army and navy for deceiving him.[17] Konoye groaned that the way things were, "Japan may have to go all the way to ultimate ruin."[18]

On April 5, Prime Minister Koiso and his Cabinet resigned en masse. He said that his Cabinet was no longer able to conduct the war, and a more powerful cabinet was needed. When the Cabinet was formed, explained Koiso, "it was planned to engage the enemy in a decisive battle in the Philippines," but when that failed, the people became "alienated from the Government."[19]

Upon the resignation of the cabinet, the emperor called on the Jushin, made up of former ministers, for advice on the make-up of the next Cabinet. The Jushin had no power other than as an advisory council. Kido, the lord keeper of the privy seal, would make the final selection on the next prime minister, and present it to the emperor.[20] Immediately after Koiso's resignation, on April 5, the Jushin assembled at the Imperial Audience Hall. It included Barons Kiichiro Hiranuma and Reijiro Wakatsuki, Admirals Kantaro Suzuki and Okada, Prince Konoye, General Tojo, and Kido. Opening the discussion, Tojo said that two opinions existed within the country: "fight to the last" or "speedily bring about peace."[21] "There is no other way but to fight on at any price," said Hiranuma.[22] "We must win at all costs," said Hirota.[23] Wakatsuki reminded them that the emperor had summoned them to select the next cabinet leader, not "to debate whether we should fight to the last or conclude peace."[24] Hiranuma, Konoye, and Kido argued that the next prime minister should be a former service man, Admiral Suzuki. He would, they said, "command popular confidence," and it was "imperative that a weighty Cabinet worthy of the people's trust be formed."[25]

Tojo disagreed. The enemy was about to invade, he argued and he wanted someone who was in active military service. He believed this would better enable the person to coordinate both state and military affairs to "act in unison." "You will need to exercise the greatest caution," he warned. "Otherwise the Army may turn its back, and the Cabinet will collapse the moment the Army turns its back on it."[26]

Okada grew angry. The army's responsibility, he said, was to defend the country, not to turn its back on the person appointed by an "Imperial Command."[27] "I just called your attention to it," replied Tojo.[28] The prime minister, said Kido, must be a man "of deep sincerity and enormous courage," and that man was Suzuki.[29]

In the end, the elder statesmen except for Tojo, agreed on Suzuki. The feeling, said Kido, was that the war should end and that "Suzuki alone had the deep conviction and personal courage to stand up to the military and bring the war to an end."[30]

Later that evening, Hirohito asked Suzuki to become prime minister. At first, he was reluctant to accept the position. At seventy-eight years old, he argued that he was too old, partially deaf, and politically inexperienced. "I think there are many other proper persons who are fond of politics," Suzuki said, "and I leave it to your imagination why a man like me, a mere sailor, has to come out at this critical juncture."[31] But Hirohito insisted that he take the post, and Suzuki could not refuse the emperor.

Suzuki's Government

On April 7, 1945, Suzuki became prime minister of Japan. Born in Osaka, a graduate of the Naval Academy and Naval War College, Suzuki was a popular war hero. At seventy-eight years old, his face lined, with bushy arched eyebrows, shaggy mustache, and huge ears, he was a portrait of "wisdom, dignity, and courage." He saw action in the Sino-Japanese (1894-95) and the Russo-Japanese (1904-05) wars. He later became principal of the Naval Academy and commander of the Kure Naval Station. In 1923, he rose to admiral and in 1925 became chief of the Naval General Staff. In 1929, he became grand chamberlain to the emperor, but he resigned from his post on February 1936 after being seriously wounded during an attempted army coup. After recovering from near death, he became a hero to the people, who respected his "personal courage and integrity and loyalty to the throne."[32]

Suzuki's goal was to end the war, and he had the emperor's blessing to do it. "It was the Emperor's desire to make every effort to bring the war to a conclusion," said Suzuki, "and that was my purpose."[33] A big problem, however, was to keep the military from sabotaging his peace efforts. If he publicly opposed the war, he feared a military coup or assassination."[34] Privately, through diplomatic channels and other means, he would try to negotiate an end to the war. "There was no sudden change in policy," said Konoye. "It was more subtle but there was a drastic reduction in the intensity of propaganda, and it began to turn gradually."[35]

Suzuki was practicing *haragei*, the Japanese art of "hidden and invisible technique," the wary and prudent approach. The word is composed of *hara*, or "mind, intention, spirit," and gei or "art or accomplishments." A person who uses *haragei* says one thing but means another. Suzuki advocated the continuation of the war with "clenched fists" but concealed his *hara*, his real intention with "sealed mouth."[36]

To seek peace, Suzuki's biggest problem was the United States' continued insistence on unconditional surrender. Honor was important to the Japanese, and unconditional surrender gave Japan no honorable way to surrender. "What is the meaning of the phrase 'unconditional surrender?'" asked Japan's Soviet ambassador Naotake Sato. "There are virtually no precedents from history to provide the answer to this question."[37]

Suzuki's first task was to choose the Supreme Council for the Direction of the War. Besides the prime minister, Suzuki picked Shigenori Togo to serve as foreign minister. Because of the similarity in their names Togo and Tojo were often confused by the Allies, but they were far apart in personality and political views. With his broad face, flat nose, and scowling lips under a well-trimmed mustache, Togo's appearance seemed "chiseled in ice." An individual who did not fit into the niche of community consensus, Togo was faithful to his wife—no concubines, no geishas. He avoided social gatherings, and his own subordinates often found him distant. He sometimes sent his daughter to solicit their views. Neither was he a man to practice *haragei*. He was outspoken in his opposition to continuing the war, but he would not push the military too far, knowing when to compromise before the "danger signal flashed."[38]

For Suzuki, who wanted to end the war, Togo was a natural choice as foreign minister. After serving in numerous diplomatic posts in Asia, Europe, and the United States, Togo became ambassador to Germany in 1937 and to the Soviet Union in 1939. In the latter posts, he helped settle Japanese fishing and territorial disputes with the Soviet Union. As foreign minister under Tojo's 1941 Cabinet, Togo participated in the unsuccessful prewar negotiations with the United Sates. In 1942, he argued that Japan should withdraw its troops from China after securing special trade rights. He said that Japan should remain flexible and avoid commitments that would hamper later peace negotiations with the West.[39] When Tojo refused his advice, Togo resigned in frustration.

At sixty-two years old, Togo was uncertain whether to accept Suzuki's offer to again become foreign minister. He did not like Suzuki's public statements in support of the war. Chief Cabinet Secretary Hisatsume Sakomizu explained that Suzuki could not speak of an early peace without "undesirable repercussions," and that Togo should call on him at his official residence. In the course of their conversation, Suzuki said that "so far as the prospect of the war is concerned, your opinion is quite satisfactory to me; and as to diplomacy, you shall have a free hand."[40] With that, Togo accepted the position.

Suzuki had to be careful in dealing with the army and navy ministers. The two services nominated their own ministers. They could bring down a government by ordering their ministers to resign and keep a new government from being formed simply by refusing to nominate a new one.

A Jushin member, Admiral Mitsumasa Yonai, was the navy minister. After graduating from the Naval Academy, he served in numerous important navy posts. He became commander in chief of the combined fleet in 1936 and full admiral the following year. As navy minister in three previous Cabinets, he firmly opposed the army's proposal for an alliance with Germany and Italy, the Axis powers. He was convinced that a war between Britain and Germany would bring in the United States, and Germany would lose, leaving Japan to fight the United States alone.[41] In January 1940, he became prime minister, and despite pro-Axis pressure from the army, he tried to steer a moderate course. Because of this, in July 1940, the army forced him out. By 1945, he recognized the need to end the war quickly.[42]

General Korechika Anami was the army minister, a post often referred to as the war minister. At fifty-eight years old, Anami, standing stiffly erect, his powerful chest thrust out, looked like a general. He dressed immaculately. His uniform hung on his muscular frame without a wrinkle, his jackboots shone like glass, and his long-hilted sword gleamed at his side. A master of martial arts, he was an expert archer, swordsman, and Kendo fencer who could also manipulate bamboo stakes with remarkable skill. Although not of "great intelligence," with little capacity to analyze long-range strategic problems, he often made the right tactical decisions through instinct "honed by rigorous Zen training."[43]

Born in 1887, on the southern Japanese island of Kyushu, Anami was headstrong as a young boy, and his parents sent him to a military academy to learn discipline. He learned quickly, and the army became his life's calling. After graduating from the Army Academy, he rose quickly to general, served as aide de camp to Hirohito for four years, and then became vice minister of war. Before becoming war minister in 1945, he commanded units in China and served as chief of army aviation.

Unable to accept unconditional surrender, Anami agreed with the army's sentiments that Japan should get out of the war with its honor intact. He enjoyed the full confidence of the younger, more passionate officers, who regarded him "as a symbol of determination to fight the war to the bitter end."[44] But he would not undercut the imperial will or go against a direct order from the emperor.

The two chiefs of staff were Yoshijiro Umezu of the army and Teijiro Toyoda of the navy. Umezu, who had earned the nickname "the ivory mask," had a face that was often devoid of expression or emotion. But despite his impenetrable manner, he had a pleasant personality that attracted many followers. A 1903 graduate of the Army Academy, he served as commander of the Japanese forces in Manchuria, called the Kwantung army, which patrolled the outer Mongolian-Manchurian border. In 1944, he became chief of staff of the army. Able and forceful, Toyoda had directed operations as commander in chief of the combined fleet. His appointment as chief of staff of the navy in May 1945 caused some anxiety because of his "almost morbid dislike of the Army." But he agreed with the army on continuing the war. The navy was divided on the issue, with Yonai among the foremost advocates of peace and Toyoda representing the war faction.

The Supreme Council agreed to deliberate mainly on the urgent problem of war and peace and to meet in secret, leaving the younger, more intractable officers in the dark.

Lord Keeper of the Privy Seal Kido was the conduit between the Supreme Council and Emperor Hirohito. At fifty-two, Kido, a small man with a neatly trimmed mustache, did not look like a great political force, but he was one of the most powerful men in Japan. As the emperor's chief advisor, he kept him informed on all domestic and foreign issues. Kido met with the emperor for at least one hour every day, and only the ministers of the war and navy could meet with him without Kido's approval.

The emperor had little direct influence on government. By tradition, although he could issue a direct order, he would do so only in a grave emergency. He merely approved of government decisions, whether he agreed with them or not. But political leaders were cautious about defying the emperor's will, and Kido was the one to make the emperor's will known to them. By 1945, both the emperor and Kido wanted to war to end.

Germany's Surrender

As the Allies closed in, Japanese diplomatic and consular officials and their staffs fled in all directions. Some escaped to the Soviet Union, Switzerland, and Sweden; others were captured by the Seventh Army.

On May 8, 1945, Germany surrendered to the U.S. 7th Army. When German radio played Wagner's "Twilight of the Gods," an American intelligence officer commented that an appropriate song for Japan would be "Don't Fence Me In," since "Nippon now a lone ranger astride a white horse, rides dolefully toward the last round-up."[45]

In a radio address, Suzuki declared that Germany's surrender would not cause "the slightest change." But privately many Japanese understood that Japan's position, always precarious, was becoming desperate. Japan was isolated, without allies, and with the total resources of the United States, Britain, and China arrayed against it. With Germany's collapse, the Soviet Union, nominally neutral, might move east and join the coalition against Japan.

Even before Germany's collapse, Japan had been pursuing peace. The Japanese looked to a neutral country to mediate the war and persuade the United States to modify its demand for unconditional surrender so that Japan could retain Emperor Hirohito and save its honor. Without this concession, the Army was determined to "fight to the end."[46]

Japanese Peace Feelers

On April 7, 1945, acting Foreign Minister Shigemitsu Mamoru approached Swedish ambassador Widon Bagge in Tokyo. He appeared sympathetic to Japan's wartime situation. "I cannot bear to think of the ruin of Japan," he told Shigemitsu, "which has such a glorious past."[47] After careful thought, Shigemitsu asked Bagge "to ascertain what peace terms the United States and Britain had in mind," but he emphasized that unconditional surrender was unacceptable because it would mean "dishonor," and that "the Emperor must not be touched."[48] Bagge relayed the message to the United States, but Secretary of State Edward Stettinius told the U.S. ambassador in Sweden to "show no interest or take any initiative in pursuit of the matter."[49]

On May 7, 1945, the Japanese sent a peace signal through Portugal, Masutard Inoue, counselor of the Japanese legation in Portugal, approached a U.S. undercover agent of the Office of Strategic Service (OSS). Inoue asked the agent to get in touch with the U.S. embassy and "find out what exactly they plan to do in the Far East." He feared that U.S. bombers would "smash Japan," but he emphasized that "there can be no unconditional surrender."[50] The agent relayed the message, but nothing came of it.

Three days later, the Japanese again sent a signal through Sweden. General Onodera, Japan's military representative in Sweden, attempted to arrange for a member of the Swedish royal family to approach the Allies for a settlement. He too stressed that Japan would not accept "unconditional surrender" and that it must be allowed to "save face."[51] The United States urged the Swedish not to pursue the matter.

On July 12, Japan sent a peace signal through Switzerland. Kojiro Kitamura, a representative of the Yokohama Specie Bank in Switzerland, approached Per Jacobson, a Swedish national and economic adviser to the Bank for International Settlements. Kitamura said that he wanted to open up contact with U.S. representatives, and that the only condition that Japan would insist on was retention of the emperor. He was acting with the consent of Shunichi Kase, the Japanese minister to Switzerland, and General Kiyotomi Okamoto, chief of Japanese European intelligence, and they were in direct contact with Tokyo.[52]

Two days later in Wiesbaden, Germany, Jacobson met with OSS representative Allen Dulles. Jacobson relayed the message that the Japanese group in Switzerland was in direct contact with Tokyo, and Japan's main demand was the "retention of the Emperor."[53] Although Dulles had no formal authority to speak for the United States, he worked out a suggested reply. Undoubtedly, he said, there would be sympathy for retention of the emperor but "no advance commitment by the United States Government on this point." He added that the best way Hirohito could ensure his continuation as ruler was "to take the lead in proclaiming and enforcing the surrender."[54]

Dulles relayed the information to Secretary of War Henry Stimson, but he refused to act on it. The Japanese group in Switzerland received no encouragement from the government. By this time, the Japanese were channeling their peace efforts through the Soviet Union.

The Soviet Union and Japan

On February 11, 1945, Stalin, Roosevelt, and Churchill signed a secret agreement at Yalta, on the southern tip of the Crimean. Stalin agreed to enter the war against Japan three months after Germany surrendered. In return, the Allies would allow the Soviets to regain their former holdings in Manchuria taken by Japan in the 1904 Russo-Japanese War. These included the southern part of Sakhalin as well as the islands adjacent to it; the internationalization of the commercial port of Dairen; the leasing of Port Arthur as a Soviet naval base; and joint Chinese and Soviet operations of the Manchurian railroads. The Soviets would also acquire the Kunile Islands and were assured of the preservation of the status quo in Outer Mongolia.[55]

The Japanese were apparently, unaware that the Soviet Union and the United States had made a deal at Yalta, yet fairly "wide knowledge of the fact" existed.[56] This lapse illustrated the poor judgment of Japan's intelligence services, and its political leaders' lack of astuteness in foreign affairs.

Shortly after the Yalta Conference, on February 22, Japan's Ambassador Naotake Sato in Moscow met with Soviet foreign minister Vyacheslav Molotov. Sato was looking for any change in attitude of the Soviet Union toward the Soviet-Japanese Neutrality Pact. Under this pact, signed on April 25, 1941, if either country was at war with a third power, the other would remain neutral. The five-year pact would be automatically extended for five years unless denounced before April 25, 1945.

Sato proposed that the two countries renew the Neutrality Pact. Our two countries must maintain peace, he said, "in a world now sick of the roar of cannon and the blast of bombing." But Molotov wanted to postpone discussion of it. This question, he said, pertains not only to European problems but to "many other problems as well."[57] Sato wanted to know the exact meaning of "many other problems," but for the moment, knowing that Molotov was a "difficult man to deal with," he decided to postpone the issue.[58] The meeting ended inconclusively.

On April 5, Molotov called a meeting with Sato. It was brief, lasting only twenty minutes. Molotov announced to a stunned Sato that the Soviet Union would not renew the Neutrality Pact when it expired in April 1946. He said that the neutrality pact had lost its meaning and that its extension had become impossible. Since the signing on April 25, 1941, Germany had invaded the Soviet Union, and Japan, an ally of Germany, "had been helping Germany in her war against the United States and Britain, Allies of the Soviet Union." When Sato asked if the pact would remain valid another year, Molotov replied that the Soviet Union's attitude would have to be "set accordingly."[59] He quickly added, however, that notification of abrogation had "not brought about any change in the existing situation.[60]

Shortly thereafter, the Soviet press adopted an "unceremonious attitude toward Japan." *Izvestia* outlined two decades of Japan's "unsatisfactory character." It reviewed Japan's intervention in the Soviet Far East between 1918 to 1922 and its occupation of Vladivostok and Northern Sakhalin, and emphasized three times that Japan had been "helping Germany," Russia's enemy.[61] Sato was particularly disturbed with the matter of "helping Germany." He had not heard Molotov mention it before. Its "knell-like repetition was unsettling."[62]

In response, the Japanese adopted a policy of avoiding offense. Fearing the "calamity of a declaration of war," Sato argued that Japan should openly accept the Soviet decision "with submissiveness" and "do nothing to make matters worse."[63] Suzuki agreed and instructed Japanese embassies to avoid emotional comment, expressions of irritations, or impressions of any shock and not to use the word "abrogation" in connection with the Neutrality Pact.[64]

Despite all indications that the Soviet Union was unfriendly, if not moving toward belligerency, the Supreme Council for the Direction of the War decided in mid-May 1945 to turn to the Soviets for help in mediating an end to the war. The Supreme Council hoped that power-politic considerations would determine the Soviet attitude. With Germany out of the war, the Allied alliance would break, and the Soviets, distrusting the West, would want a strong Japan as a buffer to keep the United States and Britain out of East Asia.

Togo was the lone dissenter; he said it was "too late." The Allies had forged a wartime coalition "incapable of being rent asunder."[65] But Anami was against opening up direct negotiations with the United States as long as it insisted on "unconditional surrender."[66] The rest agreed, particularly Suzuki, who had to be careful in dealing with the war minister, who could have broken the Cabinet at any time simply by resigning.

In return for mediation, the Supreme Council decided that Japan must make a generous offer to the Soviet Union. Ambassador Sato warned that Japan "will be forced to dance to whatever tune strikes the Russian fancy."[67] Members of the military, however, were "frightened out of their wits" at the thought of war with the Red Army and "were willing to pay the heaviest price to prevent it."[68] This price included the dissolution of the 1905 Portsmouth Treaty, ending the 1904 Russo-Japanese War; a return to Russia of South Sakhalin; concessions on Far Eastern fishery rights; and neutralization of Manchuria in exchange for Soviet oil, coal, and iron ores. To look for a clash between the Soviets and Americans, said Toshikazu Kase, Togo's secretary, is "mere wishful thinking."[69] The Soviet Union will not "sacrifice her relations with the Allies for anything we can offer."[70]

In mid-May, Togo asked Koki Hirota, a former prime minister, to meet with Yakov Malik, the Soviet ambassador to Japan, at his resort hotel in Gora, in the Hakone Mountains near Tokyo. Togo wired Ambassador Sato in Moscow, "Hirota will keep a close watch on Soviet tendencies and will try to lead the Russians along the lines we desire."[71]

On June 3, Hirota traveled to Gora and stayed with an acquaintance near the Gora Hotel where Malik was staying. That evening Hirota went for a walk and "accidently" bumped into Malik, who invited him for dinner. Over coffee and liqueurs, Hirota assured Malik that it was "the universal desire of both the Japanese Government and the Japanese people to have friendly relations with Russia."[72] Malik offered no comment, and the rest of the evening was spent in amenities.

The next evening Hirota again sounded out Malik's views on friendly relations between the two countries. "The Soviet Union," said Malik, "had endeavored to promote friendly relations with Japan but had failed because of strong opposition in Japan to rapprochement," and this "had produced a feeling of distrust and lack of safety." If such an attitude toward the Soviet Union ever existed, said

Hirota, it had disappeared, and "the Japanese people now had a likely appreciation of the USSR."[73] But Malik was again non committal. Two days later, Hirota sought another meeting, but Malik declined, pleading "indisposition."

Meanwhile, conditions appeared to deteriorate between the Soviet Union and Japan. In March 1945, the Soviets began shifting troops from the European theater to Eastern Russia near the Manchurian (Manchukuo) border. In late May, alerted by Tokyo, Japanese couriers and diplomats reported "an average of thirty east-bound trains a day carrying troops, tanks, guns, planes, and supplies," and on at least three occasions, Soviet planes were reported on reconnoitering missions over the Sea of Japan and south Sakhalin.[74] By June and early July, this shift had dramatically increased, with reported sightings of 166 eastbound trains carrying self-propelled guns, rocket guns, U.S. tanks, Stalin heavy tanks, and 2,932 cars carrying troops.[75] Ambassador Okamoto Suemasa in Sweden forwarded to Tokyo an intelligence report suggesting that the Soviet shift in military strength eastward was only "a gesture to England and the United States, not signifying that the Soviet Union will enter the war against Japan."[76]

This was wishful thinking by the Japanese, but they had to do everything they could to ensure tranquility on their Manchurian border. To reinforce the home front, the military had already transferred the bulk of its highly trained Manchurian army to the mainland of Japan. This left Manchuria thinly defended. "Should the Soviet Union strike at us," said Kase, "it would mean the instant collapse of our entire front, as we were hard pressed everywhere."[77]

In what seemed to the Japanese as petty matters, Soviet diplomats adopted an "intransigent attitude." They began pressing for a settlement of questions long in dispute, such as Tsarist buildings in Manchuria, and lodged heated protests and demands regarding current incidents. These included expropriation by the Japanese military in Shanghai of apartments occupied by Soviet citizens; alleged violations on the Mongolian frontier by Japanese planes; the "arbitrary and barbarous" action of Japanese police in arresting Metropolitan Sergei, heads of the Russian Orthodox Church in

Tokyo; delay of more than a year in constructing a still incomplete air raid shelter for the Soviet embassy in Tokyo; and shadowing of Soviet consular officials at Dairen.[78] At the same time, Soviet radio and press brought up Japan's past aggressions against Russia in Manchuria, the Kwantung Peninsula, Sakhalin, and Port Arthur, and its latest transgression—"helping Germany."[79]

"The salient feature of Russo-Japanese relations since the abrogation of the neutrality pact," said U.S. intelligence reports, "has been the fulfillment of fears expressed at the time by Japanese ambassador Sato at Moscow, that Russia would attempt to coerce Japan into adopting "a policy of obsequiousness based on fear."[80]

Plan for "Last-Ditch Defense"

On June 6, the Supreme Council for the Direction of the War met to discuss the army's plan for conducting the war, the Basic Policy for the Future of the War. It said that victory could be achieved by using suicide planes to destroy a quarter of the enemy forces at sea, destroying another quarter during the attempted landing, and annihilating the remaining half after it had established a beachhead on Japanese soil.[81] But the army did not consider a tactical victory realistic. The United States had the industrial and military capability to regroup and attack again and again until achieving victory. By dealing the heaviest blow possible on the initial invasion, the Japanese army hoped that the Americans would find additional casualties unacceptable and sue for peace on terms other than unconditional surrender.[82]

Togo considered the army's plan unrealistic. It was "mere day dreaming," he said, and Japan could not afford to indulge in it[83] "That is not to say that anyone there expressed the opinion that we should ask for peace," said navy chief of staff Toyoda, "for when a large number of people are present like that, it is difficult for any one member to disagree."[84]

Meanwhile, the Japanese were feverishly* preparing for the anticipated invasion. In October 1944, they began building defense lines along the home islands. Most were "primitive and toylike," compared with the steel and concrete fortifications that the Allied armies confronted in Europe. "Those that I inspected were hand-made and crude," said one Japanese official. "No materials existed for modern fortifications."[85] The army dug caves in the mountains, said Konoye, "and their idea of fighting on was fighting from every little hole or rock in the mountains."[86] The military even gave teenage girls wooden sticks and told them, "If you don't kill at least one enemy soldier, you don't deserve to die."[87]

The military situation was hopeless. "The time had come to terminate the war," said Navy Minister Yonai,[88] but the army would not retreat from its position. "Give us a last opportunity to prove our worth," said the army, and "vindicate our honor."[89]

On June 7, the Cabinet rubber-stamped its approval of the army's war plan. The last step was to hold an imperial conference to obtain the emperor's consent.

The next day the conference was held at the Imperial Household in Tokyo. In the presence of the emperor, the Supreme Council and its aides presented the army's war plan. It called for "supreme self-sacrifice" and "the honorable death of a hundred million" rather than surrender.[90] "We must fight to the last," said Suzuki, "Unconditional surrender will only mean that our national structure and our people will be destroyed."[91] The plan said nothing about the supreme Council's earlier decision to seek Soviet mediation to end the war, and no one, not even Togo, brought it up.

"Nobody expressed his real feelings," said Hisatsune Sakomize, chief Cabinet secretary, but "we couldn't actually advocate the stopping of the war because the military police were still around."[92]

The meeting lasted one hour and fifty minutes. Hirohito had said nothing throughout the conference. By tradition, the emperor's silence meant his official sanction of whatever the Cabinet and Supreme Council had already endorsed. Its discussion over, the Supreme Council and its aides rose and bowed, and the stone-faced emperor, solemnly withdrew from the chamber.

Despite his silence, Hirohito seemed upset with the decision to carry on the war. Throughout the conference, Toyoda noticed that "discontent was written all over him," and afterward, Kido "was struck by the shadows of deep concern which he found lingering in the Imperial countenance."[93]

Deeply alarmed, by the army plan and the emperor's dismay, Kido decided to draw up his own plan for saving the situation. "It was crystal clear," said Kido, that the army was "bent upon making the innocent people share in their dark fate, which they knew was staring them squarely in the face."[94]

Kido's Peace Proposal

On June 8, immediately after the imperial conference, Kido drew up a peace proposal, the Measures for Managing the Situation. This confidential memorandum set forth in bold terms Japan's urgent need to end the war immediately. In it, Kido reviewed Japan's desperate military situation: Okinawa will fall; the incendiary bombing will "sweep away" all the cities; shortages of provisions and foodstuffs will lead to "serious unrest" among the people; and "the situation will be beyond salvation."[95] He argued that Japan must immediately negotiate peace. "If she waits," said Kido "Japan may share Germany's fate," and the Imperial Household will fall.[96]

At the end, Kido called upon the emperor to end the war. He advocated that the emperor send a personal message to the Soviet Union to ask it to act as an intermediary for peace negotiations. The message should make clear that the throne would offer to bring the war to a close by offering "very generous terms." These terms would include evacuation of army and navy forces in occupied areas, even "giving up their arms on the spot" and reduction of armaments to "a minimum defense."[97] There is no other way to "save the situation," said Kido. Only the emperor could break the deadlock and open the door to peace.[98]

On June 9, Kido showed his peace proposal to Emperor Hirohito, who gave him an imperial sanction to consult the Cabinet on it. Armed with imperial consent, Kido spent the next ten days trying to persuade Cabinet members to accept his peace proposal. When he told Yonai that the emperor "was satisfied with my memorial," Yonai blamed Suzuki for "tying his hands."[99] But to Kido's surprise, Suzuki "was perfectly in sympathy with me."[100] Togo reminded Kido that the Foreign Office would find it difficult to implement his plan in the face of the June 8 decision to follow the army plan. He suggested another Supreme Council meeting to discuss the situation and persuaded Suzuki to set one up.

On June 18, the Supreme Council assembled to review the situation. All agreed that resistance must continue as long as the United States insisted on unconditional surrender.[101] Anami, Umezu, and Toyoda wanted to abide by the June 8 decision to implement the army's plan. They argued that diplomatic negotiations should begin only after they had dealt the enemy a decisive blow.[102] Still, they said they would not hinder the earlier decision to seek Soviet mediation.

The next day, June 19, Togo met with Hirota at Kugenuma, a seaside resort forty miles from Tokyo. Togo pressed Hirota to continue conversations with Malik to obtain peace terms other than unconditional surrender. It was necessary, he said, to secure peace terms before the United States, Britain, and the Soviet Union met for their summit conference at Potsdam, Germany.[103] At the same time, he urged Ambassador Sato in Moscow that "it was a matter of extreme urgency to miss no opportunity to talk with the Soviet leaders" to induce them to help mediate negotiations.[104]

On June 20, Togo received an audience with the emperor. Togo informed him of the Supreme Council's mid-May decision to approach the Soviets and the Hirota-Malik conversations. This was the first time that the emperor had heard of the Soviet initiative. Giving his approval, he added that it was imperative "that the war stop as soon as possible."[105] Togo agreed to comply with his wishes.

The next day Okinawa fell to the Americans. The situation was desperate.

Hirohito Presses for Soviet Initiative

On June 22, on his own initiative, Hirohito summoned the Supreme Council to another imperial conference. Departing from the usual procedure, Hirohito opened the meeting. "With regard to the termination of the war," he said, "you are desired to make definite studies on it and exert yourself to attain it without being trammeled by past ideas."[106] Although Hirohito had not directly repudiated the army's plan, he had, in effect, undermined it by asking the Supreme Council to look at other alternatives.

Hirohito's remarks sparked a lively discussion. With the Soviet initiative, said Togo, steps were now being taken to end the war.[107] Although Anami did not object to attempts "to save the situation," and "expose her weakness to the enemy."[108] Army chief of staff Umezu added that a peace proposal should be treated with "the utmost caution" and only after a "thorough deliberation."[109] Time was short, said the emperor. Thrown off by this rebuke, Umezu replied, "I do not oppose peace."[110]

Without further argument, Hirohito asked that a special envoy be sent to the Soviet Union. Togo replied that an envoy should be sent before the Potsdam Conference convened in early July.[111] No further discussion occurred, and the emperor left after confirming that no one else desired to state an opinion.

After the conference, Suzuki appeared more determined to end the war. "Today," he said, "the emperor said what everyone wanted to say, but yet was afraid to say."[112] Even Anami accepted an "increased tempo" to pursue the Soviet initiative. He could have broken the Suzuki Cabinet at any time by simply resigning. "It shows his character," said Sakomizu, "that he didn't despite what he knew of our negotiations."[113]

On June 23, Togo met with former Premier Hirota. He told him what had happened at the imperial conference and urged him to press on with the Malik negotiations, which had been left pending since June 4. "It would be a bad idea," said Hirota, "to give the Soviets the impression that Japan was in a great hurry."[114] The current situation, replied Togo, "made haste an absolute necessity," and if the Soviets were not interested, Japan needed to know so that it could "speedily consider other measures."[115]

The next evening Hirota and Malik held two meetings at Gora. At the first meeting, Hirota explained that Japan sought "to iron out all sources of friction with Russia." He offered to reconsider Russo-Japanese political and economic relations in Manchuria, arrive at some agreement on the question of China, and supply Russia with commodities from the southern areas.[116] Somewhat jestingly, Hirota added that the combination of the Imperial navy and the Red Army would produce "an invincible alliance."[117] Displaying indifference toward Hirota's proposals, Malik insisted that the Soviets would do nothing until the expiration of the Neutrality Pact. "Our future relations," he said, "will have to be based on concrete actions."[118]

At the second meeting Hirota became more specific. He would trade rubber, tin, lead, tungsten, and other commodities from Southern Asia for Russian oil. "Russia had no oil to spare," replied Malik.[119] Growing desperate, Hirota said that "Japan sought an early peace," but Malik replied that Russia was not a belligerent in the East: "His Excellency Mr. Hirota must be well aware that peace there did not depend on Russia."[120]

After the two meetings, Hirota was frustrated and ready to give up, but Togo insisted that negotiations had to be speeded up.

Five days later, on June 29, Hirota met with Malik at the Soviet embassy in Tokyo for the fourth and last time. This time Hirota submitted proposals in writing. In a memorandum, Japan proposed a treaty of non-aggression and mutual assistance in the maintenance of peace in the Far East. The memorandum said that Japan was ready to neutralize Manchuria. When the war ended, it said, Japan would withdraw its troops from Manchuria, and Japan and the Soviet Union would agree to respect Manchuria's territorial integrity and sovereignty. It further said that Japan would renounce its fishing rights off the coast of Soviet Asia in return for Soviet oil. Finally, it said that Japan was willing to discuss any matter the Soviets wanted to bring up.[121]

Malik promised to convey Japan's proposals to his government and to resume conversations upon receipt of instructions. At first, Hirota's spirits were raised, for this was the first time Malik had made a commitment. But in the next two weeks, although Hirota tried to see Malik again and again, Malik refused on the grounds of illness. Finally, Hirota conveyed his "condolences for the Ambassador's ill health" and negotiations ceased.[122] "The whole episode, "said Kase, "was like angling in waters where no fish lived."[123]

In the days before the Potsdam Conference, set for July 16, the Supreme Council expected some answer from the Soviets. If unfavorable, the Supreme Council concluded that the only choice would be to open up direct negotiations with the United States.[124] Not until July 6, when China's foreign minister T. V. Soong visited Moscow, did the Supreme Council become suspicious of Soviet intentions. Soong was received well by the Soviets and conferred with Stalin. "It is even reported," said Togo, "that the Soviet Union would soon enter the war against Japan."[125] Even at this late date, the Japanese did not realize that the Soviets had already made that decision seven months earlier.

On July 7, the emperor requested a meeting with Suzuki. Time was running short. The Potsdam Conference was soon to begin, and nothing had occurred on the Soviet initiative. Clearly anxious, the emperor urged Suzuki to make haste. "We may miss a precious opportunity," said Hirohito, "while we are trying to ascertain the attitude of the Soviet Union."[126] He brought up his previous suggestion of sending a special envoy to the Soviet Union. The envoy, he added, would be entrusted with a personal letter from himself requesting the Soviets to mediate peace negotiations.[127]

On July 12, Emperor Hirohito summoned Konoye, a former prime minister, to the Imperial Palace. When the emperor came out of an air raid shelter to the temporary audience room, Konoye was shocked by his appearance. The emperor's hair, usually neatly combed, was unkempt, and he looked "pale and terribly haggard."[128] Immediately, Hirohito asked Konoye's views on the war. Konoye did not place much confidence in the army's capability for continuing it, and the morale of the people was not high.[129] "It will be necessary," he said, "to terminate the war without delay."[130] Hirohito asked Konoye to become his special envoy to the Soviet Union. But because Konoye distrusted the Soviets, he was reluctant to accept the job. Hirohito then recalled the "joys and sorrows" he felt during Konoye's two Cabinet administrations.[131] Very touched, with tears in his eyes, Konoye accepted, stating that "he would give his utmost, at the risk of his life, were it the imperial command."[132]

Hirohito emphasized the urgency of the situation. He instructed Konoye "to secure peace at any price, notwithstanding its severity."[133] To Konoye, this might include terms tantamount to unconditional surrender, which the army would not accept. This convinced Konoye that he must take "extraordinary measures" similar to his plan of the summer of 1941. At that time, the United Sates, along with Britain and the Dutch, had clamped an oil embargo on Japan, hoping to force it out of China. To get the embargo lifted, Konoye had intended to settle the China question by meeting with President Franklin Roosevelt at a summit conference in Honolulu, Hawaii. Knowing that the army might not approve the terms of settlement, Konoye would sign the agreement only after cabling to the emperor directly for his sanction. He hoped the army would not go against the emperor's ultimate authority. But the plan fell through because Roosevelt, for reasons still unclear, would not agree to a summit.

Again, with Hirohito's help, Konoye was prepared to resort to the same method on his mission to the Soviet Union. "The plan," said Konoye, "was to present no definite terms to the Soviet Union in advance, leaving these terms to be fixed by negotiation in Moscow and to wire the terms agreed upon to the Emperor for sanction."[134] The emperor would then issue an order to accept them. In this way, the generals would be presented with a fait accompli. It would allow them to save face, for no one would expect them to refuse an imperial order.

Togo-Sato Despatches

On July 10, Ambassador Naotake Sato in Moscow met with vice Commissar Alexander Lozovsky. Sato urged an "immediate reply" to Hirota's June 29 proposal made at Tokyo to Soviet ambassador Malik. Lozovsky's reply was vague and noncommittal. "The Russian Government has not yet given full consideration to Hirota's proposal," said Lozovsky. "It is naturally difficult to predict what my Government's reply will be."[135] Changing the subject, Sato asked about Chinese foreign minister Soong's visit to Moscow. The newspapers, said Sato, interpret Soong's visit as a mission involving discussion of Manchuria and the greater East Asian war. "One should pay no particular attention to newspaper rumors," said Lozovsky.[136]

The next day Sato had a twenty minute interview with Foreign Commissar Vyacheslav Molotov. Sato again asked about the Soviet attitude concerning Hirota's June 29 proposal. "Japan's proposal," said Sato, "is simple and clear, and I hope that it will result in the furtherance and improvement of Russo-Japanese relations."[137] Like Lozovsky, Molotov was non committal. "We shall study Japan's proposal very carefully and make up our minds," he said.[138] He was also vague on the purpose of Soong's visit. "Newspaper and radio reports are full of contradictions," said Molotov. "One can hardly get the truth from them."[139]

On the same day, Togo sent Sato a cable marked "very secret." "You are not to confine yourself," wrote Togo, "to the objective of a rapprochement between Russia and Japan, but are to sound out the extent to which it is possible to make use of Russia with regard to the termination of the war."[140] He added that Japan had no intention of annexing areas occupied as a result of the war: "We hope to terminate the war with a view to establishing and maintaining lasting world peace."[141]

The United States knew about Togo's secret cable about as quickly as Sato did in Moscow. Before the war, U.S. navy cryptographers had broken the Japanese codes. Togo's cable was forwarded to President Harry Truman who was en route to Potsdam. At the Potsdam Conference, Soviet Premier Josef Stalin also reported the Japanese peace feelers to Truman.[142]

On July 12, Sato, totally frustrated with the Soviets, sent a telegram to Togo replying to his July 11 cable. You state, said Sato, that "Japan has not the slightest intention of annexing or keeping in its possession the occupied territories," but the fact remains that Japan has already lost Burma, the Philippines, and Okinawa, the tip of the empire. "How much of an effect do you expect our statements regarding the non-annexation of territories which we have already lost or are about to lose will have on the Soviet authorities?"[143] The Soviets consider Japan's very existence as "problematical," said Sato. "It is no exaggeration to say that the possibility of getting the Soviet

Union to join our side and go along with our reasoning is next to nothing."[144]

Sato insisted that Japan must make the "great decision" to end the war. Once that resolve was taken, he said, "there may be some hope of setting the Soviet Government into motion."[145] But, he added, Japan "has no choice but to accept unconditional surrender or terms closely approximating them."[146]

U.S. navy cryptographers immediately picked up Sato's message. "However sound Sato's views may be," said the intelligence report, "he seems to be, as far as Japanese policy is concerned, merely a voice crying in the wilderness."[147]

That evening, July 12, Togo sent Sato a cable. He informed him that the emperor sought a "swift termination of the war," but since the United States insisted on unconditional surrender, Japan had "no alternative but to see it through in an all-out effort for the sake of survival and the honor of the homeland."[148] Nonetheless, the emperor intended to send Prince Konoye to Moscow bearing his personal letter. Togo instructed Sato to obtain an agreement from the Soviets for Konoye's visit. Since it was not possible for Konoye to reach Moscow before the Russian authorities leave for Potsdam, said Togo, arrangements should be made to meet him as soon as they return from Moscow. Togo requested that Sato submit the request to Molotov.

Fears and Anxieties

On July 13, Sato requested an interview with Molotov. He was told that Molotov "simply could not manage it," and "any matters of importance" should be communicated to Lozovsky.[149] Later that day, Sato met with Lozovsky. He told him that the emperor would send a special envoy bearing an imperial letter to be given to Molotov and Stalin. "I should like to give you a speedy reply," said Lozovsky, but Molotov is leaving "with Stalin for Potsdam this very night." In any case, Lozovsky agreed to send the letter to Molotov in Berlin "without loss of time."[150]

Sato heard nothing until July 18, when Lozovsky told him that his government could not reply because the Japanese request was too vague. "I thought it very strange," said Togo, "that on the ground of being occupied with preparations for a trip, the Soviets would refuse to see at the Berlin conference our special envoy; but stupidly, I failed to imagine the truth."[151]

Shortly after the Lozovsky visit, Sato sent a cable to Togo. He again emphasized the need to make the "great decision" to end the war. If the special envoy goes "no further than we have gone in the past," and lacks any "concreteness beyond abstract words," said Sato, the Soviets will express "feelings of dissatisfaction at the Japanese government's lack of good faith" and thus bring "evil upon the Imperial Household"[152] He added that further interviews were "utterly meaningless" and that there was "absolutely no hope" of effecting the desired favorable attitude." He called for a policy of "watchful waiting" to see what developed at the Berlin conference.[153]

On the eve of the July 17 Potsdam Conference, U.S. leaders were aware of Japan's peace initiative by way of the Soviet Union. U.S. naval intelligence reported that Japan "officially if not publicly" recognized its defeat and turned to the twin aims of "reconciling national pride with defeat" and "finding the best means of salvaging the wreckage of her ambitions."[154]

"It was a difficult and delicate situation," said Secretary of the Navy James Forrestal, "how best to deal with the situation and coordinate Soviet and American aims with the possibility that if pressed too hard, the Japanese would still choose to go down in a suicidal defense."[155]

2.

Truman and the A-Bombs

Political Background

On the eve of America's entry into World War II, U.S. scientists feared that Germany's leaders, familiar with new research on nuclear fission, would order their scientists to build an atomic bomb. Concerned that Germany would develop it first, American scientists, with the help of Albert Einstein, persuaded President Franklin D. Roosevelt to undertake its development. Roosevelt entrusted the task, called the Manhattan Project, to a special unit of the Army Corps of Engineers headed by Major General Leslie R. Groves and J. Robert Oppenheimer, the distinguished physicist from the University of California. The Manhattan Project soon became a joint British-American endeavor to beat the Germans in a race for the atomic bomb. By April 1945 the United States had spent $2 billion on research and development of the bomb, but the date of its completion remained uncertain.

On April 12, 1945, Roosevelt complained of a severe headache, lost consciousness, and died of a massive cerebral hemorrhage. That evening Vice President Harry S. Truman, a former senator from Missouri, took the oath of office to become the thirty-third president of the United States.

Although Truman did not look presidential, his record was a steady rise to the top. A shy man who wore bow ties and spoke with a high-pitched twang, he had a high forehead, pointed nose, thin lips, short graying hair and wore oval-shaped glasses. After serving in World War I, where he saw action at St. Mihiel and the Argonne offensive, he married his childhood sweetheart Bess, whom he described as "the girl with the tanned skin, blond hair, golden as sunshine, and the most beautiful blue eyes I've ever seen."[1] He went on to lose his savings in an oil venture, went bankrupt in a haberdashery, and became county judge and then presiding judge of Jackson County under Thomas Pendergast, the political boss of Western Missouri. In addition, he served two terms as U.S. senator. In 1944, after Vice President Henry A. Wallace had been rejected by the Democratic convention as a candidate for re-election, Truman supported James F. Byrnes of South Carolina for that office. But the convention delegates turned to Truman as a compromise candidate and elected him.

On April 12, the day of Roosevelt's death, a short Cabinet meeting was held at the West Wing of the White House. Afterward, as the members silently filed out, Secretary of War Henry L. Stimson remained behind. In a "low, tense voice," he asked to speak to Truman about a most urgent matter. Stimson described a weapon of tremendous power that the United States had been working on for years. Without identifying it as an atomic bomb, he gave "a general description of the weapon's power and its possible impact on the war."[2] "That was all he felt free to say at the time," said Truman, "and his statement left me puzzled."[3]

Although Truman implied that this was the "first bit of information" that had come to him, he must have suspected that the government was building an atomic bomb. Before becoming vice president, he was chairman of a Senate committee to investigate wasteful military spending. When he started investigating the atomic energy installations in Tennessee and the State of Washington, Stimson told him to stop because "it was the top secret thing of the whole country."[4] "Many of the people who are actually engaged in the work have no idea what it is," said Stimson, "and we who do would appreciate your not going into those plans."[5] Truman backed off from his investigation. He did this, he said, because he knew Stimson to be "an honorable man."[6]

After the April 12 meeting, Stimson was uncertain whether Truman was up to the job of handling the "atomic secrets." In his diary that night, he wrote that Truman "made the impression on me of a man who is willing and anxious to learn," but he is "laboring with the terrific handicap" of becoming president "where the threads of information were so multitudinous that only long previous familiarity could allow him to control them."[7]

Shortly thereafter, General George C. Marshall told Stimson, "We shall not know what he is really like until the pressure begins to be felt."[8]

On April 25, Truman's twelfth day in office, Stimson, along with Groves, who headed the Manhattan Project, or S-1, as it was sometimes called, met with Truman first while Groves waited in an adjoining room outside the president's office.

At seventy-eight years old, Stimson looked like a statesman. With his reserved manner and distinguished appearance, people instinctively trusted him. He looked like a patrician gentleman, with a heavy gold watch chain spread across his high-buttoned vest. He wore starched collars, kept his mustache neatly cropped, parted his short grayish hair in the middle, and spoke in faintly scratchy old man's voice. A graduate of Yale and Harvard law schools and a lifelong Republican, he had served six presidents with distinction. President William H. Taft had named him secretary of war; Calvin Coolidge appointed him governor general of the Philippines; Herbert Hoover made him secretary of state; and Franklin Roosevelt made him secretary of war again in 1940.

Alone with Truman, Stimson took from his briefcase a type-written memorandum of several pages and handed it to the president to read. Stimson had written it that morning. It did not deal with whether the bomb should be used in the war but rather with its long-range political meaning. Although the United States was at present the only country capable of making the bomb, the memorandum said that this situation would not last indefinitely, and "Russia could enter into production within a few years."[9]

Stimson was pessimistic about whether the world could control such a terrible force. "The world," said the memorandum, "in its present state of moral advancement compared with its technical development would be eventually at the mercy of such a weapon" and "modern civilization might be completely destroyed."[10] It added that the question of sharing knowledge of the atomic bomb and the terms upon which it could be shared were central foreign policy issues. Two paths would emerge: in one, the United States would bear "very serious responsibility for any disaster to civilization" that might occur; in the other, if proper use of the weapon were made, it could "bring the world into a pattern in which the peace of the world and our civilization can be saved."[11]

Groves then entered the room through a private door. He presented another report, twenty-four pages long and crammed with scientific data. It stated that a bomb would be tested in mid-July and would yield an equivalent force of about 500 tons of TNT.[12] (It turned out, however, to be 20,000 tons of TNT.) "We answered Truman's questions," said Stimson, "and told him all about the process and about the problems that are coming up."[13]

Truman and Groves decided to form an Interim Committee to study the question of using the atomic bomb against Japan. When secrecy was no longer needed, they agreed, Congress would establish a permanent body to regulate and control the entire field of nuclear energy.[14] The Interim Committee would be made up of leading atomic scientists, Cabinet officials, and a personal representative of the president. Although Truman would make the final decision, the Interim Committee would have more to do with that decision than any other group.[15] "The impression that some people have," said

Margaret Truman, daughter of the president, "that my father made a snap decision to use the bomb, could not be farther from the truth."[16] But according to Stimson, "it was our common objective to be the first to produce an atomic weapon and use it."[17]

Initial Interim Committee Meetings

The Interim Committee was made up of eight men: Stimson as chairman; George L. Harrison, president of the New York Life Insurance Company, who acted as Stimson's special assistant; James F. Byrnes, who served as personal representative of the president; Ralph A. Bard, undersecretary of the navy; and three scientists, Vannevar Bush, Karl T. Compton, and James B. Conant.

A panel of four scientists was to advise the Interim Committee: Enrico Fermi, Arthur E. O. Lawrence, J. R. Oppenheimer, and Arthur H. Compton. All four were top nuclear physicists and worked on the atomic project from the beginning. They were free to discuss the technical matters and political aspects of the problem.[18]

Between May 9 and May 30 the Interim Committee held several meetings. At its first meeting, Byrnes said that the committee's primary purpose "was to make recommendations on the preparation of a test explosion in New Mexico and, if this proved successful, on the use of the bomb against Japan."[19] Stimson added that the project might "mean the doom of civilization or it might mean the perfection of civilization; that it might be a Frankenstein which would eat us up or it might be a project by which the peace of the world would be helped in becoming secure."[20]

Apparently, the Interim Committee never seriously considered not using the bomb. As various members later said, the talk centered on the "assumption that the bomb would be used against Japan," and not "whether but how to use it."[21] As Byrnes heard the scientists predict the destructive power of the bomb, he became "thoroughly frightened." He was almost afraid that the Soviets would develop such a bomb, but "no one seemed too alarmed at the prospect" because "the consensus was that they would have the secret in two or three years, but could not actually produce a bomb in less than six or seven years."[22]

Byrnes-Szilard Meeting

Leo Szilard was one of the most outspoken scientists against the use of the atomic bomb on Japan. At forty-seven years old, Szilard, who was slightly overweight and had a round pixyish face, had "unlimited faith in the human spirit."[23] He was described by Edward Shils, a friend and colleague, as a man of "unresting sensitivity and intelligence, immensely energetic and controlled, and yet with great ease and gentleness of manner."[24] "Japan was essentially defeated," said Szilard, and "it would be wrong to attack its cities with atomic bombs as if atomic bombs were simply another military weapon."[25] Yet this man who argued that the bomb not be dropped was largely responsible for its creation.

Born in Budapest, Hungary, in 1898, Szilard studied biology and electrical engineering as a young man and then enrolled in the Institute of Technology in Berlin, where he studied theoretical physics under Albert Einstein. The two became friends and took out a joint patent in the late 1920s on an electric contrivance for pumping liquid metals. During this time, Szilard became fascinated with the idea of atomic energy after reading H. G. Wells' science fiction books predicting the release of such energy, and its consequences for warfare. "If we could find an element which is split by neutrons," wrote Wells, "and which would emit two neutrons when it absorbed one neutron, such an element, if assembled in sufficiently large mass could sustain a nuclear chain reaction."[26]

While visiting the United States, in 1939, Szilard learned that two German physicists had discovered nuclear fission in uranium. On borrowed equipment, Szilard and Enrico Fermi set up experiments at Columbia University and determined that uranium would sustain a chain reaction. "That night," said Szilard, "I knew that the world was headed for trouble."[27] Realizing that war was approaching, Szilard drafted a letter to President Roosevelt describing his findings and persuaded Einstein to sign it. This convinced Roosevelt to set up the Manhattan Project to develop and build an atomic bomb.

During the war, Szilard was among several scientists working on plutonium production at the Chicago Metallurgical Laboratory. But by 1944, he realized that the Germans were not developing atomic bombs and would soon be defeated. He was now concerned that the United States would drop the bomb on Japan, "when her defeat seemed assured."[28]

Concerned with the scientists' isolation from policymakers, Szilard persuaded Einstein to write Roosevelt another letter dated March 25, 1945. In it, Einstein requested Roosevelt to receive Szilard, "who proposes to submit to you certain considerations and recommendations," and "that he now is greatly concerned about the lack of adequate contact between scientists who are doing this work and those members of your Cabinet who are responsible for formulating policy."[29] In conclusion, Einstein hoped "that the President would give his personal attention to what Dr. Szilard had to say."[30]

Fearing that Einstein's letter would not reach Roosevelt through regular channels, Szilard sent the letter to Eleanor Roosevelt, asking her to arrange a meeting between the president and himself. He received an appointment for May 8, 1945.

Szilard then prepared a memorandum for the president outlining his views against using the atomic bomb. He warned that dropping it on Japan would precipitate an atomic arms race between the United States and the Soviet Union. Each nation, he wrote, would accumulate "vast quantities of atomic bombs" and risk "the possibility of the outbreak of a 'preventive' war."[31] He advocated a system of international control of atomic energy and asked for the formation of a separate Cabinet-level committee made up of scientists so they could express their views to the government.[32]

Szilard showed the memorandum to Arthur H. Compton, who headed the Chicago project phase for developing the atomic bomb. Since he was an "establishment man," Szilard expected him to object to much of the memorandum. "I was therefore much relieved," said Szilard, "when he told me that he hoped I would get the memorandum into the hands of the President and that it would receive the attention of the President."[33] Back at his office, Szilard was met by his assistant, Norman Hilberry. "We have just heard over the radio that President Roosevelt died," said Hilberry.[34]

With Roosevelt dead, Szilard now faced the problem of getting in touch with Truman. Through contacts in Kansas City, Missouri, Szilard obtained an invitation to the White House to see Matt Connelly, Truman's appointment secretary. Szilard and his friend Walter Bartky, associate director of the Chicago project, immediately left for Washington. When Connelly received the two men, Szilard handed him a copy of Einstein's letter and memorandum. After carefully reading them, Connelly said, "The President thought that your concern would be about this matter, and he asked me to make an appointment with you to visit James Byrnes in Spartanburg, South Carolina."[35]

Szilard agreed but wondered why Truman wanted him to see Byrnes, who was out of government and living as a private citizen. "Clearly, Truman was going to give Byrnes a position in the government," said Szilard, "but what position?"[36]

James F. Byrnes had been in politics since 1910. He had served in Congress, the Senate, and on the Supreme Court. After the attack on Pearl Harbor, he left the Court and became director of Economic Stabilization and then director of War Mobilization, one of the most powerful jobs in Washington.

Byrnes was a short, balding man, with an easy Irish charm, intense eyes that could slant downward shyly with a stranger or bore straight into a foe. He was Truman's main rival for vice president at the 1944 convention. In a complicated convention power play, Roosevelt at first convinced Byrnes that he would be the choice for vice president and then betrayed him to pick Truman. Although some hard feelings remained between the two rivals, Truman respected Byrnes, a tough and shrewd politician who would shortly become his secretary of state.

Szilard, accompanied by Bartky and physicist Arthur H. Compton, met with Byrnes on May 28 at Spartanburg. Although Byrnes had a reputation as a southern gentleman, Szilard did not find that to be the case; neither did Byrnes find Szilard to be the perfect guest. "His general demeanor," said Byrnes, "and his desire to participate in policymaking made an unfavorable impression on me."[37] If the United States used the bomb against Japan, said Szilard, "we might start an atomic race between America and Russia which might end with the destruction of both countries."[38]

Byrnes was skeptical. He told Szilard that General Groves "had informed him that Russia did not have any uranium," and if that were the case, it couldn't build an atomic bomb.[39] Szilard argued that Russia had access to uranium ore in Czechoslovakia and most probably in Russia, too.[40]

Szilard argued that the government should postpone testing the bomb until it had developed a policy "on the issue of how to cope with the problem that the bomb would pose to the world."[41] Byrnes replied that the government had spent two billion dollars making the bomb, "How would you get Congress to appropriate money for atomic energy research," said Byrnes, "if you do not show results for the money which has been spent already?"[42]

Byrnes was also concerned about Russia's postwar behavior. Russian troops had moved into Hungary and Romania, he said, and "you come from Hungary. You would not want Russia to stay in Hungary indefinitely?"[43] He continued: "It would be very difficult to persuade Russia to withdraw her troops from these countries," and "Russia might be more manageable if impressed by American military might."[44] Szilard was "completely flabbergasted" by Byrnes's assumption that "rattling the bomb might make Russia more manageable."[45]

Szilard was depressed by the meeting. Byrnes failed to see that the main problem was preventing an arms race, not throwing America's weight around to justify the bomb's expense or to make Russia more manageable. "How much better off the world might be had I been born in America and became influential in American politics, and had Byrnes been born in Hungary and studied physics," said Szilard. "In all probability there would have been no atomic bomb, and no danger of an arms race between America and Russia."[46]

Groves was upset with the meeting. He knew of it because one of his intelligence agents had been following Byrnes, "as they followed others connected with the project."[47] Groves considered the visit a "grave breach of security."[48]

Interim Committee Conference

To settle the question of using the atomic bomb, the Interim Committee held a two-day conference from May 31 to June 1. Fourteen men were present, including the four advisory scientists and Generals Marshall and Groves. Although the final decision rested with Truman, the conference gave its "fullest consideration of whether and in what manner the bomb should be used."[49] By this time, Germany had surrendered. The fighting for Okinawa was at its most critical phase, and it would be another seven weeks before the first test of an atomic bomb could be made.[50]

On the first day of the conference, the Interim Committee discussed a broad range of topics dealing with the use of the atomic bomb. It started with the question of whether to share atomic secrets with the Soviets. We should open up the subject with them, said Oppenheimer, "in a tentative fashion and in the most general terms without giving them any details of our productive effort."[51] Compton advocated a "cooperative understanding" with the Soviet Union.[52] We should avoid rigid security over the project, he said, which "would result in a certain sterility of research and as very real competitive disadvantage to the nation."[53]

Bush advocated caution. "Even the British," he said, "do not have any of our blueprints on plants."[54] The Soviets' uncooperative attitude in military matters, said Marshall, stemmed from their need to maintain security, and he had accepted this reason in dealing with them.[55] The United States should stay ahead in production and research, said Byrnes, and "at the same time make every effort to better our political relations with Russia."[56] All agreed with this view.

The committee turned to a discussion on the use of the bomb. Compton brought up the idea of demonstrating the bomb before foreign observers, but the committee rejected it. Some said that the Japanese would not send representatives to see the new weapon.[57] Others said that the reliability of the bomb's electronic devices had not yet been proved, and failure would be counterproductive.[58]

"Even the New Mexico test," said Stimson, "would not give final proof that any given bomb was certain to explode when dropped from an airplane," and "nothing would have been more damaging to our effort to obtain surrender than a warning or a demonstration followed by a dud."[59]

The committee then discussed the idea of warning the Japanese about the murderous potential of the new weapon, and when and where it would be dropped. But there were objections to this, too. The idea was rejected, said Stimson, because "we felt that American prisoners of war would be brought into the designated area."[60] Some committee members feared that the Japanese would concentrate their fighters to intercept planes carrying atomic bombs.[61]

Groves raised the issue of "undesirable scientists." Since the program's inception, he said, it had been plagued "by the presence of certain scientists of doubtful discretion and uncertain loyalty."[62] All agreed that nothing could be done with them until the United States dropped the bomb, and then "steps should be taken to sever them from the program," and "to proceed with a general weeding out of personnel no longer needed."[63]

On June 1 the Interim Committee unanimously agreed on three basic recommendations for the use of the atomic bomb. First, it should be dropped on Japan as soon as possible. Second, it should be used on a dual target, "a military installation or war plant surrounded by or adjacent to houses and other buildings most susceptible to damage." Finally, it should be used without prior warning.[64] Bard was the only member to dissent from these recommendations. Thus, the committee recommended that the target be both a military one and surrounded by houses, and implicit in this was "the realization that many civilians would be killed."[65]

On the same day, Byrnes communicated the Interim Committee's recommendations to Truman. While members were reluctant to use the atomic bomb, he told Byrnes, there was no way of avoiding it.[66] "I had realized," said Truman, "that an atomic bomb explosion would inflict damage and casualties beyond imagination." But the Interim Committee concluded, "We can propose no technical demonstration likely to bring an end to the war; we see no acceptable alternative to direct military use."[67] Unlike the Interim Committee, however, Truman knew about Japan's Soviet peace initiative, and he knew that the Japanese would not accept unconditional surrender terms or the loss of their emperor.

A few days later, Stimson finally presented Truman with the Interim Committee's recommendations. "The conclusions of the committee were similar to my own," said Stimson. "I felt that to extract a genuine surrender from the emperor and his military advisers, they must be administered a tremendous shock which would carry convincing proof of our power to destroy the Empire."[68]

The Franck Report

In early June, Compton returned to the University of Chicago's Metallurgical Laboratory where work on building the atomic bomb was continuing. He was anxious about having to face Szilard and other scientists who were against dropping the bomb on Japan. Compton was most concerned about physicist James Franck. Because Franck was sensitive to the moral implications of the bomb, he agreed to work at the Metallurgical Laboratory if he could present his views on using the weapon to the nation's leaders before they made the decision to use it. Compton had agreed to Franck's terms.

Although the Interim Committee had decided to use the bomb without warning, Compton summoned the Chicago scientists and asked them if they would like him to present their views on the bomb to the Interim Committee's scientific panel. They agreed, and Compton named Franck to become chairman if the Committee on Social and Political Implications to coordinate ideas and write a report for him, Compton, to give to the scientific panel.

The new committee was made up of seven Chicago physicists, but only three of them formulated the report. Franck, a German, wrote up the initial notes, but his English was too poor to write the report. He gave his notes to Eugene R. Rabinowitch, another committee member, but it was Szilard who shaped the Franck Report.

Although the scientists on this project do not presume to speak "authoritatively on problems of national and international policy," the Franck Report began, they urge that the political problems arising from the mastering of nuclear power "be recognized in all their gravity." The report offered some suggestions to the solution of these grave problems.[69]

It stressed the importance of considering the use of nuclear bombs as a problem of long-range policy rather than for short-range military advantage and urged placing them under international control. It said that the United States would not be able to retain a monopoly of nuclear weapons for more than a few years. The fundamental facts of nuclear power were "common knowledge," and the scientists working on it were scattered in too many universities and research institutions throughout the country to effectively control atomic secrets.[70] A quantitative advantage in numbers would not protect the United States from sudden attack. "Just because a potential enemy will be afraid of being 'outnumbered and out-gunned'," said the report, "the temptation for him may be overwhelming" to strike "a sudden unprovoked blow."[71]

The report also called for an international organization for peace. It said that the existence of nuclear weapons was the most compelling argument for "an international authority which would make all resort to force in international conflicts impossible."[72] In the absence of an international authority, however, nations could still be diverted from "total mutual destruction" by international agreements banning a nuclear arms race. But if the United States dropped an atomic bomb on Japan, it would destroy the chances for international arms agreements. "It will be very difficult to persuade the world that a nation which was capable of secretly preparing and suddenly releasing a weapon, as indiscriminate as the rocket bomb and a thousand times more destructive, is to be trusted in this proclaimed desire of having such weapons abolished by international agreement."[73]

If the bomb had to be used, the report advocated a demonstration before the eyes of all the "United Nations" on a desert or barren island. It warned that if an international agreement was not concluded after the demonstration, it would mean "a flying start toward an unlimited arms race." If this race was inevitable, "we have every reason to delay its beginning as long as possible in order to increase our head start still further."[74]

If the United States dropped the atomic bomb on Japan, the report concluded, it would lose world support, precipitate an arms race, and diminish the possibility of an international agreement on controlling atomic weapons. Much more favorable conditions would result from revealing the bomb to the world by a demonstration in an uninhabited area.[75]

All seven members of the Franck committee approved the report, but they didn't know what to do with it. No one on the committee trusted the scientific panel. They decided to give the report to Stimson in the hopes that it would influence his decision, and he, in turn, would persuade Truman not to drop the bomb on Japan. Since Compton was going to Washington shortly, the committee asked him to deliver it. He agreed on the condition that he could include a cover note.

Perhaps the committee assumed Compton's note would be favorable, but it included two points that contradicted the report. "It was necessary," said Compton, "to point out that the report, while it called attention to difficulties that might result from the use of the bomb, did not mention the probable net saving of many lives, nor that if the bomb were not used in the present war the world would have no adequate warning as to what was to be expected if war should break out again."[76] However, he added, the importance of the problem and the weight of the arguments presented "for never permitting the bombs to be used in war," are such that the report deserves Stimson's attention.[77]

Still, the committee did not really trust Compton, and Franck traveled with him to Washington. The two men went to Stimson's Pentagon office, but he was not there. Instead, they gave the report and Compton's cover note to R. Gordon Arneson, the assistant to George Harrison, who was Stimson's special assistant. Arneson handed the documents over to Harrison who showed them to Stimson. Whether Stimson read them was unclear. He told Harrison that they should be given to the scientific panel and the Interim Committee, the two bodies that had already decided that the bomb should be dropped without warning. Harrison gave the documents back to Compton to give to the scientific panel.[78]

Reply to Franck Report

In mid-June, Compton met with the scientific panel in Los Alamos, New Mexico. He did not bring the Franck Report with him. Instead, he interpreted it for the panel. The discussion centered on whether a demonstration of the bomb was feasible. Lawrence argued the hardest for a demonstration. But in the end, all were against it, and on June 16 the panel gave the Interim Committee its reply to the Franck Report: "We can propose no technical demonstration likely to bring an end to the war; we see no acceptable alternative to direct military use."[79]

"On the whole," said Oppenheimer, "you are inclined to think if it was needed to put an end to the war and had a chance of doing so we thought that was the right thing to do."[80] Much later, however, he said, "The physicists have known sin, and this is a knowledge which they cannot lose."[81]

On June 21, the Interim Committee met to review the scientific panel's reply to the Franck Report. Like the scientific panel, the committee did not see a copy of the report that it was judging. Apparently, there was little discussion on the issue. The Interim Committee just reaffirmed its position agreed at the May 31 and June 1 meetings: The weapon should be used against Japan at the earliest opportunity, without warning, and on a military target surrounded by homes.[82]

The discussion turned to the upcoming "Big Three" conference and informing the Soviets about the atomic bomb. The committee agreed that the United States needed Soviet cooperation in future international controls over atomic energy.[83] It also agreed that Truman should tell Soviet premier Josef Stalin that the United States was working on the atomic bomb and expected to use it against Japan. If Stalin pressed for more information, Truman should say that "we were not ready to furnish more information at present."[84] In addition, he should say that the United States would discuss this matter in the future to ensure "that the weapon would become an aid to peace."[85]

Continuing Debate

The debate on the use of the atomic bomb continued throughout the summer of 1945. James B. Conant, chairman of the National Defense Research Committee and a member of the Interim Committee, recommended to Stimson that "the bomb must be used," for what was "the only way to awaken the world to the necessity of abolishing war altogether. No technical demonstration could take the place of the actual use with its horrible results."[86]

"We were all afraid of the future," said Donald Hurnig, a scientist at the Los Alamos Laboratory, "but as to its immediate use, we thought then that it would have the effect of ending the war."[87]

"I had no doubt about the desirability of using it," said Vannevar Bush. "I knew that it would end the war and that in doing so it would save very many American lives."[88]

"I wanted to end the war," added Arthur Compton. "I knew all too well the destruction and human agony the bombs would cause," but "I wanted the war to end."[89]

Generals Groves and Marshall were adamantly opposed to a demonstration. To Groves, it was difficult to understand how anyone could ignore the effect of the "overwhelming surprise of the bomb" on the Japanese people and their government: "To achieve surprise was one of the reasons we had tried so hard to maintain our security."[90] The bombs were the perfect weapon, said Marshall, for "shock action."[91] Stimson and Byrnes agreed that "an actual combat demonstration" would make "a far greater impression" on the Japanese and on those who needed to be "persuaded that postwar international control of the atomic bomb was in their long-range interest."[92]

Other scientists and members of government advocated a test demonstration of the bomb. "I would have been much happier if we had first demonstrated the bomb," said physicist Edward Teller. "The misconceptions has gotten around that we had only two bombs," he said. "We had at least the capability to produce more bombs before any planned invasion."[93]

"There should have been a demonstration," said former President Herbert Hoover.[94] Admiral Lewis L. Strauss advocated a demonstration over Japan's redwood forest. "The war was very nearly over," he said. "The Japanese were nearly ready to capitulate."[95]

Farrington Daniels, the director of the Metallurgical Laboratory at the University of Chicago, polled 150 scientists working on the atomic bomb. His results, released on July 12, 1945, showed that 124 scientists "favored some kind of demonstration" before using the bomb against Japan.[96]

Although Undersecretary of the Navy Bard had previously agreed with the other seven members of the Interim Committee on a quick use of the atomic bomb, on June 27, he wrote Truman a memorandum advising another course. Because the United States is a humanitarian nation, he wrote, "Japan should have some preliminary warning for say two or three days in advance of use."[97] At the same time, he added, Truman should offer assurances "with regard to the Emperor of Japan and the treatment of the Japanese nation following unconditional surrender," which might present "the opportunity which the Japanese are looking for."[98]

In early July, Groves ordered the Chicago staff not to contact Los Alamos. To Szilard, who by now suspected Compton of treachery, this could only mean that Los Alamos was getting ready to test the bomb, and Groves wanted to hide it from Chicago. If the test was successful, Szilard feared, this would convince Truman to use the bomb against Japan, if he was not already convinced. Szilard wanted the scientists to go on record opposing such action, not as the Franck Report argued, on the grounds of expediency, but on moral grounds.[99]

Szilard framed a petition to the president, arguing that atomic bombs were primarily a means to destroy cities: "Thus a nation which sets the precedent of using these newly liberated forces of nature for purposes of destruction may have to bear the responsibility of opening the door to an era of devastation on an unimaginable scale."[100] He concluded by calling for outright rejection of the use of atomic bombs on moral considerations. But he soon realized that more scientists would sign the petition if it had a milder conclusion. He changed it to read that "the United States shall not resort to the use of atomic bombs in this war unless the terms which will be imposed upon Japan have been made public in detail and Japan knowing these terms has refused to surrender."[101]

Szilard wrote a cover letter to each potential signer, explaining that the petition was based on purely moral considerations. "However small the chance might be that our petition may influence the course of events," wrote Szilard, "I personally feel that it would be a matter of importance if a large number of scientists who have worked in this field went clearly and unmistakably on record as to their opposition on moral grounds to the use of these bombs in the present phase of the war."[102] He added that many people had criticized individual Germans for not speaking out against the Nazis, although they could not protest without risking the loss of liberty or life: "We are in a position to raise our voices without incurring any such risks even though we might incur the displeasure of some of those who are at present in change of controlling the work on 'atomic power.'"[103]

Szilard sent a copy of the petition to all the group leaders in the Metallurgical Laboratory and asked them to circulate it within their groups. Grover C. Thompson, a resident intelligence agent, saw a copy and informed Groves, who became enraged and ordered the petition stopped, but Szilard refused to obey. "We did not yield to the army's demand," said Szilard. "The right to petition is anchored in the Constitution, and when you are a naturalized citizen you are supposed to learn the Constitution prior to obtaining your citizenship."[104]

Groves moved carefully because he didn't want to press the issue of civil liberties with Szilard. He ordered that Szilard could show the petition only "to those possessing the extent of information possessed by Leo Szilard and who knew as much information as was contained in the petition."[105] Since Szilard knew more than most of the other scientists, this greatly reduced the effectiveness of the petition.

Szilard circulated his petition at the Chicago laboratory and the laboratories at Oak Ridge and Los Alamos. Security officials blocked its circulation at the former, and Oppenheimer made sure the petitions were not circulated at the latter.

Sixty-seven Chicago scientists signed Szilard's petition, dated July 17. Szilard wanted to forward it directly to Truman, but the other scientists insisted on going through regular channels. "I did not like this idea," said Szilard, "because I was just not sure whether the regular channels would forward the petition or whether they would sabotage it by filing it until the war was over."[106] He finally yielded, however, and handed the petition to Compton, who gave it to Colonel Nichols, Groves's deputy, who then transmitted it to Groves on July 25. Groves kept it until August 1 and then sent it by messenger to Stimson's office.[107] By this time, Truman was at the Potsdam Conference and did not see it.

When Groves received the petition on July 25, he feared that even with Truman in Potsdam, Szilard might somehow get a copy to the president. After all, he had contacted Roosevelt when he wanted the bomb built. Hoping to strengthen his case against a demonstration, Groves asked Compton to supervise an opinion poll among the scientists. He drew up a questionnaire with five alternatives. The first advocated dropping the bomb without warning; the second advocated a military demonstration in Japan; the third advocated an experimental demonstration in the United States with representatives from Japan present; the fourth advocated a public experimental demonstration in the United States; and the fifth advocated refraining from its use in the war.[108]

The first two proposals contained much ambiguity. The first one did not specify the manner of using the atomic bomb, and the second was unclear on what a military demonstration meant. Did it mean "full use" of the weapon on people or on an uninhabited area of Japan?

Compton polled only the Chicago scientists and not those in Los Alamos, Berkeley, Oak Ridge, or other project centers. Fifteen percent of the respondents favored the first proposal; 46 percent favored the second; 26 percent the third; 11 percent the fourth; and 2 percent the fifth.[109] Consequently, 83 percent (proposals two, three, and four) presumably wanted a warning, but Compton turned the figures around to argue that 87 percent (proposals one, two, and three) voted for the bomb's military use.[110]

The final decision on whether to drop the atomic bomb on Japan rested with Truman. "Where and when to use the atomic bomb was up to me," said Truman. "I had to make the decision."[111] The next two chapters will deal with how and under what circumstances he came to make that decision.

3.

Ending the War:
The American Point of View

Debate Over Unconditional Surrender Terms

The U.S. military was aware of the burden of imposing terms of unconditional surrender on Japan. The Okinawa campaign was long, hard, and bloody, and fighting would be even worse in the invasion, subjugation, and occupation of Japan's home islands.

On May 3, 1945, the Joint Chiefs of Staff advocated that Truman issue a declaration of intentions to clarify unconditional surrender terms. The declaration would explain that unconditional surrender "does not mean the extermination or enslavement of the Japanese people" but "that the people of Japan after eliminating the burdens of militarism, can begin to earn their way back into the fellowship of peace-loving and law-abiding nations."[1] In other words, surrender would not mean "national suicide" for the Japanese nation.[2]

To the proposed declaration, the State Department wanted Truman to add a definite statement on the retention of Emperor Hirohito. This group included Undersecretary of State Joseph Grew and his assistants; Eugene H. Doorman, former counselor of the U.S. embassy in Tokyo; Joseph W. Ballantine, director of the Office of Far Eastern Affairs; George Hubbard Blakeslee, chairman of Far Eastern Area Committee. Such a statement, they said, would greatly strengthen the emperor's "peace-minded advisers," weaken the "intransigent militarists," and lead to an early surrender.[3]

"The Emperor's voice," said Grew, former ambassador to Japan, "is the only voice which the Japanese people, and probably the Japanese military forces, are likely to obey."[4]

The State Department had an uphill battle. In 1945, a U.S. public opinion poll showed that one-third of the respondents favored Hirohito's execution; another one-fifth his imprisonment or exile; one-sixth his trial by judicial process; and only 3 percent his retention as emperor.[5]

On May 8, shortly after Germany surrendered, Truman issued a press statement modifying unconditional surrender. The Japanese military and naval forces must lay down their arms unconditionally, but, he said, "we have no desire or intention to destroy or enslave the Japanese people."[6] The statement included a warning: "The striking power and intensity of our blows will steadily increase, and will bring utter destruction to Japan's war production."[7] Nothing was said about retaining Emperor Hirohito. "I knew," said Grew, "that when the time came for Japan's surrender, the emperor was the only one who could bring it about."[8]

Meanwhile, Harry Hopkins, Truman's special adviser, was in Moscow conferring with Stalin. On May 28, Stalin told Hopkins that the Allies should go through with unconditional surrender and "destroy the military might and forces of Japan once and for all."[9] As a tactic, the Allies could agree to milder terms, but once the war had ended, "give them the works."[10] He assured Hopkins that Soviet armies would be deployed on the Manchurian border by August 8 and would launch their attack during the same month."[11]

Grew's Struggle to Retain the Emperor

On May 28, acting on his own initiative, Grew called on President Truman and urged him to allow the Japanese to keep Emperor

Hirohito. He gave Truman a draft of a proposed declaration to that effect, drawn up by the State Department. It stated that the Allies would withdraw from Japan as soon as a government representative of the people of Japan was established, and "this may include a constitutional monarchy under the present dynasty."[12]

Truman appeared to be in agreement. "I had already given thought to this matter myself," said Truman, "and it seemed to me a sound idea."[13] He told Grew to discuss the proposal with Secretary of War Stimson, Secretary of the Navy James V. Forrestal, and the Joint Chiefs of Staff, and then to report to him the consensus of that group.[14]

On May 29, Grew called a morning meeting in Stimson's office at the Pentagon. In attendance were Stimson, Forrestal, Chief of Staff Marshall, and Grew's assistants Elmer Davis, Judge Samuel Rosenman, and Doorman. Admiral Ernest J. King, chief of the Bureau of Naval Operations, was absent.

Grew passed around his proposed declaration clarifying the terms of unconditional surrender. Acting on instructions from Truman, he said that the meeting's purpose was to get the attendees' views on it. If U.S. surrender terms included the retention of the emperor, said Grew, the Japanese "would see a way open to an orderly surrender and acceptance of foreign occupations," for only the emperor "could order capitulation of the Japanese armed forces."[15] The president assured me, he added, that "his own thinking ran along the same lines as mine."[16]

After an hour of discussion, Stimson, Forrestal, and Marshall agreed in principle with Grew's declaration but considered the timing wrong for the president. Because the fighting on Okinawa was still going on, they argued, the Japanese would view the declaration "as a confession of weakness."[17] However, that was not the real reason. In his diary that night, Stimson wrote, "I could not discuss the real feature which would govern the whole situation, namely S-1. We had hesitated just before they came in whether we should go on with the meeting at all on account for that feature but decided to let Grew, who was the one who really had gotten it up, to go ahead with it."[18]

Grew informed Truman that Forrestal, Stimson, and Marshall considered the timing wrong and recommended that the proposed declaration be set aside temporarily.

But Grew did not give up. Throughout June, he continued to press hard for retention of the emperor and for a clarification of un-conditional surrender terms. He appeared to have some support. Admiral William Leahy, presidential chief of staff, agreed that "a surrender of Japan can be arranged with terms that can be accepted by Japan and that will make fully satisfactory provision for America's defense against future trans-Pacific aggression."[19]

While all agreed on the demilitarization of Japan, said Stimson, "it was equally true that no one desired the permanent subjugation of Japan, the enslavement of her people or any attempt to dictate what kind of government the country should have."[20] According to General Marshall, however, unconditional surrender had "a great psychological effect on our people that we were going through with this thing to the finish."[21]

On June 16, with the fall of Okinawa imminent, Grew wrote another draft proclamation clarifying terms of unconditional surrender. He told Rosenman there was no "good reason to defer such action until the meeting of the Big Three," set for mid-July.[22] Although Truman had stated that unconditional surrender did not mean extermination or enslavement of the Japanese people, Grew added two points. First, Truman must state that the Japanese will "be permitted to determine for themselves the nature of their political structure"; and second, the United States has no wish "to deprive the Japanese of a reasonable peacetime economy to prevent starvation and to enable them gradually to work their way back into the family of nations."[23]

Two days later, he gave Truman his clarification and urged him to issue it immediately. Every appropriate step should be taken, said Grew, to encourage Japan's peace movement: "Nothing could be lost by such a step and in my opinion the sooner it was taken the better."[24]

Truman disagreed. He had decided to issue a proclamation of surrender at the forthcoming Big Three conference at Potsdam. By that time, he would know more about Soviet participation against Japan and the atomic bomb test scheduled for mid-July. If the bomb test was successful, said Truman later, "I wanted to afford Japan a clear chance to end the fighting before we made use of this newly gained power." But if it should fail, "then it would be even more important to us to bring about a surrender before we had to make a physical conquest of Japan."[25]

To Grew, Truman's delay was a missed opportunity for peace. "If the President had made a public categorical statement that surrender would not mean the elimination of the present dynasty," said Grew, "the surrender of Japan could have been hastened."[26]

At the same time, the release of a Combined Chiefs of Staff intelligence report strengthened Grew's argument. It said: "The idea of foreign occupation of the Japanese homeland, foreign custody of the Emperor, and the loss of prestige entailed by the acceptance of 'unconditional surrender' are most revolting to the Japanese."[27]

The June 18 Military Strategy Session

At the White House on the afternoon of June 18, Truman attended a special military strategy session to discuss the final plans for the defeat of Japan. Those in attendance included Stimson, Forrestal, Assistant Secretary of War John J. McCloy, Admirals Leahy and Ernest J. King, and Generals Marshall and Ira C. Eaker. Neither Secretary of State Grew nor any of his assistants were present. The final plans which were drawn up without reference to the atomic bomb, included an intensified sea and air blockade and increased bombing from bases in Okinawa, Iwo Jima, the Marianas, and the Philippines. The military planners set November 1, 1945, as the invasion date for the southern island of Kyushu and the spring of 1946 for the invasion of Honshu. Counting military and naval forces, over five million men would participate.[28]

Truman and Marshall were adamant on the need for Soviet entry into the war. To Truman, his immediate goal at Potsdam "would be to get the Russians into the war against the Japs."[29] "It was hoped," he said, "that some of Japan's forces would continue to be preoccupied in China and others would be prevented from reinforcing the home islands if Russia were to enter the war."[30]

"The impact of Russian entry on the already hopeless Japanese," said Marshall, the military leader Truman most admired, "may well be the decisive action leveling them into capitulation at that time or shortly thereafter if we land in Japan."[31] Not everyone agreed on the need for Soviet entry into the war. Admiral King and General Douglas MacArthur, army commander in the Pacific, discounted the importance of Soviet participation. There was no question, said King, that the United States "could handle it alone." To MacArthur, who was not a participant in the meeting, "any intervention by Russia during 1945 was not required" because Japan had already "been gutted," and "was now at the mercy of air raids and invasion."[32] On this issue, however, Truman did not seek MacArthur's views or comments."[33]

Casualty figures for the invasion of Kyushu were unclear. In the first month ashore, Marshall said that U.S. casualties would not exceed the 31,000 suffered in the invasion of Luzon in the Philippines.[34] "It is a grim fact," he said, "that there is not an easy, bloodless way to victory in war."[35] In Admiral King's view, the casualty rate would be higher, between 31,000 and 41,000.[36] It was estimated, said Truman later, that landing on Kyushu would mean 700,000 casualties: "250,000 killed and 500,000 maimed for life."[37]

There was some debate over whether an invasion of Japan's home islands was necessary. The invasion of the home islands was not necessary, said Admiral King, because "United States sea and air power was sufficient to defeat Japan."[38]

"It was already clear," said Stimson, "That even before the invasion we should be able to inflict enormously severe damage on the Japanese homeland by the combined application of 'conventional' sea and air power," but "the critical question was whether this kind of action would induce surrender."[39]

"I was convinced it could be done," said army air force general Henry (Hap) Arnold, who was not present at the meeting. "I did not believe Japan could stand the punishment from the air that Germany had taken."[40] Air power alone, said Marshall, was unable to defeat

Germany, and the invasion plan "offered the only way the Japanese could be forced into a feeling of utter helplessness."[41]

Forrestal sided with Marshall. "Even if we wished to besiege Japan for a year or a year and a half," he said "the capture of Kyushu would still be essential."[42]

Truman seemed to express some ambivalence about the need to invade Japan's home islands. He ordered his generals to plan for the Kyushu operation, but they were to consult with him again before its execution, and he would reserve until later his decision on whether to invade Honshu Island.[43] "The name given to our invasion plan [of Kyushu] was Olympic," said Truman, "but I saw nothing Godly about the killing of all the people necessary to make that invasion."[44] He also withheld for later consideration the idea of a prolonged occupation of Japan. Leahy hoped Truman would go against it. "The cost of such an operation," said Leahy, "will be enormous in both lives and treasure."[45]

After Truman's decision had been made, when the meeting was about to break up, McCloy turned the discussion to a diplomatic initiative, which he said should receive serious attention. "There was a submerged class in Japan," said Stimson, "who do not favor the present war," but they would "fight tenaciously if attacked on their own ground." Something should be done to appeal to them he said, before "it became necessary to come to grips with them."[46]

McCloy agreed: "The time was propitious now to study closely all possible means of bringing out the influence of the submerged group in Japan."[47]

Leahy added that he was against unconditional surrender or the need for invasion. The concept, he said, "had been approved only as it applied to Europe," not Japan, and he was sure "that a surrender could be arranged with terms acceptable to Japan" and not against America's defense interests.[48] "I was unable to see any justification from a national defense point of view," he added later, "for an invasion of an already thoroughly defeated Japan."[49]

McCloy next turned attention to the atomic bomb. He advocated warning the Japanese of U.S. possession of it.[50] Although all those in the meeting knew about the development of the atomic bomb, his uninhibited mention of it generated a sense of shock even among that select group.[51] In fact, his interference "annoyed" the generals. In principle, they were not opposed to political action, but according to McCloy, "several of the Chiefs were not too happy about it."[52] But Truman seemed to welcome the suggestion of a political initiative and asked Stimson if he had any more comments on it. Stimson replied that he needed more time to formulate his views.[53] Shortly thereafter, with the help of Grew and Forrestal, he put together a surrender proposal that would become the basis of the Potsdam Declaration.

The Importance of Soviet Participation

In February 1945, at the Yalta conference, Stalin agreed to enter the war against Japan two or three months after Germany's defeat. In return, the Soviet Union would obtain from Japan the Kuriles, South Sakhalin and adjacent islands, and from China a lease of Port Arthur as a naval base: the "preeminent interests" of the Soviet Union would be safeguarded at Dairen as well as its interests in the South Manchurian and Chinese Eastern Railways; and it would remain dominant in Outer Mongolia. At the same time, the Soviet Union pledged recognition of full Chinese sovereignty in Manchuria and indicated its willingness to conclude a pact of friendship and alliance with Chiang Kai-shek's government.[54]

The United States based its battle plan on the assumption that Japan had a huge army in Manchuria, the Kwantung army. U.S. war planners considered it to contain the cream of the enemy's troops. If this were true, the United States believed it needed Soviet participation to pin down this army as well as the additional Japanese troops on the Asian mainland fighting the Chinese.[55] Moreover, the United States had an aversion to fighting on the mainland of China. Stimson told Marshall that he did not think the country would stand for a large number of U.S. troops in China.[56]

Throughout June, despite naval intelligence messages reporting on the Kwantung army's weaknesses, U.S. planners continued to overestimate its strength. On paper, it had twenty-four divisions, but apart from three divisions brought from China proper, all the rest were newly raised divisions. The Kwantung army's morale was low; it had no anti-tank guns and less than half the authorized number of medium and light machine guns. There was a shortage of artillery and ammunition, and nearly all the infantry's guns were obsolete. Each division's average efficiency was not more than three-tenths that of a prewar front line one.[57]

The military's view on the need for Soviet entry seemed to shift back and forth. At times the generals were for it, but at other times they expressed uncertainty and ambivalence. General Marshall considered Soviet help crucial. "I was for Russia entering the Pacific war," he said. "We needed everything we could get to save American casualties."[58]

On January 23, 1945, the Joint Chiefs of Staff reported: "Russia's entry as early a date as possible consistent with her ability to engage in offensive operations is necessary to provide maximum assistance to our Pacific operations."[59] On April 24, they said that "the early invasion of the Japanese home islands represented the most suitable strategy to accomplish unconditional surrender," but "Soviet entry into the war was no longer considered necessary to make the invasion feasible."[60]

The Soviets did not need U.S. support to enter the war against Japan. Their forces, said Stimson "could in any case occupy Manchuria, Korea, North China, and South Sakhalin before the United States could do anything to prevent it."[61] Although the defeat of Japan could be accomplished without Soviet assistance, said Ambassador Averell Harriman in Moscow, "there was no way to keep Stalin from declaring war at the last moment" and invading Manchuria to regain territory taken by the Japanese in the war of 1904–05.[62]

"The Russians would enter the Far Eastern War because it suited their own interests to do so," said Foreign Secretary Anthony Eden of Britain. "There was no need for us to offer a high price for their participation."[63]

At the time of the Potsdam Conference, set for mid-July, Truman wanted the Soviets to enter the war against Japan. As stated previously, one of his immediate goals in going to Potsdam was to get the Soviets into the war as soon as possible. "There was no way for us to get troops into China to drive the Japanese from the Chinese mainland," said Truman. "Our hope always was to get enough Russian troops into Manchuria to push the Japanese out."[64]

Stalin was eager to get into the war in the Far East. He reassured Harry Hopkins that he intended to attack Manchuria in August. In addition, he agreed with America's open door trade policy in China, and said he would promote unification of China under the leadership of nationalist Chiang Kai-shek because no Communist leader was strong enough to unify the country.[65] By June, the Soviets were transporting troops to East Siberia "night and day."[66]

The Original Potsdam Declaration

At eleven o'clock on July 2, Stimson met with Truman at the White House. He handed the president a tentative draft of a declaration to be issued at Potsdam. Clarifying unconditional surrender terms for Japan, it contained thirteen paragraphs that Stimson had carefully prepared in consultation with Forrestal and Grew. It was, in fact, basically the same framework as Grew's declaration submitted to Truman on May 28. "It is important to emphasize," said Stimson later, that "it was designed to promise destruction if Japan resisted, and hope, if she surrendered."[67]

In an accompanying memorandum, Stimson pointed out Japan's desperate military situation. Japan had no allies; its navy was almost destroyed; its island was under a naval blockade; and its cities were undergoing concentrated air attacks. On the other hand, the United States had "inexhaustible and untouched industrial resources to bring to bear against her diminishing potential."[68] But the United States should not underestimate Japan's "extremely sensitive national pride" said Stimson, and when locked into battle, the enemy will fight to the death.[69]

In this respect, Stimson was hoping that the declaration would provide the liberal peace elements the chance they were looking for to offset the military hard-liners. But the declaration contained a warning. The Japanese armed forces must surrender "unconditionally," lay down their arms, or face "prompt and utter destruction."[70]

Despite the demand that the military surrender unconditionally, the declaration offered conditions for surrender. It promised that he Japanese would not "be enslaved as a race or destroyed as a nation, and they could rebuild their economy once it was purged of its militaristic influences."[71] Most important, paragraph twelve said that the new government "may include a constitutional monarchy under the present dynasty if the peace-loving nations can be convinced of the genuine determination of such a government to follow policies of peace."[72] This would, said Stimson, "Substantially add to the chances of acceptance."[73]

Stimson's declaration, however, did not mention the atomic bomb. "On the grounds of secrecy," said Stimson, "the bomb was never mentioned except when absolutely necessary, and furthermore, it had not yet been tested. It was of course well forward in our minds that the bomb would be the best possible sanction if our warning were rejected."[74] But why did Stimson argue that the atomic bomb was the best possible sanction? What about other sanctions, like continued blockade? And why keep the atomic bomb secret from the Japanese? Apparently, while still agreeing with the Interim Committee's proposal that the bomb should be dropped without warning, he had moved away from those who advocated dropping the bomb on a city first and then seeking peace, to seeking peace first, and if that failed, dropping the bomb on a city.

Truman read Stimson's declaration but would not commit himself to it. He needed to know first "what was going to be done with S-1."[75] Truman invited Stimson to the forthcoming Potsdam Conference but not to travel with him on the presidential cruiser. The Cabinet member who would travel with Truman and who became his most trusted confidant was James F. Byrnes, the new secretary of state.

On June 30, 1945, after Secretary of State Edward R. Stettinius resigned, Truman appointed Byrnes as secretary of state. Although Roosevelt had taken him to Yalta, Byrnes had little special interest or competence in foreign policy. His critics said that he lacked diplomatic subtlety and that he "was incapable of defining a consistent policy to achieve his goals."[76] His experience was mainly in domestic politics, serving in the House of Representatives, the Senate, and on the Supreme Court before resigning to become Roosevelt's chief lieutenant for the home front. Lacking a vice president, Truman understood that the secretary of state would be next in line to succeed him, and this may have been the main reason he picked Byrnes.

Nonetheless, Byrnes had Truman's ear, and he guarded that position carefully. He may have been responsible for keeping Stimson off the seven-day cruise to Potsdam and for getting rid of Charles E. Bohlen as liaison between Truman and the State Department. "Byrnes told me," said Bohlen, "that henceforth he would be dealing directly with the President."[77]

Unlike Grew or Stimson, Byrnes was not eager to keep paragraph twelve on the retention of the emperor in the Potsdam Declaration. Before he left for Potsdam, Grew gave him a copy of Stimson's declaration containing that clause. "Mr. Byrnes was already on his way out of his office," said Grew, "to drive to the airport, and his last action before leaving was to place our draft in his pocket."[78] Shortly thereafter, Grew told Forrestal that "he was afraid it would be ditched on the way over to the Potsdam Conference by people who accompany the President.[79]

The British and the A-Bomb

In the Quebec Agreement of August 1943, the British and Americans agreed not to use the atomic bomb against a third party without first obtaining each other's consent. On June 28, 1945, the British informally approved the use of the atomic bomb against Japan. They consented without hearing the arguments for its use, and without seeing the recommendations of the Interim Committee or Stimson's July 2 memorandum.[80] In World War II, Britain main goal was to defeat Hitler, and it needed America's help to do it. In the Pacific, the balance of power had changed, and the British had accepted that area as America's military sphere of influence.

On July 4, in Washington, D.C., the British gave their formal consent to the use of the atomic bomb against Japan. "This was a pretty strenuous day without a single firecracker to remind anyone that some people might be having a holiday," wrote Stimson in his diary, "We worked long and hard for nearly two hours" before obtaining "the formal consent of both our nations to use the S-1 against Japan."[81]

4.

The Potsdam Conference

Background

The Potsdam Conference was the last wartime meeting of the Allied leaders. From July 17 to August 2, 1945, President Harry S. Truman, Soviet premier Josef Stalin, and British prime minister Winston Churchill met at Potsdam, Germany, to discuss urgent European problems resulting from the Allied victory. Before the conference ended, the Allies agreed to divide Germany into four occupation zones; created the Allied Control Council to handle matters involving all of Germany; agreed to disarm Germany and destroy its ability to wage another war, to remove all Nazis from power, and introduce democratic institutions, and to try Nazi leaders as war criminals. In addition, they recognized Polish and Soviet occupation of German territory east of the Oder and Neisse rivers pending a final peace treaty.

Truman was more concerned with the Far East than with the aftermath of the European war. His immediate goal was to persuade

Stalin to renew his commitment to entering the war against Japan.[1] He was also anxious to learn about the atomic bomb test set for July 16 in the desert of Alamogordo, New Mexico.

On July 7, Truman arrived at Newport News, Virginia, to board the heavy cruiser U.S.S. *Augusta* for the eight-day voyage to Antwerp, Belgium. His presidential party included fifty-three assistants, advisers, newsmen, and helpers. The heavy cruiser *Philadelphia* accompanied the *Augusta*. These two ships formed Task Force 68, commanded by Rear Admiral Allan R. McCann. No other escort, by ship or air, was used to transport the presidential party to Europe. "It seems to take two warships to get your pa across the pond," wrote to daughter Margaret.[2]

But there was no real danger. Wartime precautions, such as following a zigzag course to avoid submarines, maintaining darkened ship lights or radio silence, were not taken. The hostilities in the Atlantic had ended, and the passage was made under normal cruising conditions. "It was a wonderful crossing," said Truman later. "There were movies every night in Secretary Byrnes' cabin," and "I was up early every morning to take some exercise on the deck and spent a good deal of time talking with the members of the crew."[3]

Throughout the eight-day voyage, Truman met daily with his advisors. They included Leahy, Byrnes, Joseph E. Davies (former U.S. ambassador to Moscow), and Charles E. Bohlen, foreign service officer and interpreter. As his closest advisors, said Byrnes, "We spend hours each day reviewing departmental memoranda and recommendations and preparing proposals for the President to consider for discussion at the conference."[4]

"We made steady progress," said Leahy. Truman "squeezed facts and opinions out of us all day long," and he "was more systematic than Roosevelt."[5] Because Truman was "somewhat nervous about confronting such awesome figures as Churchill and Stalin," said Bohlen, "he stuck to business."[6] At the Potsdam Conference, Averell Harriman, ambassador to Moscow, found Truman "astonishingly well prepared."[7]

On July 15, the *Augusta* docked at Antwerp, Belgium. To Truman, it was difficult to realize that a devastating war had just ended. "All along the riverbanks I saw very little evidence of damage caused by the war," he said later. "Everything appeared peaceful and in order, and large herds of fat cattle could be seen grazing in the green meadows along our way."[8] Once ashore, led by a forty-car caravan, General Dwight D. Eisenhower and Admiral Harold R. Stark escorted Truman on the thirty-five mile motor trip to the airport northwest of Brussels. The road was guarded by soldiers from the 137th Infantry Regiment, 35th Division—the same in which Truman had served as captain in World War I. The flight to Babelsberg took three hours and a half, and Truman landed at Gatow Airfield, ten miles from Babelsberg. In less than thirty minutes after landing, another caravan took him to his quarters at Babelsberg, a three-mile-drive from Cecilienhof Palace, where the conference would be held.

In Babelsberg, Truman stayed at No. 2 Kaiserstrasse, a three-story stucco residence named the "Little White House." The Russians had stripped the house bare, as they had done all the others, but a U.S. commander, said Truman, "caught the Russian loot train and recovered enough furniture to make the place livable."[9]

Named "10 Downing Street, Potsdam," Churchill's residence was only two blocks away, while Stalin's residence was a mile away in a vast wooded park surrounding Cecilienhof Palace. He had brought in a division from Central Asia to act as his personal guard during the conference.

Preliminaries

On the morning of July 16 Churchill visited Truman at the Little White House. This was their first meeting, and it did not go well. Churchill had aged, and he sounded "tired and disheartened."[10] "No business of the conference was discussed," said Truman later. "I did tell the Prime Minister that I had no agenda," and "asked him if he had one, but he replied, 'No, I don't need one.'"[11] In fact, Churchill had not prepared for the conference, and the reason for it was unclear. "He gave a lot of hooey about how great my country is and how he loved Roosevelt and how he intended to love me," wrote Truman in his diary. "I am sure we can get along if he doesn't try to give me too much soft soap."[12] Churchill told his friend Lord Moran that Truman "takes no notice of delicate ground; he just plants his foot down firmly on it."[13]

After the meeting with Churchill, Truman, Byrnes, and Leahy toured Berlin. The ruined city and homeless people disturbed them. "This is a hell of a place," wrote Truman to his wife Bess, "ruined, dirty, smelly, forlorn people, bedraggled, hang-dog look about them. You never saw as completely ruined a city."[14]

"Despite all we had read of the destruction there," said Byrnes, "the extent of the devastation shocked us."[15] At dinner that evening, said Leahy, "there was no mood of vindictiveness or revenge, but rather a realization brought home to those of us who fought the war from Washington of the horrible destructiveness of modern conflict."[16]

On July 16, as Truman, Byrnes, and Leahy were touring Berlin, the first nuclear explosion took place at a remote part of the Alamogordo Air Base in the desert of New Mexico. That evening Stimson received special assistant George Harrison's first message. "Diagnosis not yet complete but results seem satisfactory and already exceed expectations."[17] Upon reading it, Truman realized "that the test not only met the most optimistic expectations of the scientists but that the United States in its possession an explosive force of unparalleled power."[18] In his diary, he wrote, "I fear machines are ahead of morals by some centuries. Maybe when morals caught up it will be too late."[19] The successful atomic bomb test created a stir among the American leaders. "There was much excitement," said Truman, "and conversation about the effect on the war then in progress with Japan."[20]

"We had developed a weapon of such revolutionary character," said Stimson, "that its use against the enemy might well be expected to produce exactly the kind of shock on the Japanese ruling oligarchy which we desired."[21]

"This did not come as a complete surprise to me," said General Henry (Hap) Arnold of the army air force, "but I must admit I did not expect the test until a few days later."[22] Eisenhower expressed his hope to Stimson that "we would never have to use such a thing against any enemy because I disliked seeing the United States take the lead in introducing into war something as horrible and destructive as this new weapon was described to be."[23]

Shortly after learning of the successful test, Stimson, Assistant Secretary of War John J. McCloy, and Generals Marshall and Arnold met to discuss which city would be the best target for the atomic bomb. Stimson was adamant that Kyoto not be a target because of "its shrines and ancient monuments."[24] He eventually obtained Truman's agreement on this. General Arnold suggested that the best results would be to turn the matter over to General Carl Spaatz, commander of the Strategic Air Force, who "had planes ready and waiting out in the Pacific for the arrival of the bomb, and who knew the cities chosen for the test."[25] All agreed, and Arnold sent Spaatz a cable.

At noon, on July 17, Stalin, Foreign Commissar Vyacheslav Molotov, and interpreter V. N. Pavlov visited Truman, Byrnes, and Bohlen at the Little White House. "Promptly, a few minutes before twelve," wrote Truman in his diary. "I looked up from the desk and there stood Stalin in the doorway."[26] Although Truman was dressed in a civilian double-breasted gray suit, Stalin wore military clothes—a lightweight khaki uniform with red epaulets and red seams down the trousers. He had no decorations but a single red-ribboned gold star, the Order of the Hero of the Soviet Union, over his left breast pocket. "Stalin looked tired," said Bohlen, Truman's interpreter, "and older than he had a few months before, during the talks with Hopkins."[27]

"I got to my feet and advanced to meet him," continued Truman in his diary. "He put out his hand and smiled. I did the same, we shook, I greeted Molotov and the interpreter and we sat down."[28]

Called "the man of steel," Stalin was absolute dictator of over 180 million people of 170 nationalities in a country representing one-sixth of the earth's surface. At sixty-six, he was only five years older than Truman, but in contrast to the president, "who radiated vitality," Stalin looked and acted like an old man. His face was badly pock-marked, and he had small, yellow-gray eyes, with streaks of gray in his mustache and hair. He moved slowly and stiffly, spoke very little and in a low tone.[29] "I was surprised at Stalin's stature," said Truman. "He was not over five feet five or six inches tall."[30] He was "extremely polite," and "I liked the little son of a bitch."[31]

While Roosevelt had been warm and friendly in dealing with Stalin, Truman was pleasant and distant. But in this first meeting, he tried an "Uncle Joe" joke. According to Bohlen, "it did not draw even a hint of a smile from the dictator."[32] Truman got serious. "I am a diplomat," he said, "but usually say yes or no to questions after hearing all the arguments."[33] This pleased Stalin.

Truman turned the discussion to Japan. He wanted to know when the Soviet Union was going to enter the war. In fact, to Truman, the most "urgent" reason for going to Potsdam was "to get from Stalin a personal reaffirmation of Russia's entry into the war against Japan."[34] And here, at their first meeting, Stalin said, "The Soviet Army would come into action against Japan on August 15."[35]

Truman was extremely pleased. In his diary, he wrote, "Fini Japs when that comes about."[36] In a letter to Bess Truman he added, "I've gotten what I came for. I'll say that we'll end the war a year sooner now, and think of the kids who won't be killed."[37]

Truman and Stalin omitted all military arrangements regarding the Soviet entry into the war against Japan from the Potsdam Conference's official communiqué. According to the president, this was the only secret agreement made at Potsdam.[38] "I can deal with Stalin," wrote Truman in his diary. "He is honest—but smart as hell."[39]

While Stalin and Truman were having lunch, Stimson showed Churchill Harrison's message on the successful atomic bomb test. From the beginning, Churchill knew about the atomic bomb project because it involved the pooling of American and British scientists, but he did not know the date of the New Mexico test. "It means," said Churchill excitedly, that "the atomic bomb is a reality."[40]

"He was intensely interested," wrote Stimson in his diary, "and greatly cheered up."[41]

"Now all this nightmare picture had vanished," said Churchill. "In its place was the vision of the end of the whole war in one or two violent shocks."[42] Lord Moran, Churchill's friend, was not so cheerful. "I was deeply shocked," he said. "There had been no moment in the whole war when things looked to me so black and desperate, and the future so hopeless."[43] Upon hearing the news, General Hastings Ismay, the chief British military figure, was filled with "revulsion." "For some time," he said, "it had been firmly fixed in my mind that the Japanese were tottering."[44]

On the same day, Stalin informed Churchill that the Japanese ambassador had a message delivered to him on the eve of his departure for Potsdam asking the Soviet Union to act as mediator in ending the war. "The message," said Stalin, "contained no definite proposals and the Soviet government could take no action."[45] He did not want Truman to think that the Soviet Union wished to act as mediator, and said he, would have "no objection" to Churchill mentioning the overture to Truman.[46]

In the early hours of July 18 Stimson received a second message from Harrison on the atomic test in New Mexico's desert. It read: "Doctor has just returned most enthusiastic and confident that the Little Boy is as husky as his big brother."[47] On July 21, a courier brought Stimson a report from General Groves. The test, said Groves, was "successful beyond the most optimistic expectations of anyone," and he estimated that the energy generated was between 15,000 and 20,000 tons of TNT.[48]

Stimson immediately showed the documents to Truman and Byrnes. They were "immensely pleased" by the news and quickly assembled Admirals Leahy and Ernest J. King and Generals Marshall and Eisenhower to discuss the new developments. Despite the successful test, the military advised going ahead with the existing plans for the invasion of Japan's home islands. Truman asked Marshall how many American casualties would result in the invasion of the Tokyo plain and other islands. According to Truman, "It was his opinion that such an invasion would cost at a minimum one quarter of a million casualties, and might cost as much as a million on the American side alone, with an equal number of the enemy."[49]

At noon, Truman met Churchill for lunch at 10 Downing Street, Potsdam, and showed him the recent documents on the atomic bomb test. He wanted to inform Stalin of the new weapon. Churchill agreed that Stalin should be told this "great New Fact" but not any of "the particulars."[50] Churchill wondered how Stalin should be told. "I think," said Truman, "I had best just tell him after one of our meetings that we have an entirely novel form of the bomb, something quite out of the ordinary, which we think will have decisive effects upon the Japanese will to continue the war."[51] Churchill agreed with this method.

Churchill brought up two other issues. He told Truman about Japan's mediation offer to Stalin. "I explained to the President," he said, "that Stalin had not wished to tell him direct lest he might think the Russians were trying to influence him towards peace."[52] Truman did not respond. He already knew about Japan's mediation offer from intercepted naval intelligence reports.[53] Then Churchill turned the conversation to unconditional surrender. He brought up the tremendous cost in lives in forcing unconditional surrender upon the Japanese.[54] Again, Truman did not respond, and Churchill did not press it further.

After lunch with Churchill, Truman, Byrnes, and Bohlen paid a return call on Stalin. To the president's surprise, Stalin had a second lunch waiting. It was a meal in Truman's honor, and he couldn't refuse. Over lunch, Stalin pushed across the table Ambassador Sato's message from Japan asking the Soviets to receive Prince Konoye and help mediate an end to the war. Bohlen noticed that Stalin's disclosure of the Japanese proposal made a good impression on Truman, who saw it "as an indication that the Soviets might be prepared to deal openly with the United States."[55] To Byrnes, Stalin's motive was self-interest. "He left me," said Byrnes, "with the distinct impression that he was not anxious to see an end to the fighting until Soviet entry into the war could help secure the concessions he expected of China."[56] Stalin explained that Molotov had told Sato that "he would discuss the matter with him later."[57] Stalin's answer, wrote Truman in his diary, "was satisfactory." But he added, "Believe Japs will fold up before Russia comes in."[58]

The A-Bomb and the Need for Invasion

By mid-July 1945 Japanese army strength appeared formidable—on paper. The U.S. War Department estimated its strength as slightly under 2,000,000 in Japan's home islands; slightly over 2,000,000 in Korea, Manchuria, China proper and Formosa; over 200,000 in French Indochina, Thailand, and Burma; over 500,000 in the East Indies area, including the Philippines; and over 100,000 in the bypassed Pacific Islands.[59] In total, the Japanese army numbered about 5,000,000 men.

But these figures were deceiving. By the time of the Potsdam Conference, Japan was a beleaguered island, facing imminent defeat. Its navy and air force had almost ceased to exist; its cities were undergoing tremendous aerial bombardment; its island was blockaded; its leaders were looking for an honorable way to surrender. "The homeland was in chaos," said Churchill, "and on the verge of collapse."[60] By mid-June, said Admiral Leahy, the Japanese air force could not effectively prevent U.S. bombers from "blanketing the Japanese islands with high explosive and incendiary bombs."[61]

"I was a little fearful," said Stimson, "that before we could get ready the Air Force might have Japan so thoroughly bombed out that the new weapon would not have a fair background."[62]

Japan was "approaching the limit of its endurance," and its leaders were preparing to accept surrender, said the U.S. Strategic Bombing Survey. "The only remaining problem was the timing and terms of that surrender."[63]

Some military commanders argued that neither an invasion of the home islands nor the dropping of atomic bombs was necessary to defeat Japan. "If the United States had been willing to wait, said Admiral King, "the effective naval blockade would, in the course of time, have starved the Japanese into submission through lack of oil, rice, medicines, and other essential materials.[64] "The atomic bombs were of "no material assistance in our war against Japan," said Admiral Leahy. "The Japanese were already defeated and ready to surrender because of the effective sea blockade and the successful bombing with conventional weapons."[65]

The bombing stopped all production and normal services in Japan's sixty-six largest cities, said air force general Curtis LeMay. "Japan was finished long before either one of the two atomic bombs were dropped."[66]

"My staff," said General Douglas MacArthur, U.S. Army commander in the Pacific, "was unanimous in believing Japan was on the point of collapse and surrender. I even directed that plans be drawn 'for a possible peaceful occupation' without further military operation."[67]

To army air force general Arnold, "the bomb was not needed to win the war because conventional bombing, coupled with the blockade, had already brought the Japanese Empire to its knees."[68] On July 20, at Potsdam, General Eisenhower had urged Truman "not to use the bomb," as he had argued earlier with Stimson.[69] In all probability, said the U.S. Strategic Bombing Survey, Japan would have surrendered prior to November 1, 1945, without invasion, without the use of the atomic bomb, and without Soviet entry into the war.[70]

General Marshall was the main spokesman for invasion and the use of the atomic bomb. Bombing the Japanese with conventional weapons wasn't going to win the war, he said. "We had to go in after them," and the atomic bomb was "a wonderful weapon as a protection and preparation for landings."[71]

"Shall we invade Japan proper or shall we bomb and blockade?" wrote Truman in his diary. "That is my hardest decision to date. But I'll make it when I have all the facts."[72]

The A-Bomb and the Need for Soviet Entry

On July 21, Truman and Byrnes read General Groves' report on the atomic bomb test, which called it a "tremendous success." As mentioned earlier, Groves estimated that the bomb was equivalent to 15,000 to 20,000 tons of TNT.[73] This was much more than anticipated. Truman sad, it gave him "an entirely new feeling of confidence."[74] To Byrnes, concerned about the Soviets' takeover of Eastern Europe, the bomb would "render the Russians more manageable in Europe."[75] Stimson referred to it as Washington's "master card" in dealing with the Kremlin.[76]

Shortly afterwards, Truman went to the Cecilienhof Palace to attend the next session of the conference. There was a pronounced change in him. "He seemed much more sure of himself," said Robert Murphy, political adviser to General Eisenhower, "more inclined to participate vigorously in the discussions, to challenge some of Stalin's statements."[77]

"Truman was evidently much fortified by something that had happened, and he stood up to the Russians in a most emphatic and decisive manner," said Churchill. "He told the Russians just where they got on and off and generally bossed the whole meeting."[78] Truman wrote to his wife: "Stalin doesn't know it but I have an ace in the hole and another one showing—so unless he has threes or two pair (and I know he has not) we are sitting all right."[79]

With the successful results of the atomic bomb test positively confirmed on July 21, Truman no longer appeared anxious to get the Soviets into the war against Japan. According to Stimson, Truman began to lose interest in knowing the exact date on which the Soviets would enter the war.[80] "The President and I," said Churchill, "no longer felt that we needed Stalin's aid to conquer Japan."[81]

"Whatever views President Truman may have had of it earlier," said Byrnes, "in the days immediately preceding the dropping of the bomb his views were the same as mine—we wanted to get through with the Japanese phase of the war before the Russians came in."[82]

But Generals Eisenhower and Marshall did not think the United States could keep the Soviet Union out of the war. "Unless victory came before they could get in," said Eisenhower, "no power on earth could keep the Red Army out of that war."[83] Marshall agreed that the United States could not prevent the Russians from entering Manchuria and taking whatever they wanted.[84]

Stalin may have sensed that the Allies' attitude changed. On July 23, at dinner with Churchill, Truman, and their military chiefs, Stalin announced, for the first time publicly, "Here's to our next meeting in Tokyo." He added, "It would not be right to allow Britain and America to shed their blood there without help from the Soviet Union."[85] Turning to Stalin, Stimson said, "I hope our common effort would not only bring success, but bring it promptly," and Stalin assured him that it would "surely speed up victory" and "reduce losses."[86]

"Stalin is determined to enter the war," said Leahy later, "which is plainly to the advantage of Russia now that Japan is certain to be defeated by the Allies."[87]

The Final Military Report and Truman's Decision to Use the Atomic Bomb

On the morning of July 24 the U.S. and British Combined Chiefs of Staff met with Truman and Churchill at the Little White House. The generals presented a written report listing the strategic aims to bring about the final defeat of Japan. With the preliminary operation on Kyushu set for November 1, 1945, the report said the invasion of Japan was the main objective, and that no other operation would be undertaken that would hinder its success. Despite the changed attitude of the U.S. and British leaders, it reiterated the policy of encouraging Soviet entry into the war. Also, although the Americans would regularly consult the British, operational strategy in the Pacific would remain in the hands of the U.S. Chiefs of Staff.

No one recorded this part of the meeting, but apparently Truman at this point gave his formal consent to use the atomic bomb against Japan. "This decision had the unanimous approval of those present," said Truman later.[88] Marshall, the general Truman most trusted and respected, was the most vocal advocate for its use, arguing that the atomic bomb was the perfect complement to an invasion. It was the "shock action," and he wanted nine of them, two for three initial invasion attacks and three against Japanese reserves that would pour into the areas.[89] But he remained silent about how radioactivity would affect U.S. troops.[90]

The exact date on which Truman made up his mind to use the atomic bomb was never clear. Most likely, he never seriously considered not using it. "Napoleon made the statement that the Lord was always on the side with the heaviest artillery," said Truman at one point. "I had to make the decision as to whether the atomic bomb was just another piece of artillery."[91] And he did. "Let there be no mistake about it," he said. "I regarded the bomb as a military weapon and never had any doubt that it should be used."[92]

"No effort was made," said Stimson, "and none was seriously considered, to achieve surrender merely in order not to have to use the bomb."[93] He considered its use "as legitimate" as any other "deadly explosive" of modern war.[94]

"At any rate," said Churchill, "there never was a moment's discussion as to whether the atomic bomb should be used or not."[95]

Truman hoped the atomic bomb would make an invasion unnecessary and save U.S. lives. The figures differed in the number of U.S. casualties expected from an invasion of Japan. Sometimes Truman said 250,000 casualties, and at other times 500,000, and Byrnes said a million casualties.[96] But official military estimates appeared considerably lower than those of Truman or Byrnes.[97] "If any thought is given to the value of American lives," said General Groves, Truman's decision "will always stand as an act of unsurpassed courage and wisdom."[98] The killing of Japanese civilians, however, was not a consideration. After the fire-bombings of Tokyo and other Japanese cities, U.S. leaders "were generally inured to the mass killing of civilians."[99]

Chief of Staff Admiral Leahy disagreed with Truman's reasoning that the atomic bomb was needed to prevent an invasion of Japan and save U.S. lives. The Japanese were ready to surrender, said Leahy, "because of the effective sea blockade and the successful bombing with conventional weapons."[100] Truman's decision to use the atomic bomb, said Leahy, was made more to justify the expense of the Manhattan Project than to invade an "already thoroughly defeated Japan."[101] The making of the bomb cost $2 billion and tied up huge industrial firms, hundreds of thousands of workers, and the best scientists in the United States and Britain. "Truman knew that," said Leahy. "It was my reaction that the scientists and others wanted to make this test because of the vast sums that had been spent on the project."[102]

On the evening of July 24, Truman received a written directive containing the order to drop atomic bombs on Japanese cities. Largely prepared by General Groves, the directive was addressed to General Carl A. Spaatz of the Twentieth Air Force and signed by Marshall's deputy, General Thomas T. Handy. It read: "The 509

Composite Group, 20th Air Force, will deliver its first special bomb as soon as weather will permit visual bombing after about 3 August 1943, on one of the targets: Hiroshima, Kokura, Niigata, and Nagasaki," and "additional bombs will be delivered on the above targets as soon as made ready by the project staff."[103]

Truman, Stimson, and Marshall approved the directive dated July 25, 1945, which set in motion the machinery for dropping the atomic bombs. Later, Truman's critics said that the directive had no reference to the Potsdam Declaration, given on July 26, and no statement as to what should be done in the event of a Japanese offer to surrender before August 3.[104] As commander-in-chief, Truman could have countermanded General Handy's order at any time, but, said Truman, "it was necessary to set the military wheels in motion."[105]

Soviet Military Plans in the Far East

On the afternoon of July 24, the British, U.S., and Soviet chiefs of staffs assembled in Crown Prince William's palace to discuss Soviet military operations in the Far East. Soviet general A. E. Antonov said operations would begin in the last part of August but would be contingent upon an agreement with China in regard to Soviet privileges in Manchuria.[106] The Red Army's objective was to destroy the Japanese armies there and to occupy the Liaotung Peninsula, which contained Port Arthur and Dairen. After Japan's defeat, he added, "it is the intention of the Soviet Union to withdraw its troops from Manchuria."[107]

Before the meeting ended, Antonov wanted to know the answers to two questions: first, could the United States prevent Japan from reinforcing its Manchurian army (estimated by the Soviets at fifty divisions) from either China or the Japanese mainland? The enemy, said Marshall, could not transfer any troops from the home islands because of U.S. naval air operations and only a few Japanese divisions from China because of continual sabotage of the railroads by Chinese guerrillas.[108] Antonov then asked what American's intentions were in the Kurile Islands and in Korea." Admiral King replied that the United States would not be able to operate against the Kuriles, and

Marshall said that no present plans existed for amphibious landings against Korea because it could be brought under control "once our aircraft could operate from fields on the Japanese island of Kyushu."[109]

The Soviet and U.S. generals met on July 26—without the British this time. The U.S. generals "all remarked on the big change on the part of the Russians,"[110] who had agreed to all of the U.S. requests. The Soviets agreed to have U.S. personnel staff weather stations at Petropavlovsk and Khabarovsk; to exchange liaison groups, including a Soviet military mission in Washington; to make designated Siberian ports and airfields available to U.S. units for repair needs and emergency use; and to mark off areas of operation for the air and naval forces that were based in northern Korea.[111] But the Soviets "took pains" to emphasize that all agreements would become effective upon their entry into the war against Japan.[112]

Truman Informs Stalin about New Weapon

On July 24, after an evening session at the Cecilienhof Palace, Truman decided to inform Stalin about the "new weapon." Walking casually over to him, the president said the United States had a new weapon of "unusual destructive force." According to Truman, Stalin showed no special interest: "All he said was that he was glad to hear it and hoped we would make 'good use of it against the Japanese.'"[113] Truman said later, "He didn't know what I was talking about, but it didn't make any difference; I told him."[114]

The only person who directly heard the conversation between Truman and Stalin was Pavlov, the Russian interpreter. Truman had told Bohlen, his interpreter, not to accompany him "because he did not want to indicate that there was anything particularly momentous about the development."[115]

However, several persons watched the conversation from a distance. "I watched Stalin's expression," said Byrnes. "I did not believe Stalin grasped the full import of the President's statement and thought that on the next day there would be some inquiry about this 'new and powerful weapon,' but I was mistaken."[116] Across the room,

Bohlen also carefully watched Stalin's face: "So offhand was Stalin's response that there was some question in my mind whether the President's message had got through."[117] About five yards away, Churchill and Eden were covertly watching. They also had some doubts as to whether Stalin "had taken it in."[118]

Stalin was playing dumb. He already knew about the atomic bomb, and his own scientists were conducting research on it. The information came from Klaus Fuchs, a British physicist working at Los Alamos, New Mexico, who had been supplying the Russians with atomic secrets from the beginning. Marshal Georgi Zhukov overheard Stalin tell Molotov immediately after his meeting with Truman to order Igor Kurchatov, a Soviet scientist "to speed things up."[119]

Japan's Continuing Mediation Attempts

While the Potsdam Conference was taking place, the Japanese continued their efforts to get the Soviets to mediate an end to the war. At the same time, Foreign Minister Shigenori Togo and Ambassador Naotake Sato were at odds over whether to accept U.S. terms for unconditional surrender.

In a July 17 cable to Sato, Togo adamantly opposed mediation leading to unconditional surrender. "We would terminate the war," he said, "if the United States recognized Japan's honor and existence," but if it insisted on unconditional surrender, the Japanese would "fight a war of resistance to the bitter end."[120] Replying on July 18, Sato strongly advocated accepting unconditional surrender provided the United States preserved the imperial house. He added, "I want to preserve the lives of thousands of people who are about to go to their deaths needlessly."[121]

On the evening of July 18 Sato received a message from Vice Foreign Commissar Alexander Lozovsky stating that the Japanese telegram of July 13 concerning the Konoye mission was unclear. "It is therefore impossible," wrote Lozovsky, "for the Soviet Government to give a definite reply."[122] The next day Sato cabled to Togo that "the powers-that-be in Japan are out of touch with the atmosphere prevailing here," and "the rejection of the plan indicates that we cannot thus accomplish the desired objective of winning over the Russians."[123]

On July 20 Sato cabled Togo an "impassioned plea," asking again that the Japanese government accept unconditional surrender provided the United States preserved the imperial house. The military situation was hopeless, and surrender was the only way to preserve the nation, said Sato, and "save our 70,000,000 people from misery and endeavor to maintain the survival of our race."[124] He recognized that critics would charge him with "being an advocate of defeatism," but he was willing to take full responsibility for his remarks: "I will just have to put up with that, and no matter for what responsibility I am accused, I will gladly face it."[125]

On July 21 Togo sent Sato a message clarifying Konoye's mission and emphasizing that unconditional surrender was unacceptable. Togo said the emperor was sending Konoye as his special envoy "to solicit Russia's good offices in bringing the war to an end" and to negotiate "a cooperative relationship between Japan and Russia."[126] But, Togo said, Japan would not accept unconditional surrender under any circumstance: "We will stand united as one nation against the enemy if the enemy forcibly demands our unconditional surrender."[127]

"That cable, which we intercepted, depressed me terribly," said Byrnes later, "It meant using the atomic bomb."[128]

Four days later, on July 25, Togo's cable to Sato offered a solution to the deadlock on unconditional surrender. Togo said Japan had no objection to the restoration of peace on the basis of the Atlantic Charter.[129] (Issued in August 1941 by President Roosevelt, the charter included respect for national self-determination and pledged no territorial aggrandizement.) "The difficult point," said Togo, "is the attitude of the United States, who continues to insist on the formality of unconditional surrender." If it continued to insist on it, he said, "there is no solution to this situation other than for us to hold out until complete collapse because of this one point alone."[130]

On the evening of July 25, Lozovsky spoke briefly with Sato. He wanted to know if Konoye's mission was to terminate the war or to strengthen Soviet-Japanese relations. It's both, replied Sato, "to request the Russian Government to use its good offices to the full for ending of the present war" and to strengthen "relations between Russia and Japan, which are a cherished part of Japanese diplomacy."[131] Lozovsky said he would report to his government and give Sato an answer shortly. Sato reported to Togo that Lozovsky "listened to our proposal with an earnest and attentive attitude."[132]

U.S. naval intelligence, which had long ago broken Japan's code, summarized the messages between Togo and Sato. In regard to ending the war, said naval intelligence, Japan's leaders, "though still balking at the term unconditional surrender," had reached the point where they have "no objection to the restoration of peace on the basis of the Atlantic Charter."[133] It further reported: "The Japanese are playing the Russians against the Anglo-Americans and through resultant friction salvage as much as possible in terminating a war now officially recognized as lost."[134] These messages, said Lewis L. Strauss, assistant secretary of the navy, "indeed stipulated only that the integrity of the Japanese Royal Family be preserved."[135]

Churchill and the British Election

On July 25 the Potsdam Conference was put on temporary hold. Churchill and Foreign Secretary Eden left for London to learn the final results of the July 5 general election.

Before he left for London, popular sentiment at the conference was that Churchill, a conservative, would beat the Labour Party's Clement Attlee by a large vote. "We had numerous bets among us on how big his sweep would be," said General Arnold.[136] According to Churchill, Stalin told him that "all his information from Communist and other sources confirmed his belief that I should be returned by a majority of about eighty."[137] Churchill told Byrnes that the British gamblers were "confident that the Conservatives were in by a substantial margin" and that Attlee agreed "with this prediction."[138]

Privately, Churchill and Eden had doubts about the election results. When Churchill woke up on July 25 he told Lord Moran he had an unpleasant dream: "I dreamed that life was over. I saw—it was very vivid—my dead body under a white sheet on a table in an empty room. Perhaps this is the end."[139] Earlier, Churchill had told Moran that the election "hovers over me like a vulture of uncertainty in the sky."[140]

Eden particularly worried about how the soldiers would vote. "In one of my son Simon's last letters from Burma," he said, "he had hinted that many of the fighting forces were not likely to vote for us and, from the contacts I had in the army, I shared his opinion."[141]

On July 26 the news came from London that the Labour Party had won. Clement Attlee was now prime minister, and Ernest Bevin became his foreign minister. The British electorate had defied predictions, and everybody at Potsdam was surprised. According to General Arnold, "his defeat came as a great surprise not only to the Americans but also to our British colleagues."[142]

"We were all shocked by Churchill's defeat," said Bohlen.[143]

With the arrival of Attlee and Bevin, the conference resumed on July 28. Although they followed the same policies as Churchill and Eden, the "quiet mousy" Attlee and the "tough guy" Bevin had very different personalities. To his sister Margie, Truman described the two as "sourpusses," and Attlee was "not so keen as old fat Winston," and "Bevin looks rather round to be a Foreign Minister."[144] General Zhukov described Attlee as "rather more reserved" than the talkative Churchill.[145]

"Stalin lost interest after the departure of his arch-rival," said Robert Murphy, Eisenhower's political adviser. "There was a touch of condescension in the Soviet dictator's unvarying politeness to Attlee, a contrast to his sharp interchanges with Churchill."[146]

The Potsdam Declaration and the Retention of Emperor Hirohito

The Potsdam Declaration was a warning to Japan, an ultimatum whose goal was to clarify for Japan the meaning of unconditional surrender. Written, revised, and agreed upon by Grew, Stimson, and Forrestal, it contained thirteen paragraphs. But to the Japanese, paragraph twelve would be the most important. It said that the Allied occupying forces would be withdrawn from Japan as soon as the

Japanese established "a peacefully inclined responsible government of a character representative of the Japanese people," which "may include a constitutional monarchy under the present dynasty if the peace-loving nations can be convinced of the genuine determination of such a government to follow policies of peace."[147] This offered the best hope to the Japanese that they could keep Emperor Hirohito, their main surrender term.

On July 2, Stimson gave a copy to President Truman before he left for Potsdam. Truman turned it over to Byrnes, the new secretary of state.

Just before leaving for Potsdam, Byrnes, still feeling insecure in his new post, telephoned Cordell Hull, former secretary of state under Roosevelt. Over the phone, Byrnes gave Hull the substance of the proposed Potsdam Declaration, including paragraph twelve. Grew, Stimson, and Forrestal had approved it, said Byrnes, but Hull was not impressed, particularly with paragraph twelve. It "seemed too much like appeasement," said Hull, "especially after the resolute stand we had maintained on unconditional surrender."[148] He wanted to strip the emperor of "all extraordinary privileges" and place him on the same level of the law as everybody else.[149] According to Truman, "Hull had the most reason for vindication against the Japanese. He was secretary of state when the Japanese bombed Pearl Harbor."[150]

On July 8 Allied intelligence reported that the Japanese equated unconditional surrender with "national extinction" and would not accept foreign custody of the emperor. The official report said that "the idea of foreign occupation of the Japanese homeland, foreign custody of the person of the Emperor, and the loss of prestige entailed by the acceptance of unconditional surrender are most revolting to the Japanese."[151] If the Allies allowed the Japanese to retain their emperor, the report concluded, they might agree "to withdraw from all the territory they have seized on the Asiatic continent and in the Southern Pacific" and "to the practical disarmament of their military forces."[152]

On July 16, at a Combined Chiefs of Staff meeting, British chief of staff Alan Brooke argued for the retention of the emperor. The emperor was necessary, he said "to order the cease-fire in outlying areas, whereas if the dynasty were destroyed, the outlying garrisons might continue to fight for many months or years."[153] Because the issue was primarily a political one, Leahy suggested that Brooke ask Churchill to raise it with Truman.[154]

Two days later, Churchill again brought up the subject of unconditional surrender with the president. Although Churchill did not mention retention of the emperor directly, he said there should be no rigid insistence on unconditional surrender, "apart from what was necessary for world peace and future security," and the Japanese should be left "some show of saving their military honor and some assurance of their national existence."[155] Truman replied "bluntly" that the Japanese did not have "any military honor after Pearl Harbor."[156] According to Churchill, Truman then became "quite sympathetic," and he spoke of the "terrible responsibility that rested on him in regard to the unlimited effusion of American blood."[157]

Later at the conference, Forrestal asked Bevin his views on retention of the emperor. "There was no sense in destroying the instrument through which one might have to deal in order to effectively control Japan," said Bevin. Then he made a surprising statement: "It might have been better for all of us not to have destroyed the institution of the Kaiser after the last war," and "far better to have guided the Germans to a constitutional monarchy rather than leaving them without a symbol and therefore opening the psychological doors to a man like Hitler."[158]

On July 16, the day of the successful atomic bomb test, Byrnes received a telegram from Hull. In it, he repeated his objections to the emperor and advised postponing the declaration "to await the climax of Allied bombing and Russia's entry into the war."[159] Shortly thereafter, Byrnes sent Hull a reply, "agreeing that the statement should be delayed, and that, when it was issued, it should not contain this commitment with regard to the Emperor."[160]

The Joint Chiefs of Staff, disregarding the July 8 Allied intelligence report calling for the retention of the emperor, informed Truman on July 18 that they favored no commitments or definite references to the future structure of Japanese politics. Specifically, they did not like the last sentence of paragraph twelve: "This may include a constitutional monarchy under the present dynasty if the peace-loving nations can be convinced of the genuine determination of such a government to follow policies of peace which will render impossible for future development of aggressive militarism in Japan."[161] They wanted the last sentence changed to read: "Subject to suitable guarantees against further acts of aggression, the Japanese people will be free to choose their own form of government."[162]

The argument that the Joint Chiefs of Staff gave for the change was ambiguous and unclear. They argued that the original wording of the last sentence in paragraph twelve would misconstrued by divided opinion in Japan. The devotees of the emperor would see it as an attempt "to depose or execute the Emperor" or "install some other member of the Imperial family," while the radical elements would see it as a commitment to keep the emperor and "Emperor worship."[163] To the Joint Chiefs of Staff, the revised statement "would be more likely to appeal to all elements" of the Japanese people.[164] But what elements of the Japanese people would not want the emperor? In an apparent contradiction of their proposed change, the Joint Chiefs of Staff said that it was "inadvisable to make any statement or take any action at the present time that would make it difficult or impossible to utilize the authority of the Emperor to direct a surrender of the Japanese forces in the outlying areas as well as in Japan proper."[165]

At this point, as advocated by the Joint Chiefs of Staff, Stimson accepted the revision of paragraph twelve. On July 20 he sent Truman a note: "I concur in the revised form of paragraph 12 suggested by the Joint Chiefs of Staff in their memorandum to you 18 July 1945."[166]

On July 23 Truman and Byrnes showed Stimson their final revision of paragraph twelve to be included in the forthcoming Potsdam Declaration. It neither mentioned the emperor's status nor included the Joint Chiefs of Staffs' proposed revision. It now read: "The occupying forces of the Allies shall be withdrawn from Japan as soon as these objectives have been accomplished and there has been established in accordance with the freely expressed will of the Japanese people a peacefully inclined and responsible government."[167]

Although Stimson had concurred with the Joint Chiefs of Staffs' revision, he now argued for the original provision that permitted the continuance of the dynasty. "I had felt that the insertion of that in the formal warning was important," said Stimson later, "and might be just the thing that would make or mar their acceptance."[168]

He told Truman. "I hoped that the President would watch carefully so that the Japanese might be reassured verbally through diplomatic channels if it was found that they were hanging fire on that one point." Truman replied that he had that in mind, and that he "would take care of it."[169] He and Byrnes were not "obdurate on it," said Stimson, "but thought they could arrange it in the necessary secret negotiations which take place after any armistice."[170]

The Potsdam Declaration

During the early morning of July 26 the Potsdam Declaration, bearing the names of Truman, Churchill, and Generalissimo Chiang Kai-shek went out through diplomatic channels and was released to the press. But in a diplomatic snub, no formal text was submitted to the Japanese via a neutral country.

The Potsdam Declaration contained thirteen paragraphs. It warned that the "prodigious" military might of the United States, Britain, and China was "poised to strike the final blows," and that Japan had to decide between "annihilation and reason." Its terms of Allied enforcement included setting up a non-militaristic government, limiting Japanese sovereignty to the four main islands, and disarming Japan's military forces. Its conditions for surrender said that the Allies would not enslave the Japanese or destroy their nation but mete "stern justice" to all war criminals. In addition, it said the Allies would remove all obstacles to democracy, set up safeguards to basic human rights, and allow Japan to have non-military, sustaining industries. Paragraph twelve, Byrnes' and Truman's revision, did not mention the emperor, and the words "unconditional surrender" appeared only once, in the final paragraph. It proclaimed the unconditional surrender of all Japan's armed forces but not of its government. The alternative, it warned, was "prompt and utter destruction."[171]

The fate of Emperor Hirohito was left out of the declaration. "I did not say anything about disowning the Emperor of Japan," said Truman.[172] Byrnes argued that paragraph twelve "implied" that surrender would not involve the downfall of the dynasty by saying that Allied forces would be withdrawn as soon as "there has been established in accordance with the freely expressed will of the Japanese people a peacefully inclined and responsible government."[173] But to the Japanese, said Grew, this was not "a categorical undertaking regarding the dynasty," and it did not comply with Stimson's suggestion that "it would substantially add to the chances of acceptance if the ultimatum should contain a statement that we would not exclude a constitutional monarchy under the present dynasty."[174]

Without knowledge of the successful atomic bomb test in New Mexico on July 16, would Truman and Byrnes have worded the Potsdam Declaration differently? Would they have mentioned the development of the atomic bomb or included the retention of Emperor Hirohito? No one knows, but according to General Groves, "with the news of our success in hand, President Truman and Mr. Churchill were able to see it dispatched with a great deal more confidence than otherwise might have been the case."[175]

Japanese Reaction to the Potsdam Declaration

At 6:00 a.m. on July 27, Tokyo time, a radio-monitoring station in Chofu, a Tokyo suburb, picked up a broadcast from San Francisco announcing the Potsdam Declaration. Seiichiro Katsuyama, the radio operator, described the event: "Suddenly the words 'Potsdam Proclamation' sounded in my earphones. This seemed to be a communication of considerable importance, so I made six recordings of it; and then I typed it out, jumped on my motorcycle, and made my way as fast as I could to the foreign ministry."[176]

Meanwhile, over Japan's twelve major cities, U.S. planes were dropping thousands of leaflets explaining the Potsdam Declaration. They said the Allies did not consider the Japanese people the enemy but rather the military, who "had plunged the country into this disastrous war." But, they said, Japan must surrender immediately or the U.S. air force would bomb Otaru, Akita, Hachinoke, Fukushima, Urawa, Takayama, Iwakumi, Tottori, Imabaru, Yawata, Miyakonojo, and Saga.[177] But the cities targeted for the atomic bomb—Hiroshima, Nagasaki, Kokura, and Niigata—were not on the list.

When Togo received the declaration, he hurriedly met with Suzuki and Cabinet Secretary Hisatsune Sakomizu. According to Sakomizu, "we felt that the declaration must be accepted as the final terms of peace, whether we liked it or not."[178] While sympathetic, Togo still had faith in the Soviet Union's eventual agreement to mediate the conflict.[179] With Soviet mediation he hoped to enter into negotiation with the Allies to obtain clarification and revision of the declaration. "It was evidently not a dictate of unconditional surrender," said Togo, but it was vague concerning the eventual form of the Japanese government, disarmament, and war criminals.[180]

Shortly thereafter, Togo met with Emperor Hirohito. "The declaration," said Togo, "must be treated with utmost circumspection, both domestically and internationally; in particular, I feared the consequences if Japan should manifest an intention to reject it."[181] The declaration, said Hirohito, was "acceptable in principle."[182] First, said Togo, Japan should wait for the Soviet response to the Konoye mission, and "our attitude toward the declaration should be decided in accordance with that outcome."[183] And yet, despite Sato's doubts about Soviet intentions, Togo continued to trust the Soviet Union with the fate of Japan.

On the same day, Prime Minister Kantaro Suzuki assembled the Supreme Council for the Direction of the War to discuss the Potsdam Declaration. War Minister Korechika Anami, General Yoshijiro Umezu, and Admiral Teijiro Toyoda said that the terms were "too dishonorable."[184] They argued that "it would undermine the morale of the rank and file" and urged that the government issue a "trenchant statement" against it.[185] Although leaning toward acceptance, Suzuki, Togo, and Admiral Mitsumasa Yonai agreed that the unsettled status of the emperor needed clarification.[186] In the end, all agreed with Togo, who argued that the government should not make any decision until it received the Soviet response to the Konoye mission.[187] The Supreme Council would give the press a text of the Potsdam Declaration but with no comment.

On the afternoon of July 28 Suzuki held a scheduled press conference at his official residence in Tokyo. After answering questions on various government policies and expressing a "strong conviction of sure Japanese victory," someone asked, "what is the Prime minister's view regarding the Joint Proclamation by the three countries?"[188] It is "a thing of no great value," said Suzuki. "The declaration is simply an adaptation of the Cairo Declaration" an Allied statement of December 1943 setting forth unconditional surrender as the terms for peace, and "we have decided to '*Mokusatsu*' it.[189]

Mokusatsu was a word with many different meanings. *Moku* means "to keep silent," and *satsu* means "to kill." Taken together, the word literally means "to kill with silence." But it can be translated to mean "take no notice of," "treat with silent contempt," "ignore," or "remain in a wise and masterly inactivity."[190] In idiomatic English, it could mean "no comment at this time" or "pending further information."[191] Sakomizu said later that "no comment" would have accurately expressed Suzuki's true meaning.[192] But War Minister Anami told the Information Board, which cleared all news, that Suzuki meant "reject by ignoring," and the head of the board went on the radio to explain this.[193]

The next morning the Tokyo newspaper reported that the government had decided to ignore the Potsdam Declaration. Togo was "desolate" and immediately protested to the Cabinet, "pointing out that the report was at variance with our decision."[194] But it was too late. On July 30 the *New York Times* banner headline said, JAPAN OFFICIALLY TURNS DOWN ALLIED SURRENDER ULTIMATUM.[195]

Down to the Wire

On July 28, as the tenth session at the Cecilienhof Palace convened, Stalin enlivened the proceedings by announcing that he had received two messages from Japan. The first, received on July 18, requested the Soviet Union to mediate an end to the war and included a proposal to send a royal prince of Japan to Moscow as chief of the mission. "The proposal was too vague," said Stalin, "to warrant [his] approving a meeting with the proposed mission."[196] The most recent message received this day, said Stalin, made the matter clearer: Konoye's mission was to ask the Soviet Union to mediate an end to the war; to negotiate with respect to Soviet-Japanese relations during and after the war; and to convey to the Soviet Union that "it was exclusively the desire of His Majesty to avoid more bloodshed by the parties engaged in the war."[197] Japan, said Stalin, "would receive a more definite answer than was the case the last time, and the answer would be in the negative."[198] Truman thanked Stalin.

On several occasions, Stalin said Soviet troops would be ready to enter the war by August 8. But this meant the Soviet Union would have to violate the terms of the Soviet-Japanese Neutrality Pact of 1941, which was binding until April 5, 1946. In 1941 the Soviet Union had had a similar pact with Germany, but it was the latter that violated it. Soviet violation of the Neutrality Pact with Japan would expose it to the same charge that the Soviets had once leveled against Germany—that she could not be trusted to honor treaties.

Stalin and Molotov came up with a solution. On July 29 Molotov informed Truman that Stalin instructed him to ask that the Allies address a formal request to the Soviet Union to enter the war. Although Truman said he would consider it, he was "disturbed" because he was reluctant to request that a country break a treaty. But to Truman and Byrnes, there was a more important issue. According to Byrnes, "We had, of course, begun to hope that a Japanese surrender might be imminent and we did not want to urge the Russians to enter the war."[199]

Leahy told Truman, "I did not think he should ever consider complying. The British and ourselves were fully capable of defeating Japan without assistance."[200]

Two days later, Truman handed Stalin a letter in response to the Soviet's attempt to request the Soviet Union to enter the war against Japan. In his letter Truman did not formally request the Soviet Union to enter the war. Instead, he pointed out that the Soviet government's duty under the U.N. agreements was to assist in preserving world peace.[201] However, Stalin considered Truman's reply a request to enter the war. And on August 8, 1945, when the Soviets officially declared war on Japan, they said that the Soviet Union "had acceded to the Allied request to join in hostilities in the Far East."[202]

On July 28 Togo wired Sato an urgent dispatch imploring him to meet with Molotov without delay. He instructed Sato to find out the Soviet position on the Potsdam Declaration and whether there was some connection between it and Japan's mediation proposal. He was also to find out whether the Soviets had informed the Americans and British about Japan's proposal and about the attitude the Soviets would take toward Japan in the future.[203]

On July 30, with Molotov still away, Sato again met with Vice-Commissar Lozovsky. He repeated the points that Togo had instructed him to present. Lozovsky remained noncommittal. Just before leaving, Sato remarked, "What I fear is that the 3-Power Joint Declaration may prevent good offices of the Russian Government for which Japan hopes."[204] Lozovsky would not be drawn out, and Sato again left empty-handed.

In his dispatch on July 30 Sato argued for immediate acceptance of the Potsdam Declaration. The Allies, he said, have no intention of softening the declaration, and Stalin "would bring full and heavy pressure" on the Allies in regard to Manchuria, China, and Korea: "There is no necessity for Stalin now, of his own free will, to make a treaty with Japan."[205]

This was not what Japan's leaders wanted to hear. By pinning their hopes on the Soviet initiative, however, they had backed themselves into a corner. They needed to know the Soviet attitude on the Konoye mission before taking a position on the Potsdam Declaration or whether to open up negotiations directly with the United States.

Meanwhile, America's leaders had taken Suzuki's July 28 *Mokusatsu* statement as a rejection of the Potsdam Declaration and final justification to use the atomic bomb against Japan. "There was no alternative now," said Truman. "They just as good as told me where I could go."[206]

"In the face of this rejection," said Stimson, "we could only proceed to demonstrate that the ultimatum had meant exactly what it said," and for that purpose, "the atomic bomb was an eminently suitable weapon."[207]

Byrnes said, "I recognized then that our hope of avoiding the use of the bomb was virtually gone."[208] And yet, he said later, "I and a good many others will always feel that had the President issued as far back as May 1945 the recommended categorical statement that the Japanese dynasty would be retained the atomic bomb might never have to be used at all."[209]

Late in the evening of July 30 U.S. officials at Potsdam received and decoded an urgent top secret cable from Washington. Addressed to Truman, it was from Stimson, who had returned to Washington five days earlier. Because Truman was sleeping, officials did not give it to him until the next morning. It stated that the atomic bomb was ready for delivery but needed Truman's final order to be dropped: "The time schedule on Groves' project is progressing so rapidly that it is now essential that statement for release by you be available not later than Wednesday, 1 August."[210] On the back of the pink message, Truman wrote large and clear with a lead pencil: "Suggestion approved. Release when ready but no sooner than August 2."[211]

"I did what I thought was right," said Truman later. "Death is an inevitable part of every order that a wartime leader gives."[212]

On August 2 Togo cabled Sato with another urgent message. Under the circumstances, he said, "there is a disposition to make the Potsdam Declaration the basis of our study concerning terms," but the Japanese must not let a single day slip by or "the present situation may result in a thousand years of regret."[213] In a cable marked "extremely urgent," Sato replied the next day. "The days are numbered," he said, "and this causes us to feel very deeply the pressure of time." Because of this, Prince Konoye was to bring concrete plans for ending the war; otherwise, he will "return with empty hands, and I fear the results obtained would be worse than if he had not been sent at all."[214]

U.S. naval intelligence reported: "With regard to Russo-Japanese relations, Japan is in the increasingly uncomfortable position of the pursuing female who has been left 'waiting at the church' for a marriage of her own arranging, while the chosen bridegroom consorts alarmingly, if discreetly, abroad."[215]

On August 2 OSS Director William Donovan reported that Japanese officials in Switzerland would soon clarify the meaning of Suzuki's July 28 response to the Potsdam Declaration. Donovan's agents informed him that the Allies should not take "too seriously" what was said on Tokyo Radio, for that was merely "propaganda to maintain morale," and the Japanese would transmit the "real reply" through some "official channel."[216] How Truman and his advisers responded to Donovan's report was unclear, but it clearly reinforced naval intelligence's intercepted messages from Togo and Sato indicating Japan's willingness to negotiate a surrender.

5.

The Atomic Bombings

Background

On July 14, 1945, a closed black truck, escorted by seven cars filled with heavily armed security agents, left Santa Fe for Albuquerque, New Mexico. Disguised as field artillerymen, Major Robert R. Furman from General Groves's office and Captain James F. Nolan, a radiologist at the Los Alamos base hospital, were inside the truck guarding a large box, about the size of two orange crates, and a small metal cylinder. Inside these holding devices were the final assembly parts, including the crucial uranium 235, for the atomic bomb.

The motorcade speeded into Albuquerque, where two air force C-54 cargo planes waited for the flight to Hamilton Field outside of San Francisco. After military men lifted the holding devices into one of the planes, the pilots were "flabbergasted" to learn that two C-54s were needed to carry only a few hundred pounds of cargo and in only one of the planes. Groves, however, had insisted on two planes. If the one carrying the uranium 235 crashed, the other would spot and radio the location of the crash site.[1]

After landing at Hamilton Field, military men took Furman, Nolan, and their cargo to Hunter's Point, where they boarded the heavy cruiser U.S.S. *Indianapolis* for the trip to Tinian Island in the South Pacific. Because their mission was the "most important assignment of the war," Oppenheimer had instructed them to keep an eye on their cargo at all times. If torpedoed by the Japanese, the captain was under orders, before rescuing survivors, to have the first motor launch or life raft save the "special cargo."[2] However, the trip was uneventful.

On July 26 the *Indianapolis* arrived at Tinian, discharged its cargo the same day, and then left for the Philippines. However, for all the precautions taken, the *Indianapolis* was a poor choice to carry the uranium 235 to Tinian. It had no underwater sound equipment, and its design was so poor that a single torpedo could quickly sink it.[3] Four days out to sea, on July 30, a Japanese submarine torpedo sank it with some 900 of its crew.

At Tinian, a small island in the Marianas taken from the Japanese in 1944, the army had built an airfield with four parallel 8,500-foot runways. Far away from the other military personnel, the government had built a small cluster of Quonset huts where the scientists and technicians, led by Brigadier General Thomas F. Farrell, were assembling the atomic bomb. Most of its parts had arrived by air transport. The *Indianapolis* had brought the last of the fissionable material needed to complete the assembly. Called Little Boy, the atomic bomb was fourteen feet long, five feet in diameter, and weighed 10,000 pounds. The scientists set it to go off at 1,850 feet above ground. At that moment, a small chunk of uranium 235 would move forward at 5,000 feet per second and strike another piece of uranium. In an instant, a space of time too small to measure, the bomb would explode.[4]

Once assembled, the scientists concealed Little Boy under canvas, and technicians took it to a loading pit where soldiers kept it under armed guard.

The 509th Composite Group

On December 17, 1944, the air force created a self-sustaining bombing unit called the 509th Composite Group for the purpose of dropping atomic bombs. At Wendover Field, Utah, Generals Henry Arnold, the unit's commanding officer, and Groves shared responsibility for organizing, equipping, and training the unit's 225 officers and 1,542 enlisted men. The air force gave the 509th fourteen of its best B-29 models, equipped with fuel injection engines and electrically controlled reversible propellers. General Arnold said "No one would ever be able to say that the Air Force did not do its utmost to support the Manhattan Project."[5]

Arnold and Groves agreed that Lieutenant Colonel Paul Tibbets, one of the air force's best pilots, would fly the plane that would drop the first atomic bomb. As operation officer of the 97th Bombardment Group in the North African and European theater of operations, he had flown numerous combat missions, tested B-29s, and written the instructions for its use in combat. "He was a superb pilot of heavy planes."[6]

Under him, Tibbets commanded seventy-five of the best pilots in the air force and an equal number of top supporting airmen. But besides Tibbets, only navy captain William S. Parsons, weaponeer and tactical commander, knew the real purpose of the 509th Composite Group's mission.

Forty-four-year-old Parsons, called "Deak" by his friends, was a handsome man with "intelligent eyes and a melancholy smile." The navy considered him one of its finest gunnery engineers. Before working on the development of the atomic bomb, he had pioneered the development of radar and the proximity fuse. As chief of the Ordnance Division in the Manhattan Project, he had supervised the design and assembly of Little Boy and was familiar with every part of it. A sensitive man who "loathed the idea of creating an object of mass destruction," he argued, after the war ended, that the United States should have warned the Japanese before dropping the atomic bomb.[7]

Although Tibbets would pilot the aircraft, Parsons was the tactical commander with the power of decision on all matters involving the use and emergency disposal of the bomb.

Throughout the winter and spring of 1944–45 the pilots trained over the Utah desert. Having rejected radar as inaccurate, they practiced making visual drops, using one bomb and maneuvering the B-29 into sharp diving turns to make as quick an exit from the point of explosion. The pilots did not know the purpose of their training. "They were given 43 seconds to get away 10 miles after the drop which to them was curious," said Truman later. "And they were practicing to drop only one bomb which to them was funnier still."[8]

In the spring of 1945 the 509th composite Group arrived on Tinian Island. Now under the command of General Curtis E. LeMay, who headed the 21st Bomber Command, the 509th formed tiny three-plane formations and flew into Japan and back, dropping a single bomb, called "Pumpkin," over an enemy target. The arms technicians designed the Pumpkin, containing 5,500 pounds of explosives, for blast effect only. Groves explained: "We hoped that analysis of the results obtained by the use of the Pumpkins might help us to refine the ballistic data for the real bomb."[9]

On Tinian, the regular air force pilots, who risked their lives daily in mass raids on Japan, ridiculed the pilots of the 509th for leading a "soft life." Their geographical separation, rigid security measures, and failure to participate in ordinary combat missions brought them the ridicule usually reserved in the military world for the "abnormal unit." This ridicule earned the 509th a poem by some unknown satirist, entitled "Nobody Knows" that had the refrain, "For the 509th is winning the war."[10]

The Targets

Earlier, a special Target Committee had reserved Kyoto, Hiroshima, Kokura, and Niigata for the atomic bomb. Because an untouched city was necessary to measure more accurately the effects of the bomb, orders came down for the air force to bypass them.

Kyoto was Grove's first choice. Its war industries included machine tools, precision ordnance and aircraft parts, radio fire control and gun direction equipment. But equally important to Groves, it had a population of over a million, and "it was large enough in area for us to gain complete knowledge of the effects of an atomic bomb."[11] Groves considered it ideal for psychological reasons, too. It was the ancient capital of Japan, with "exquisite temples, shrines, and palaces," and it would satisfy the Target Committee's need for a city "sufficiently spectacular for the importance of the weapon to be internationally recognized when publicity on it was released."[12]

On June 12 Stimson asked Groves for the list of cities targeted for the atomic bomb. Going over the list, he immediately objected to Kyoto. "It had been the ancient capital of Japan," he said, "and was a shrine of Japanese art and culture."[13] He feared the Japanese would never forgive the United States, and the world would disapprove of bombing a religious and culturally significant city. But Groves continued to press it: "I suggested that he might change his mind after he had read the description of Kyoto and our reasons for considering it to be a desirable target.[14]

Stimson agreed "it was a target of considerable military importance," but the other considerations for not bombing it took precedence.[15]

Still afraid that Groves might get his way on Kyoto, Stimson brought up the issue with Truman at the Potsdam Conference. To his surprise, Truman readily agreed with him. "Stimson was the best informed man I ever had around me," said Truman later. "He was very anxious that I not order the bombing of Kyoto, which is the religious center of Shintoism in Japan, and I didn't."[16]

The new list of target cities for the atomic bomb, included Hiroshima, Kokura, Nagasaki, and Niigata.

Hiroshima

On August 2 Tibbets and Major Thomas Ferebee, the bombardier who would make the drop, reported to General LeMay's headquarters on Guam. Showing them a map of Hiroshima, the primary target, LeMay asked Ferebee to pick an aiming point. After closely studying the map, he placed his index finger on the T-shape of the Aioi Bridge near the center of the city.

Except for Kyoto, Hiroshima was the largest city still undamaged by air attacks, extending twenty-six miles. Most of its 245,000 people lived within seven miles of the city's center. Located on the underside of Honshu Island, Hiroshima was built on the broad fan-shaped delta of the Ota River, whose seven mouths divided the city into six islands that projected finger-like into Hiroshima Bay on the Inland Sea. A highly developed bridge system with eighty-one important bridges joined the islands.

Hiroshima was the headquarters of the Japanese Second Army and the Chugoku Regional Army. It had once been the foremost military shipping point for troops and supplies. By August 1945, however, its shipping activities had virtually ceased because of the destruction of the Japanese navy and the mining of the Inland Sea.[17] Although Groves described Hiroshima as a "beehive" for war production, it had no great manufacturing plants for munitions or aircraft, the chief targets for heavy bombing.[18]

Throughout the war the United States had left Hiroshima almost untouched by bombs. Various rumors circulated among the Japanese that it was being spared because so many Christians lived there; because many Japanese-Americans were from there; because the city was a famous beauty spot; because Truman had a relative living there. These reasons were "fantastic," said others; the United States was saving Hiroshima for "something big."[19]

On August 4 Parsons briefed the seven B-29 crews on their special bombing mission. Leaving out the words "atomic" or "nuclear," he did not reveal the exact nature of the bomb. All of the pilots knew, however, that they would be dealing with a different kind of bomb. Still, they were surprised to hear his description of it. "The force of the explosion," he said, "would be equivalent to that of twenty thousand tons of TNT."[20] And when he showed a film of the New Mexico test explosion, the men "were stunned." Even Tibbets, who knew about the test, was "overwhelmed."[21]

All seven B-29s had a specific task. One was a spare, housed at Iwo Jima, where facilities had been set up for unloading and reloading the bomb in case of an abort. In advance of the attack, three warplanes would fly to each target. The main force consisted of three

B-29s. Tibbets's *Enola Gay*, named after his mother, would carry the atomic bomb. Loaded with cameras and scientific instruments, Major Charles W. Sweeney's *The Great Artiste* and Captain George W. Marquandt's *No. 91*, the two observation planes, would carry military and civilian observers. While the Twentieth Air Force would provide sea and air rescue service, no planes besides those on the mission were to approach within fifty miles of the target from four hours before to six hours after the strike—even for rescue. Afterward, two F-13s would perform photographic reconnaissance.

Shortly after midnight, August 6, a final briefing took place, followed by a pre-flight breakfast, and by religious services. At 12:37 a.m. the three weather scout planes took off. At 2:00 a.m. the crews of the *Enola Gay* and its escort planes arrived in trucks to their B-29s. Immediately, an army film crew, accompanied by photographers and tape recorders, surrounded them. To Parsons, it all "seemed obscene." The crew was not opening a new play but dropping an atomic bomb.[22]

At 2:27 a.m. Tibbets taxied the *Enola Gay* onto the runway, turned it in the direction of Japan, and to gain the momentum necessary to lift the extra load, pulled back the wheel virtually at the water's edge. The time was 2:45 a.m. Fifteen minutes later, while over the Pacific Ocean, Parsons and his assistant, Morris R. Jeppson, armed the bomb.

The flight was uneventful. At 4:55 a.m. the two observation planes joined the *Enola Gay* to create a V-formation. The weather report was the key. If cloud cover hid Hiroshima, Kokura, and Nagasaki, Tibbets was to abort the mission. At about 8:00 a.m. the weather plane over Hiroshima, Major Claude Eatherly's *Straight Flush*, bearing a cartoon of a Japanese soldier being flushed down a toilet, radioed that cloud cover was less than three-tenths at all altitudes. He advised, "Bomb primary." This sealed "Hiroshima's doom."[23]

Tibbets positioned the plane for the drop. *The Great Artiste*, the instrument plane, dropped back 1,000 yards. The other escort, *No. 91*, positioned itself to take photographs. At this point bombardier Major Thomas W. Ferebee, navigator Captain Theodore J. Van Kirk, and radar operator Sergeant Joe A. Stiborik took controls. At 8:15

a.m. Ferebee dropped the bomb. The plane was then at 31,600 feet. Tibbets immediately took back the controls, executed a violent turn of 150 degrees, and nosed down to gain speed.

At 8:16 a.m., fifty-one seconds after it had left the plane, Little Boy exploded at a height of 1,850 feet, 200 yards from the T-shaped Aioi Bridge that spanned the widest of the seven streams at Hiroshima. Almost immediately, two shock waves hit the *Enola Gay*, which by now was fifteen miles from the burst. In his record book, Captain Robert A. Lewis, the copilot, described the blast: "The initial burst and 'ball of fire'; the cloud mass; the rapidly ascending column which eventually mushroomed and continued its climb to 50,000 feet." He added, "My God, what have we done?"[24]

At the hypocenter, the blast's impact lifted the Aioi Bridge, a modern steel and concrete structure 100 yards in length spanning the Ota River, into the air and then dropped it back, "twisted by the heat," in almost the same place. The bomb's "shock wave" moved outward from the hypocenter, forming concentric circles. Then the blast reversed itself and the air began moving back toward the center. This produced a kind of whirlwind, flattening buildings over four square miles from the hypocenter.[25]

The initial blast illuminated the city with a yellowish light that possessed, for a fraction of a second, a temperature of a million degrees. According to eyewitness accounts, the bomb exploded with a "tremendous flash" and "intense glare and heat," followed by a "tremendous pressure wave" and "a rumbling sound."[26] Directly under the bomb's explosion, those in the open were so severely burned that their skin was "charred dark brown or black," and they died within a few minutes or hours.[27] Drawing in air from all directions, fires sprang up simultaneously over the city's wide flat area, generating a firestorm with a wind velocity of 40 miles an hour, almost completely burning out over four square miles of the city's center."[28]

Those who directly survived the blast and fire appeared "aimless," "hysterical," and "terror-stricken." "The primary reaction to the bomb was fear," said the Strategic Bombing Survey, "uncontrolled terror, strengthened by the sheer horror of the destruction and suffering witnessed and experienced by the survivors."[29]

"The entire population had been reduced to a common level of physical and mental weakness," said Dr. Michihiko Hachiya, a survivor. "They were so broken and confused that they moved like automatons."[30] To the survivors, the sudden nonexistence of Hiroshima was "unnatural." In re-creating the scene, survivors would describe "a single stretch of wasteland," or "the citizens were annihilated," or "it is the city of the dead," or simply, "I can't express what I feel."[31]

Many of those who survived the initial blast and fire later died from the effects of the bomb's radioactive fallout. Within 3,000 feet of the blast, said the Stategic Bombing Survey, 95 percent of the survivors suffered from radiation disease.[32] Often a lingering illness, its first symptoms were loss of appetite, lassitude, general discomfort, inflammation of the gums, mouths, and pharynx, followed by fever. If the fever subsided, the person might recover. Otherwise, the disease continued, with loss of hair, decrease in sperm count, and loss of white blood corpuscles, which affected the bone marrow and destroyed the human process of resisting infection.[33] Death followed thereafter. "This new weapon," said Leahy, "is a poisonous thing that kills people by its deadly radioactive reaction more than the explosive force it develops."[34]

Hiroshima's death toll was difficult to determine. The circumstances of fire, flight of entire families, destruction of official records, mass cremation, and identification of the dead made an accurate estimate impossible. The Japanese estimated 71,000 dead and missing and 68,000 injured.[35] The Strategic Bombing Survey estimated 70,000 to 80,000 dead and an equal number injured.[36] The British mission to Japan estimated the number killed at between 70,000 and 90,000. In comparison, the British pointed out that the overall number killed by German air attacks throughout Britain, including London, was 60,000.[37] After an extensive study, Professor Shogo Nagaoka, the first curator of the Peace Memorial in Hiroshima, and Doctors Naomi Shohno and K. Sakuma concluded that at least 200,000 died as a result of the atomic bomb, and twenty-three of them, including several women, were U.S. prisoners of war.[38]

Response and Reaction

On the morning of August 6 Truman and his party were on board the *Augusta* on their way home from Potsdam. The ship had entered the Gulf Stream, south of Newfoundland. The sun was out, and the sea was calm. Truman was below deck having lunch with some of the crew. Captain Graham, one of the map room officers, rushed in with a Japanese map and a decoded message from Stimson. It read, "Big bomb dropped on Hiroshima August 5 at 7:15 p.m. Washington time. First reports indicate complete success which was even more conspicuous than earlier test."[39]

Truman immediately telephoned Byrnes aboard ship: "It's time for us to get home."[40]

Truman was "exuberant." Greatly moved, he said to a group of sailors near him, "This is the greatest thing in history."[41] Then, tapping on a glass with a fork, he called for the crew's attention. "Keep your seats, gentlemen," he said in a voice tense with excitement. "I have an announcement to make to you." As the officers waited, excited and puzzled, Truman said, "We have just dropped a bomb on Japan which has more power than 20,000 tons of TNT. It was an overwhelming success."[42]

Everyone broke out in applause and cheers. "Surprise in war is the greatest asset," said Truman later. "We were able to surprise the Japanese and all the rest of the world."[43]

At his Pentagon office on August 6 General Marshall assembled Groves and Arnold to discuss the prewritten presidential press statement for release at 11 a.m. Freshly shaven and looking crisp in a clean uniform, Groves, like Truman, was "exuberant" over the atomic bombing. Marshall said to him: "We should guard against too much gratification over our success because it undoubtedly involved a large number of Japanese casualties."[44]

Clearly annoyed, Groves replied, "I was not thinking so much about these casualties as I was about the men who had made the Bataan death march."[45] (Beginning on May 7, 1942, between 7,000 and 10,000 U.S. and Philippine soldiers died of starvation, disease, beatings, and executions as their Japanese captors marched them to Bataan after the surrender of Corregidor.) In the hall afterward,

Arnold slapped Groves' back and said, "I am glad you said that—it's just the way I feel."[46]

At the White House that morning everything was rather hum-drum. The White House had informed the press that it would issue a press release at 11 a.m., but White House correspondents were accustomed to such notices, and their interest was not aroused. Many sent their assistants instead of going themselves. At the appointed hour, a spokesman read: "Sixteen hours ago an American airplane dropped one bomb on Hiroshima, an important Japanese army base. That bomb had more power than 20,000 tons of TNT. It is an atomic bomb."[47] At that instant, according to Groves, "there was a tremendous rush of reporters for the press releases."[48]

The news brought "astonishment," but not all were enthusiastic. "We are the inheritors to the mantle of Genghis Khan," said *New York Times* editorial writer Hanson W. Baldwin, "and all of those in history who have justified the use of utter ruthlessness in war."[49]

Admiral Leahy agreed. "In being the first to use it," he said, "we had adopted an ethical standard common to the barbarians of the Dark Ages. I was not taught to make war in that fashion, and wars cannot be won by destroying women and children."[50]

Senator Richard B. Russell of Georgia argued for sterner measures. In a letter dated August 7, he wrote Truman that the United States should stop appealing to Japan to surrender. "We should continue to strike the Japanese until they are brought groveling to their knees," he said. "If we do not have available a sufficient number of atomic bombs with which to finish the job immediately, let us carry on with TNT and fire bombs until we can produce them.[51]

In a letter dated August 9 Truman replied, "I certainly regret the necessity of wiping out whole populations because of the 'pig-headedness' of the leaders of a nation and, for your information, I am not going to do it unless it is absolutely necessary."[52]

Shortly after 8:16 a.m. the Japan Broadcasting Corporation reported that the telephone line to Hiroshima's radio station was dead. Two hours later, Central Command Headquarters in Osaka reported that military communications to Hiroshima were dead. By

1:00 p.m. Tokyo authorities had learned from a Domei correspondent who had bicycled into Hiroshima that one bomb had annihilated the city. But the military refused to allow the press to release the story. Instead, the press reported the bombing as "an ordinary air raid."[53]

At about 1:00 a.m., August 7, Tokyo's Domei radio monitoring station picked up a U.S. broadcast of Truman's press release. After announcing that the United States had dropped an atomic bomb on Hiroshima, it warned the Japanese to "now accept our terms" or "expect a rain of ruin from the air, the like of which has never been seen on this earth."[54]

The news "stunned" Japan's leaders. Hirohito was "overwhelmed with grief." Although he did not order a surrender, he told Kido the war must end."[55] At a Cabinet meeting that day, Togo wanted to accept the Potsdam Declaration, but War Minister Anami was against it. "Such a move is uncalled for," Anami said. "We do not yet know if the bomb was atomic."[56] All agreed to send Dr. Hyoshio Nishina, the nation's leading nuclear scientist, to investigate Hiroshima.

Nishina and Lieutenant Colonel Seiichi Niizuma, a physics graduate of Tokyo University, flew to Hiroshima. At 8:00 p.m. August 8, Nishina telephoned Cabinet Secretary Sakomizu. "I'm very sorry to tell you this," said Nishina. "The so-called new-type bomb is actually an atomic bomb."[57] Japan's leaders could no longer deny the reality that the United States had dropped an atomic bomb on Hiroshima.

Soviet Entry

On August 7, Molotov sent Sato a note offering him an appointment at 8:00 p.m., August 8. Early the next day, he moved it up to 5:00 p.m. When Sato arrived, he greeted Molotov in Russian. Brushing it aside, Molotov got right to the point. "The Allies approached the Soviet government with a proposal to join in the war against Japanese aggression," he said. "True to its obligation as an ally, the Soviet government accepted the proposal of the Allies," and as of August 9, "the Soviet Union will consider herself in a state of war against Japan."[58]

Despite his previous misgivings about the Soviet initiative, Sato was "considerably shocked," but he maintained "a calm attitude." He asked to telegram the Soviet declaration of war to Japan at once. Molotov agreed, but the Soviets intercepted it. In addition, they disconnected all telephones at the Japanese embassy and confiscated all radio equipment. The Japanese first heard about the declaration of war from a San Francisco broadcast at 4:00 a.m., August 9, and did not receive official notification of war until August 10, when Ambassador Malik handed it to Togo.[59]

On August 8 Molotov informed Ambassador Harriman in Moscow that the Soviet Union was at war with Japan. "Although at one time it was thought that this action could not take place until mid-August," said Molotov, "the Soviet Government had now strictly lived up to its promise to enter the Pacific War three months after the defeat of Germany."[60] Previously, Stalin had said that the Soviet Union would not enter the war until it had reached an agreement with China over Soviet interests in Manchuria. But Soviet-Chinese negotiations were still far from an agreement. The Soviet move, however, did not surprise Truman. "Our dropping of the atomic bomb," he said, "had forced Russia to reconsider her position in the Far East."[61]

At midnight, August 9, over one and a half million Soviet troops, supported by 3,000 tanks, moved across the Manchurian border. A Soviet broadcast accused Japan of breaking the Neutrality Pact, recounted Japan's past aggressions, "in which she had always been very wolf-like," and delivered a "scathing indictment of Japan's right-wing imperialists who were destroying the interests of the people."[62]

For the most part, the war was over in six days. The Kwantung Army's 600,000 troops were green and ill-equipped, lacking modern antitank weapons, and supplied only with obsolescent artillery and few shells. The Red Army pushed to within 100 miles of Beijing, where it linked up with Mao's Communist Army. According to Soviet reports, 80,000 Japanese and 8,200 Soviet troops died, and the Soviets captured 600,000 Japanese military personnel and civilians.[63] Afterward, Truman said "No military contribution was made by the Russians toward victory over Japan."[64] Still, for the longest time, he had been "most insistent" that their entry was necessary to help defeat Japan.

Japan's leaders learned of the Soviet declaration of war from the Domei News Agency at 4:00 a.m., August 9. Upon hearing the news, Togo was as indignant as Secretary of State Cordell Hull had been on Pearl Harbor day. It was beyond his comprehension, said Togo, "that the Soviet Union should have suddenly declared war upon Japan without making any reply to our request for good offices made in July and without any reference to the Neutrality Pact, which was in force until 1946."[65]

"This was the most unkindest cut of all," said Toshikazu Kase. "We had asked for an olive branch and received a dagger thrust."[66]

To Japan's leaders, the Soviet entry into the war was as great a blow, if not greater, than the atomic bomb. Suzuki agreed with Togo: "The war must stop immediately."[67]

"It was a bigger blow for me," said Lieutenant General Seizo Arisu "that Russia joined the war than the atomic bomb."[68]

Admiral Toyoda said later: "Russian participation in the war against Japan rather than the atomic bombs did more to hasten the surrender."[69]

"The Government," said the Strategic Bombing Survey, "was not prepared for war with the Soviets nor the military capable of any effective counterplan."[70]

Nagasaki

The Manhattan Project had built three bombs, including the one used in the New Mexico test. After Hiroshima, it had one left. Nicknamed Fat Man, this bomb was a spherical plutonium missile, ten-feet-eight-inches long and five feet in diameter. To keep the Japanese "off balance," Admiral William R. Purnell, the navy's representative on the Manhattan Project, and Groves agreed that the second bomb should quickly follow the first. "It was Purnell who had first advanced the belief that two bombs would end the war," said Groves, "so I knew that with him and Farrell on the ground at Tinian there would be no unnecessary delay in exploiting our first success."[71]

For the drop, the 509th Composite Group would use six B-29s. Like Hiroshima, the striking force included three planes, one armed and two for observation, and a spare at Iwo Jima. Only two weather planes were needed because there were only two targets: Kokura, near the northern tip of Kyushu, and Nagasaki, on the west coast of Kyushu. Major Sweeney, who had flown an observation plane on the Hiroshima mission, would pilot the drop plane.

At 3:49 a.m., August 9, Sweeney's B-29 took off from Tinian, followed by its two observation planes. Just before takeoff, Admiral Purnell said to Sweeney: "Young man do you know how much that bomb cost?"

Sweeney replied, "About $25 million."

Purnell added, "See that we get our money's worth."[72]

Shortly after takeoff, Sweeney discovered that the fuel selector to the 600 gallons of gas in their planes bomb-bay was not working. The trapped fuel meant limited flying time. When the BP-29 weather plane over Kokura reported clear visibility, he decided to continue the mission. By the time his plane got over the city, however, smoke and haze had obscured it. Captain Kermit K. Beahan, Sweeney's bombardier, made three runs without getting a glimpse of the target. Fuel was getting low. Sweeney turned to Frederick Ashworth, the weaponeer. "We'll go on to the secondary target, if you agree," said Sweeney. Ashworth nodded.[73] Sweeney turned southwest, heading for Nagasaki. The B-29 weather plane over the city had reported little cloud cover.

Facing the East China Sea, Nagasaki was located on the best natural harbor of Western Kyushu. Spread over precipitous hills, the city extended for several miles along the narrow shores and up the valleys opening out from the harbor. Divided by a mountain spur, two rivers formed the two main valleys in whose basins the city lay. The mountain spur and the city's irregular lay out would reduce the area of destruction by the atomic bomb.

The city's built-up area was over three miles, but less than a mile of it was industrial. The city's four largest companies were the Mitsubishi Shipyards, Electrical Equipment Works, Arms Plant, and

Steel Works. These four firms employed nearly 90 percent of the city's labor force.

In 1571, the Portuguese had built Nagasaki from a fishing village to Japan's chief port of foreign trade. Despite its excellent harbor, it had declined in modern times because of its isolated peninsular position and the difficulties of transportation through the mountains by inadequate roads and railroad facilities. Sasebo had replaced it as a major military port. The Portuguese had introduced European ways and Christianity to Nagasaki. Throughout the next four centuries, Japan unsuccessfully tried to suppress both, and Nagasaki remained the most Christian and Europeanized city in the country. A blend of East and West, it had scores of Christian churches and schools and hundreds of Western-style homes.

In the previous twelve months, Nagasaki had experienced five small-scale air raids. The air force had dropped 270 tons of explosives, and fifty-three tons of incendiary, and twenty tons of fragmentation bombs, destroying or badly damaging 276 residential buildings and industrial firms.[74] But the city was still relatively intact.

By the time Sweeney's plane arrived at Nagasaki, the weather had clouded up and conditions seemed no better for visual bombings than at Kokura. But at the last second, 11:01 a.m., Captain Beahan found a hole in the clouds, synchronized aiming on a race track, and dropped Fat Man from an altitude of 29,000 feet. A minute later, the explosion came. The crew felt five separate shocks, "as if the B-29 were beaten by a telephone pole."[75] In one of the observation planes, correspondent William Lawrence wrote: "The pillar of fire became a living thing, a new species of being, born right before incredulous eyes. It seethed and boiled in white fury like a thousand geysers."[76]

The actual area destroyed was smaller at Nagasaki than at Hiroshima. Because of the cloud overcast, Beahan's drop was almost two miles northwest of the planned hypocenter, the high ground near Morimoto's Kite shop. At that point, the blast and fire would have wiped out the center of town, the port areas, and the factories of the Urakami Valley. Instead, the explosion occurred over the northwest portion of the city, exactly between the Mitsubishi Steel and Arms Works and the Mitsubishi Torpedo Factory, and confined it to the

Urakami Valley. The intervening hills protected a major portion of the city lying in the adjoining valley. In addition, no firestorm occurred, and a shift in wind direction helped to control the fires.[77]

Despite the intervening hills, the whole city felt the blast. "A tremendous roaring sound was heard," said the survivors, "and a crushing blast wave and intense heat were felt."[78] According to the Nagasaki Prefectural Report, within a radius of one mile from ground zero, everybody died, and within two to four miles, some died while almost everybody else suffered injury.[79] As in Hiroshima, many who survived the initial blast died shortly after from radiation sickness: "anemia, leukopenia, and pupura."[80] Blast and fire gutted over 80 percent of the city's hospital beds and destroyed about 90 percent of the city's industrial output. Only the Mitsubishi Dockyards were far enough from the explosion to escape serious damage.

As in Hiroshima, the casualty rate at Nagasaki was difficult to determine. The Strategic Bombing Survey estimated the casualty rate between 35,000 and 40,000 dead and an equal number injured, out of a population of around 250,000.[81] If the bomb had fallen at the hypocenter, the casualty rate would have been higher. "I was considerably relieved when I got the bombing report," said Groves, "which indicated a smaller number of casualties than we had expected, for by that time I was certain that Japan was through and that the war could not continue for more than a few days."[82]

Although Truman expressed his determination to use the atomic bombs on military targets, not women and children, the overwhelming majority of those killed were civilians. By dropping conventional bombs, the United States could have limited civilian casualties. But the fire raids had already desensitized U.S. leaders to killing Japanese women and children. Many industries had parceled out war work to home shops, which led to a blurring of the distinction between civilians and war workers, who were considered legitimate targets.

In the wake of the Soviet entry, the historian wonders why U.S. leaders were in such a hurry to drop the second bomb. The United States dropped Fat Man on Nagasaki only hours after the Soviet Union announced its entry and its one and a half million troops were crossing the Manchurian border. The United States had given Japan virtually no time to surrender before being struck by a third blow. Moreover, Truman had said numerous times that Soviet entry would end the war.

Since the spring of 1945, Japan's leaders had hoped to persuade the Soviet Union to mediate an end to the war. After intercepting the messages between Togo and Sato, naval intelligence reported this information to U.S. leaders. Despite the knowledge that the Japanese were trying to negotiate an end to the war, U.S. leaders never considered opening direct negotiations with them. Instead, they issued the Potsdam Declaration. While it clarified unconditional surrender terms, it left out the most important point for the Japanese— retention of Emperor Hirohito.

With three new blows—Hiroshima, Soviet entry, and Nagasaki— Japan's leaders, seeking a negotiated surrender, had to decide whether to hurry the process or continue to hold out for better terms.

6.

The First Imperial Decision

Deadlock

On the morning of August 9, 1945, the Supreme Council for the Direction of the War assembled at the concrete-walled air raid shelter underneath Prime Minister Kantaro Suzuki's official residence. All six members were there: Suzuki, Foreign Minister Shigenori Togo, War Minister Korechika Anami, Navy Minister Mitsumasa Yonai, Army Chief of Staff Yoshijiro Umezu, and Navy Chief of Staff Teijiro Toyoda. "The atmosphere was very gloomy and very cold," said Cabinet Secretary Hisatsune Sakomizu. "Everyone was sunk deep in his chair."[1] Events were moving rapidly: the Hiroshima bomb, the Soviet entry, and the new report from a captured U.S. pilot that Tokyo was the next target on the atomic bomb list.[2]

The Supreme Council's six members were evenly divided over surrender terms. Suzuki, Togo, and Yonai favored acceptance of the Potsdam Declaration on condition that Emperor Hirohito remained on the throne. Anami, Umezu, and Toyoda favored three additional conditions: voluntary withdrawal of Japanese overseas forces under their own commanders; no Allied occupation of Japan's main islands; and Japan's ability to conduct its own trials of those responsible for the war.[3] "This proud nation must not yield so abjectly to its enemies," said Anami. "We all want peace," but "it must be on the basis of four conditions."[4]

With Japan close to total military collapse, Togo argued that the Allies would probably reject four additional conditions for surrender. If that happened, he asked, could the armed services offer any hope of victory? Although Anami could give "no assurance of victory," he said, "Japan could still fight another battle."[5]

Togo pressed: Could the military "be certain of preventing the enemy from landing on our mainland?"

Anami said, "The army would be able to hold off an invading force."[6]

Togo was not persuaded. "The enemy would follow up with a second assault," he said. "There being no possibility of replenishing our supply of armaments, in a short period, our position would be one of defenselessness, even leaving the atomic bomb out of account."[7]

At that moment, one of Suzuki's aides burst into the room. After catching his breath, he said "Nagasaki has just been hit by a second atomic bomb."[8] The discussion, which had been rather quiet and somber, suddenly became "impassioned," but by this time, the Supreme Council was irreconcilably deadlocked, three to three. At nearly 1:00 p.m., with a Cabinet meeting scheduled for that afternoon, Togo adjourned the meeting. Nothing was resolved.

At 2:30 p.m., the Cabinet came to order. Its sixteen members debated whether to accept the Potsdam Declaration with the sole condition that Hirohito remain on the throne or to also include the three additional demands by Anami, Umezu, and Toyoda. Togo argued that "it would be inadvisable to submit so many terms at this juncture when the situation was so tense."[9] All "grave and gloomy," the civilian ministers of the treasury, agriculture, and transportation said that "the war was no longer possible."[10] Yonai, a taciturn admiral, added that "there was no chance whatsoever of victory."[11]

But Anami was adamant. "If it came to a final battle on Japanese soil," he said, "we could at least for a time repulse the enemy, and might thereafter somehow 'find life out of death'"[12]

To resolve the issue, the Cabinet was required to have a unanimous decision. When they voted, however, nine were for acceptance of the Potsdam Declaration with the sole condition that Hirohito remain on the throne; four wanted the three additional conditions included; and three were undecided.[13]

About 7:00 p.m. Suzuki, Sakomizu, and Togo assembled in the prime minister's room. Because neither the Supreme Council nor the Cabinet could reach agreement on surrender terms, Sakomizu argued that the emperor should debate the issue. "It would be better," he said, "to have the Supreme Council meet in the Emperor's presence and let all the members express personally their own views."[14] The emperor "venerated as a descendant of Amaterasu, the sun goddess who lived beyond the clouds," would then settle the issue by imperial decision.[15]

Sakomizu's proposal broke all precedent. The Supreme Council and the Cabinet were first supposed to reach unanimity on any issue brought to the attention of the emperor. Regardless of his own views on the matter, the emperor was then obligated to sanction the government's unanimous decision.[16] This protected the emperor from all responsibility for decisions of state.

To hold a Supreme Council meeting in the emperor's presence, Sakomizu had to follow procedure. He needed to give Privy Seal Marquis Koichi Kido a petition, signed by the chiefs of the army and navy. He would then present it to the emperor. To persuade Navy Chief of Staff Toyoda and Army Chief of Staff Umezu to sign the petition, Sakomizu resorted to a deception. He did not tell them that Suzuki would immediately try to arrange an Imperial Conference. Instead, he explained that "there was no telling when such an Imperial conference would have to be held—perhaps even in the middle of the night—and so the prerequisite signatures of the two chiefs would save time and trouble later on."[17] Sakomizu implied that he would not call for an Imperial Conference without first confirming the fact with them, and only if the government had reached a unanimous decision on the issue beforehand.[18]

What happened next is a little unclear. Apparently, immediately after Toyoda and Umezu signed the petition, Sakomizu gave it to Mamoru Shigemitsu, former foreign minister in the Koiso Cabinet, who handed it to Kido. At the same time, Shigemitsu asked Kido to set up a meeting with Suzuki, Togo, and Emperor Hirohito. When Kido appeared to hesitate, Sakomizu pressed: "We were hovering on the verge of an irretrievable disaster. Rather than leave matters in the hands of a government that was too weak to restrain the army, it was right and proper to invoke an imperial decision."[19] Kido agreed. At 10:50 p.m. he asked Hirohito to grant an audience with Suzuki and Togo and to allow a meeting of the Supreme Council in the emperor's presence.[20] Hirohito agreed to both recommendations.

Shortly thereafter, Suzuki and Togo met with Hirohito. They explained the government's deadlock over whether to accept the Potsdam Declaration with the sole condition of retention of the emperor or to accept the military's three additional conditions. They asked Hirohito to meet with the members of the Supreme Council, to hear their views on the matter, and then to make an imperial decision.[21] According to the ladies at court, Hirohito answered with great emotion: "I am going to stop this, and I don't care what happens to me personally."[22]

Imperial Conference

Shortly before midnight on August 9 the Imperial Conference assembled in the underground air raid shelter on the palace grounds. In attendance were the six members of the Supreme Council for the Direction of the War, its four secretaries, Chief Cabinet Secretary Sakomizu, Lieutenant General Masao Yoshizumi, and President of the Privy Council Baron Kichiro Hiranuma.

The men filed into the eighteen-by-thirty-feet conference room. Because the air conditioning was not working properly, the air was hot, humid, and damp. Drops of water stood out on the lacquered panels. Two long, narrow tables, covered with damask cloths, faced each other. At the head of the room was a much smaller table reserved for Emperor Hirohito. All present were wearing either full military uniform or formal morning dress, and all were perspiring.

As the men were taking their seats, Toyoda and Umezu spotted Sakomizu. With their "swords clanging ominously," they accused him of obtaining their signatures "under false pretenses."[23] At 11:50 p.m., Hirohito, escorted by his military aide, General Shigeru Hasunuma, entered the conference room. Immediately everyone snapped to attention and bowed from the waist. Acknowledging their bows, Hirohito sat down at the small table set up for him. Neatly dressed in an army uniform, he looked "weary," and his face was red, "a few strands of his bristly black hair hung down, uncharacteristically, on his forehead."[24]

Outside, Tosahikazu Kaze, Togo's secretary, was sitting in a parked car. "Quietly shining in the moonlight," he said later, "the palace was silhouetted against the sky, where, undisturbed, dim constellations moved on in majestic silence, propelled, I thought, by the prophetic soul of the wide world dreaming on things to come.[25]

Suzuki opened the conference by asking Sakomizu to read the Potsdam Declaration. The words stuck in his throat. "It was very hard to do," he said, "because the words of the declaration are very hard; the contents were not cheerful things to read in the presence of the Emperor."[26] Next, Suzuki stated that the Supreme Council was evenly divided over two surrender proposals. The first, advocated by Suzuki, Togo, and Yonai, called for acceptance of the Potsdam Declaration, with the sole condition that Emperor Hirohito remain on the throne. The second, advocated by Anami, Umezu, and Toyoda, called for three additional conditions.

Suzuki called on each member of the Supreme Council to make a statement. Togo was the first to speak. Despite the heat and humidity, he appeared self-possessed. In a firm voice, he said, "We must now end the war by accepting the Potsdam Declaration in accordance with the first alternative."[27] Admiral Yonai sided with Togo.

In opposition to Togo and Yonai, Anami said he would accept surrender if the three conditions were added to the first alternative.[28]

Otherwise, he said "when invasion of the homeland was undertaken, it would be possible to strike a damaging blow against the enemy," and then Japan could end the war "on more favorable terms than those offered by the Potsdam Declaration."[29]

Backing him up, Umezu added, "Since many brave men had gladly fought and died for the Emperor, it would be inexcusable to surrender unconditionally."[30]

Admiral Toyoda was next in line, but Suzuki passed him up, either by mistake or design. Instead, he called on Baron Hiranuma, an ultranationalist who could go either way. Hiranuma asked a series of pointed questions: "What had happened to the proposed Soviet negotiations? Why had the Soviet Union declared war? Just whom did the Allies mean when they spoke of war criminals? Would such persons be turned over to the Allies? Would they be tried in Japan? Would the Allies agree to let Japan disarm her own troops?[31] The task fell to Togo to respond. He did a fair job, but the questions did not have easy answers—except that Japan had lost the war.

Hiranuma next brought up the military situation. He discussed the daily air raids, decline in morale, destruction of transportation facilities, lack of food, atomic bombs, and the Soviet entry. Turning to Umezu and Toyoda, he asked, "Do the army and navy have any true confidence in their ability to continue the war?"

Both men were optimistic. Umezu said that "anti-aircraft measures could prevent further atomic bomb attacks. Toyoda added, "We have been preserving our strength for future use. We are now prepared to counterattack."[32]

"Is there anything more you could do that you are not doing?" asked Hiranuma. "I think both in the army and in the navy we are doing our best under the circumstances," said Toyoda. Umezu nodded in agreement.

"That is no doubt true," said Hiranuma. "But it is now quite clear that your best is not good enough and has not been good enough for some time."[33]

Hiranuma's blunt criticism of the military left an uneasy silence. The intense heat and dampness made everyone uncomfortable. The men's faces were wet with perspiration; mosquitoes buzzed in the air while some tried to brush them away.

In the end, Hiranuma's position was unclear. He first leaned toward acceptance of the Potsdam Declaration with the sole reservation of retention of the emperor, but he then argued that the government should negotiate with the Allies for the army's demands. He agreed, however, that the Allied terms were a "very grave matter," and the emperor's views "should be sought." Looking at Hirohito, he made one final observation: "Your Imperial Majesty is also responsible for preventing unrest in the nation. I should like to ask Your Majesty to make Your decision with this point in mind."[34]

Admiral Toyoda was the last to speak. "We cannot say that victory is certain," he said, "but at the same time we do not believe we shall be positively defeated."[35] When he finished, the men squirmed in their seats. After two hours, the conference was still deadlocked. Togo and Yonai favored the first alternative; Anami, Umezu, and Toyoda wanted the second alternative; Hiranuma was on the fence; and Suzuki had remained silent.

The time was now 2:00 a.m., August 10. Slowly, Suzuki got to his feet. Perhaps now, some thought, he would reveal his convictions. Instead, he made an electrifying announcement. "We have discussed this question for a long time, and everyone has expressed his own opinion sincerely without any conclusion being reached. The situation is urgent. I am therefore proposing to ask the Emperor his own wish and to decide the conference's conclusion on that basis."[36]

Suzuki's proposal was unprecedented. The emperor's role at an Imperial Conference was to sit quietly and not to take an active part. The government made decisions and the Imperial Conference was held merely to maintain the fiction that the emperor sanctioned them in person.[37] But to break the deadlock, Togo and Suzuki, with Sakomizu's knowledge, had worked out this maneuver with Hirohito beforehand.

His speech shocked the men in the conference room. Before they had time to react, Suzuki slowly turned and approached Hirohito. The men gasped. Even Togo and Sakomizu, who were expecting Suzuki's move, were awed. Anami cried out, "Mr. Prime Minister!"

Suzuki kept on until reaching Hirohito's table. "I present myself humbly at the foot of the throne," he said, "and I request Your Imperial Majesty's opinion as to which proposal should be adopted— the one stated by the Foreign Minister or the one containing the Army's conditions."[38] Nodding, Hirohito gestured to Suzuki to return to his seat.

When the emperor arose from his chair, everybody snapped to attention and bowed in his direction. With "visible emotion welling up within him," Hirohito began to speak. "I agree with the first opinion expressed by the Foreign Minister," he said. "Thinking about the world situation and the internal Japanese situation, to continue the war means nothing but the destruction of the whole nation." He was gazing thoughtfully at the ceiling now while wiping his glasses with a white-gloved thumb. "To continue the war now means that cruelty and bloodshed will still continue in the world and that the Japanese nation will suffer severe damage."[39]

At this point, tears flooded Hirohito's eyes, and everyone in the room broke down crying. A few had "thrown themselves forward— arms outstretched, prostrate on the tables, sobbing unashamedly."[40]

"When I think about my obedient soldiers abroad," the emperor said, "and of those who died or were wounded in battle, about those who have lost their property or lives by bombing in the homeland; when I think of all those sacrifices, I cannot help but feel sad."[41] Choked with emotion, Hirohito was forced to stop.

Sakomizu wanted to cry out: "We now all understand His Majesty's wishes. Please do not condescend to say another word."[42]

Hirohito concluded: "I cannot stand the disarming of loyal and gallant troops and punishment of those responsible for the war," but "the situation of today calls upon us to bear the unbearable."[43]

As if burdened with intolerable weight, Hirohito left the room. Suzuki immediately turned to the others. "The imperial decision has been expressed," he said. "This should be the conclusion of the conference."[44] The members of the Supreme Council agreed, including Anami, that they could not go against an imperial decision. However, it had no legal binding until the Cabinet sanctioned it.

Japanese Reaction

At 3:00 a.m. the Cabinet assembled at Suzuki's official residence. He wasted no time in getting to the purpose of the meeting. The Supreme Council just met with the emperor at the palace, he said. "His Majesty expressed the opinion that this government should accept the terms of the Potsdam Declaration with one stipulation—that our national polity and our imperial system be maintained."[45] The Cabinet members listened in silence; some appeared to be in shock. Togo presented a motion that the Cabinet accept the terms of the Potsdam Declaration "with the understanding that the said declaration does not comprise any demand which prejudices the prerogatives of His Majesty as a sovereign ruler." Togo said that the emperor's authority stood above the laws of the country, and the word "prerogatives" helped clarify this.[46]

Suzuki asked for a vote on Togo's motion. All hands were raised in favor of it, but as the written motion circulated for signatures, Home Minister Genki Abe "showed considerable reluctance to put his signature to the decision."[47] Apparently, he had a personal concern. If there was a rebellion among the people or a revolt by the army officers, all those who signed the motion would be in danger. Kozo Ota, the education minister, prodded Abe. "You must sign," said Ota. "The procedure is necessary."[48] Slowly, Abe picked up his brush, dipped it in ink, and signed. The government had taken the first official step toward surrender.

Immediately after the Cabinet meeting, Togo and Kaze hurried to the Foreign Ministry. Togo drafted a telegram notifying the Allies of the imperial decision, and Kase translated it into English. It comprised three short paragraphs. The first summarized the emperor's desire for a "speedy termination" of the war and his desire "to restore the general peace." The second contained the imperial decision, and the final paragraph was one sentence, asking that the reply "be speedily forthcoming."[49]

By 7:00 a.m., August 10, cables announcing Japan's conditional acceptance of the Potsdam Declaration were on their way to Tokyo's embassies in Switzerland and Sweden, from there to be forwarded to the United States, Britain, the Soviet Union, and China.

With regard to the Soviet Union, Togo took out "double in-surance." On the morning of August 10, he met with Soviet ambassador Yakov Malik in the guest room of the House of Peers. In one of the most surprising diplomatic meetings in the annals of diplomacy, Malik handed Togo the first official Soviet notice of declaration of war against Japan. In return, Togo handed Malik a copy of Japan's conditional acceptance of the Potsdam Declaration.[50]

The morning of August 10 was hot and muggy as General Anami arrived at army headquarters on Ichigaya Heights. At 9:30 a.m. he met with fifty high-ranking officers, generals, colonels, and lieutenant colonels. He spoke quietly, trying to restrain his emotions. At an Imperial Conference meeting yesterday, he said, "His Majesty told us with tears in his eyes that he felt the time had come when we must bear the unbearable. It was his wish that we seek peace immediately."[51]

"No! No! No!" they shouted.

"Since it is the wish of His Imperial Majesty that we accept the Potsdam Proclamation," said Anami, "there is nothing that can be done." When several officers again started to protest, he slapped his riding crop against his palm for emphasis: "If anybody disobeys Anami's order, he will have to cut Anami down."[52]

Lieutenant Colonel Masao Inaba of the Military Affairs Bureau approached Anami with a plan to keep order in the army. "Regardless of whether we end the war or not," said Inaba, "we must send out instructions to keep fighting, particularly with the Soviet troops advancing in Manchuria."[53] Anami told Inaba to write his plan out.

Meanwhile, the Cabinet decided to issue a vague statement to help prepare the people for surrender. Written by President Kainan Shimomura of the Information Board and his staff, the message indicated that Japan was about to face an unprecedented situation. "In truth, we cannot but recognize that we are now beset with the worst possible situation," said the statement. "Just as the government is exerting its utmost efforts to defend the homeland, safeguard the polity, and preserve the honor of the nation, so too must people rise to the occasion and overcome all manner of difficulties in order to protect the polity of their Empire."[54]

Inaba's statement, titled "Instruction to the Troops," offered no hint of surrender. He wrote: "We are determined to fight resolutely even if that involves nibbling grass, eating earth, and sleeping in the fields. It is our belief that there is life in death."[55] He sent a copy to Anami for approval. But shortly thereafter, Inaba learned that the Board of Information would release a statement hinting at surrender. Because he believed this would confuse and weaken the morale of the troops, he decided not to wait for Anami's approval. Turning his wastebasket upside down, he retrieved the original draft and released it in Anami's name to all local radio stations and newspapers.

That evening, August 10, news broadcasters read first the so-called Anami Proclamation and then the Board of Information's statement. In the following morning's newspapers, both statements appeared side by side. Because the government's formal notes informing the Allies of Japan's willingness to surrender were still moving through the diplomatic channels of Sweden and Switzerland, Togo feared that the Allies would take the Anami Proclamation to mean that Japan would continue the war.[56]

Acting quickly, Togo decided to bypass the military and get Japan's surrender proposal directly to the United States and England. Although the army's censors were everywhere, its agents did not monitor the Domei News Agency's Morse Code broadcasts. On the evening of August 10 Togo persuaded the editor at Domei to use Morse Code to beam the Imperial Conference's statement directly to the United States and England.[57]

Washington received the message at 7:33 a.m., August 10. It read: "The Japanese Government is ready to accept the terms enumerated in the joint declaration which was issued at Potsdam with the understanding that said declaration does not compromise any demand which prejudices the prerogatives of His Majesty as a sovereign ruler."[58]

The Allies Reply

At 9:00 a.m. on August 10 President Truman summoned his key aides to his office. These included Secretary of State Byrnes, Secretary of War Stimson, Secretary of the Navy James V. Forrestal, and

Admiral William Leahy, chairman of the Joint Chiefs of Staff. After showing them Tokyo's Morse Code radio message, Truman asked each in turn: "Were we to treat this message from Tokyo as an acceptance of the Potsdam Declaration?"[59]

Stimson and Leahy readily agreed. The Allies would need Hirohito's help to get the scattered Japanese armies to surrender, said Stimson. This would, he said, "save us from a score of bloody Iwo Jimas and Okinawas all over China and the New Netherlands."[60]

While having "no feelings about little Hirohito," Leahy agreed with Stimson that "it would be necessary to use him in effecting the surrender."[61]

But Byrnes disagreed. "Since the Japanese were patently anxious to surrender," he said, "it was not the time for them to present conditions."[62] Acceptance of Japan's qualifying statement, he added, would leave the United States open "to the criticism that we had receded from the totality and severity of the Potsdam Declaration."[63]

"The question of the Emperor was a minor matter," said Leahy, "compared with delaying a victory in the war which was now in our hands."[64]

Forrestal offered a solution. "We might in our reply," he said, "indicate willingness to accept yet define the terms of surrender in such a matter that the intents and purposes of the Potsdam Declaration would be clearly accomplished."[65] Truman asked Byrnes to draft a reply that would convey such an understanding.

Just as the meeting was ending, Stimson, concerned over the continued loss of life, advocated an immediate halt to the bombing. "It would be a humane thing," he said, and "might effect the settlement if we stopped the bombing during this time."[66]

Forrestal agreed: "We must remember that this nation would have to bear the focus of the hatred by the Japanese."[67] Rejecting the proposal, Truman said he would wait until Japan's official surrender came through diplomatic channels.[68]

Right after the meeting, Byrnes left for the State Department. He met with lawyer Benjamin Cohen, Far Eastern experts Joseph W. Ballantine and Eugene H. Doorman, and former acting Secretary of State Joseph C. Grew. After showing them Japan's message, Byrnes asked for their help in writing a reply. According to Ballantine, Cohen saw "the point in three minutes." He changed the Japanese condition, "with the understanding that said declaration does not compromise any demand which prejudices the prerogatives of His Majesty as a sovereign ruler," to that of "the Japanese Emperor's authority and that of his government to rule the state would be subject to the authority of a Supreme Commander of the Allied Powers."[69] Cohen's change acknowledged the fact that the emperor would continue to rule, but it did not guarantee him ultimate authority.

At 2:00 p.m. on August 10 Truman convened an emergency meeting of the Cabinet. By this time, he had received the official text of the Japanese surrender from the Swiss embassy. Byrnes read the American reply. Cohen's part read: "From the moment of surrender the authority of the Emperor and the Japanese Government to rule the state shall be subject to the Supreme Commander of the Allied Powers who will take such steps as he deems proper to effectuate the surrender terms."

Byrnes added: "The ultimate form of government of Japan will, in accordance with the Potsdam Declaration, be established by the freely expressed will of the Japanese people."[70]

The reply reassured the Japanese about the future position of the emperor, but on America's terms. Stimson liked its conciliatory tone: "I thought it was a pretty wise and careful statement and stood a better chance of being accepted than a more outspoken one."[71]

"They wanted to keep the Emperor," said Truman. "We told 'em we'd tell 'em how to keep him, but we'd make the terms."[72]

First, the Allies had to give their approval to the American reply. The United States cabled copies to its ambassadors in London, Chungking, and Moscow with a request that they secure quick compliance. Britain and China accepted the reply almost immediately. The Soviets, however, had a problem with the Japanese surrender offer.

At midnight, August 10, Ambassador Harriman and British ambassador Clark Kerr met with Molotov in his office in Moscow. He told them that the Soviet government was "skeptical" about the Japanese surrender offer. "The Soviets did not consider it unconditional surrender," said Molotov, "and the Soviet forces, therefore, were continuing their advance into Manchuria."[73] While Kerr remained silent, Harriman, not satisfied with Molotov's response, pressed for a quick answer to the American reply. Molotov promised an answer the following day, but Harriman wanted it before the night was out. "Harriman was dealing with a government that was plainly anxious to maintain its forward drive in Manchuria," said Byrnes later.[74]

At 2:00 p.m., August 11, Molotov called Harriman and Clark Kerr back to his office. He handed them a statement. "In case of an affirmative reply from the Japanese Government," it read, "the Allied Powers should reach an agreement on the candidacy or candidacies for representation of the Allied High Command to which the Japanese Emperor and the Japanese Government are to be subordinated."[75] To Harriman, the statement appeared ambiguous. He asked for clarification. "There was not a combined command in the Far East," said Molotov. "Therefore it would be necessary to reach agreement as to the Allied representative or representatives who would deal with the Japanese."[76]

Harriman asked, "Would MacArthur be acceptable?" Molotov thought so; however, he suggested that the high command might consist of both a U.S. and a Soviet general. He named Marshal A. M. Vasilevsky, commander of Soviet forces in Manchuria, to the post.[77]

Harriman was angry. The United States had carried the main burden of the Pacific war for four years and had kept the Japanese off Russia's back, he said. "The Soviet Union had been in the war but two days and it was only just that an American should be the Supreme Commander—any other solution was unthinkable."

Molotov, too, became heated: "He did not wish to make a reply as he would have to refer to the European war."[78] (The Soviets were bitter that the Allies had waited until 1944 before opening up a second front in France.) Molotov said he would consult with Stalin and the meeting ended.

Harriman was following America's set policy. "We wanted Japan controlled by an American Commander," said Truman. "I did not want divided control or separate zones."[79]

Harriman went back to his office and found Pavlov, Molotov's secretary, on the telephone. "There had been a misunderstanding," said Pavlov, "and that only consultation had been intended and not the necessity of reaching an agreement."[80] Stalin's bid had failed. Perhaps he knew that it would. He now retreated and accepted the U.S. reply.

With the approval of the Allies, Secretary Byrnes handed the completed text of the Allied note, dated August 11, to Herr Max Grassli, chargé d'affaires of the Swiss legation for transmission to Tokyo by way of Berne, Switzerland. "I was confident the Japanese would accept," said Byrnes, "but the feeling of responsibility for thousands of lives was inescapable."[81] At the same time, the White House released the text of the Allied note to the American press and radio, which would make it known to the Japanese eighteen hours before they received it through official channels on the morning of August 13.

After the Swiss had sent the Allied note, Stimson and Forrestal again tried to persuade Truman to stop all air and naval action against Japan as a humane gesture. Truman agreed to suspend further atomic attacks unless Tokyo's reply was unsatisfactory. (On Tinian two more atomic bombs were ready for drops, tentatively scheduled for August 13 and 16.) Otherwise, he said, he would continue to press the war "with all possible vigor."[82]

The pounding continued. The Third Fleet raided northern Honshu again and struck at the Kurils and then turned south. On August 13, 1,000 carrier planes attacked Tokyo.[83] In the last seven and a half months of the war, the air force destroyed 2,846,932 tons of Japanese shipping, 1,375 aircraft, dropped 100,000 tons of bombs, and flew over 150,000 sorties. "Never in history," said General Douglas MacArthur, "had one nation been the target of such concentrated air power."[84]

FDR authorized atomic research in 1939 before the United States had entered the war.

Ambassador Joseph Davies was sent by Roosevelt to maintain good relations with Stalin and Molotov in 1943 before the conference at Teheran.

Secretary of War Henry Stimson with General George C. Marshall, Chief of Staff. Stimson, one of a handful to know about the secret weapons research, was the main proponent of using the atomic bomb to end the war.

Missouri Senator Harry Truman, selected by Franklin D. Roosevelt as his running mate in 1944, at one of his few meetings with the ailing president. FDR never informed his new vice president about the atomic bomb.

Joseph Davies, Admiral Leahy, and Harry Hopkins with President Truman examine a document from Joseph Stalin after Hopkins' return from the USSR in June 1945.

The crew of the *Enola Gay* B-29 Superfortress bomber that dropped the first atomic bomb on Hiroshima on August 6, 1945.

The Nagasaki bomb explosion.

The devastation at Nagasaki after the August 9, 1945, bombing.

Harry Truman is sworn in as president on April 12, 1945.

Emperor Hirohito during the early 1940s.

President Harry Truman.

Captain Paul Tibbetts taking off on his mission from Tinian Island.

The Hiroshima bomb known as "Little Boy."

The Nagasaki bomb known as "Fat Man."

Churchill, Truman and Stalin meet at the Potsdam Conference in July 1945.

The conference table at Potsdam where Truman told Stalin about the new weapons.

Truman announces the Japanese surrender, August 15, 1945.

Stimson, Marshall, and Truman holding up the Japanese surrender document.

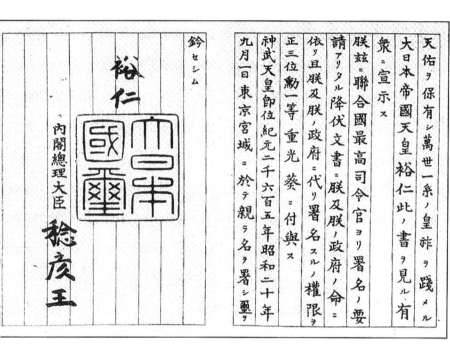

天佑ヲ保有シ萬世一系ノ皇祚ヲ踐メル
大日本帝國天皇裕仁此ノ書ヲ見ル有
衆ニ宣示ス
朕ハ茲ニ聯合國最高司令官ヨリ署名ノ要
請アリタル降伏文書ニ朕及朕ノ政府ノ命ニ
依リ且朕及朕ノ政府ニ代リ署名スルノ權限ヲ
正三位勳一等重光葵ニ付與ス
神武天皇卽位紀元二千六百五年昭和二十年
九月一日東京宮城ニ於テ親ラ名ヲ署シ璽ヲ
鈐セシム

裕仁

内閣總理大臣
稔彥王

Emperor Hirohito's signature.

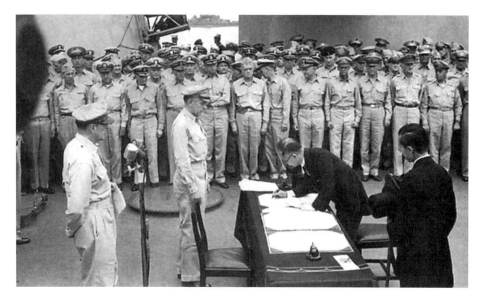

Formal surrender ceremony on board the USS *Missouri* on September 2, 1945. General MacArthur, at left, watches as the Japanese envoys sign.

Truman congratulates Henry Stimson on his retirement as secretary of war, 1945.

7.

The Second Imperial Decision
and Its Aftermath

Japanese Reaction to the Allied Reply

While the Byrnes reply was officially forwarded to Japan through Switzerland, the United States broadcast it to Tokyo by short-wave radio from San Francisco. Tokyo's Domei radio monitoring station picked it up about a half-hour after midnight on August 12. Domei immediately notified the Foreign Ministry and Cabinet Secretary Sakomizu.

At 1:30 a.m., August 12, Vice Minister for Foreign Affairs Shunichi Matsumoto arrived at the prime minister's official residence, where he met with Tosahikazu Kaze, Togo's secretary and English language expert, Sakomizu and Saiji Hasegawa, a Domei reporter. Matsumoto noticed "deep disappointment and concern" in all three faces. "I'm afraid," said Sakomizu, "we have no choice."

Pacing the floor, Matsumoto pondered the problem for several minutes. "All right," he said. "Let's try to push it through as it is."[1] Shortly afterward, they talked with Togo and Suzuki, who agreed that "we must end the war."[2]

Meanwhile, Kido showed a transcript of the message to Emperor Hirohito. He said that the clause calling for Japan's ultimate form of government to be set "by the truly expressed will of the people" could mean the end of the monarchy. "That is beside the point," said Hirohito. "It would be useless if the people did not want an Emperor. I think it's perfectly all right to leave it up to the people."[3]

At 8:00 a.m. Hirohito met with Umezu and Toyoda at the Imperial Palace. The reply, said Umezu, could not be accepted. "The Emperor would become subordinate to the Allied commander," and that, he contended, "could not be countenanced."[4] In addition, he said, "it is not possible to foretell the reaction of certain elements in the army and navy."[5]

Hirohito was well aware of the volatile nature of young Japanese military officers. In February 1936 he intervened personally to put down a coup attempt by young military officers. Although he had already reached a decision to accept the Allied reply, he decided that at the moment stalling the military was the safe thing to do. "When we receive the Allied reply formally," he said, "we can probably make further inquiry about those points still in doubt."[6]

Later that morning, at 11:00, Togo visited Hirohito. He said that the Foreign Office recommended acceptance of the Allied surrender position. Hirohito agreed that they "should accept it as it stood," and he instructed Togo to convey his wishes to Suzuki.[7] Togo was gratified. This would give him the advantage he needed at the afternoon's Cabinet and the next morning's Supreme Council meetings.[8]

At 2:30 p.m., War Minister Anami was in his office preparing to leave for a 3:00 p.m. Cabinet meeting when Colonel Masahiko Takeshita burst in with no delegation of officers. He demanded that Anami reject the Allied reply and help them stage a coup d'état. If you refuse, said Takeshita, "you should commit hara-kiri!"[9] But Anami remained noncommittal. He bowed gracefully and hurried to the door. "The situation was growing very unquiet," said Togo. "The police guard of my house was greatly increased."[10]

Stalemate and Deadlock

At 3:00 p.m., August 12, the Cabinet assembled at the second-floor meeting room of the prime minister's official residence to discuss the Allied reply. Togo, the first to speak, advocated its acceptance. "Although the authority of the Supreme Commander of the Allied Powers would be paramount," he said, "the position of the Emperor nevertheless remained, in principle, unimpaired." He reminded the Cabinet that the idea of establishing the form of government "by the freely expressed will of the people" appeared in the Atlantic Charter and the Potsdam Declaration.[11] Even if submitted to a referendum, he added, "it was impossible to conceive that the overwhelming loyal majority of our people would not wish to preserve our traditional system.[12]

While Yonai sided with Togo, Anami and Hiranuma opposed his position. The Allies are proposing "to thwart the Sovereign's prerogatives," said Anami. "I maintain that we fight on to the bitter end."[13]

Hiranuma said that "divine will" ordained the emperor and that "the freely expressed will of the people" could not possibly alter it.[14]

But "if we persist in enlarging our demands," said Togo, "the Allies might abolish the imperial dynasty outright instead of leaving the decision to the Japanese people."[15]

Suzuki, who had been quiet, suddenly spoke out against accepting the Allied reply. It was unsatisfactory, he said, "because it did not guarantee the preservation of Japan's polity," and unless the Allies conceded on this point, "there would be no other way than to fight it out."[16]

Stunned by Suzuki's reversal, Togo leapt to his feet. He paused, got his anger under control and decided not to argue with Suzuki in front of the full Cabinet which might only harden Suzuki's reversal. Togo said, "The prime minister's remarks are worthy of careful consideration," but "as the official reply of the Allies has not yet arrived, we had better continue our discussion after receipt of it."[17] Togo then adjourned the meeting.

Suzuki immediately left the room and went directly across the hall to his private office. To his surprise, Togo had followed right behind, closed the door, and let out his anger, "Togo said he could not possibly understand why the premier, of all people, was taking such an attitude, especially when the Emperor was of the opinion that the war could not go on."[18] Suzuki made a gesture of resignation. "If the opinions of the Premier and the Cabinet should incline to continuation of the war," warned Togo, "I might be compelled to report individually to the throne my dissenting view."[19] This was a serious threat. According to the Constitution, a personal appeal of a minister to the throne dissenting from the prime minister would cause an immediate fall of the Cabinet.[20]

After Togo informed Kido of the complication that had arisen, he summoned Suzuki to his office at 9:30 p.m. Kido said that the emperor's wish was to accept the Potsdam Declaration "courageously."[21] To Kido's surprise, Suzuki, who always appeared ambivalent, either from emotion or design, immediately reverted to his original position. "Yes, let us do it," he said.[22]

At 8:30 a.m., August 13, the Supreme Council met in the stuffy air-raid shelter under Suzuki's official residence. The main point of discussion was the Allies' reply, which placed the emperor in a position subordinate to that of the supreme commander of the occupation forces.[23] Togo insisted, "We should consider the positive aspect that the Emperor would be assured of remaining on the throne."[24]

Anami, Umezu, and Toyoda repeated that they "could wage another battle" but could offer no promise of final victory.[25] After several hours of debate, the meeting deadlocked, three to three: Suzuki, Togo, and Yonai argued for acceptance of the Allies' reply while Umezu, Anami, and Toyoda were against it.[26]

From 4:00 p.m. to 7:00 p.m., August 13, the Cabinet reassembled to discuss again the Allies reply. "Further delay," warned Togo, "would only increase the suspicions of the Allies, now growing every hour, and destroy the chance of peace."[27] This time, the Cabinet confined the discussion almost entirely to the stipulation that the people should decide the ultimate form of government. "Some said that this meant acceptance of our proposal," said Sakomizu, "while others said that it was a refusal."[28] Although Anami was the most adamant against acceptance, he seemed "to have less zest" for the debate.

Togo recalled, "Often I felt wearied with fighting, but conditions were too tense to permit any personal feeling to degenerate from the utmost sincerity in arguing the issues preoccupying us, and my personal relations with General Anami remained unclouded to the end."[29]

At one point, a messenger disrupted the meeting. He handed Suzuki a copy of an army communiqué that the army would immediately release to radio and newspapers. It read: "The army, upon receipt of a newly issued imperial command, has renewed offensive action against the United States, the United kingdom, the Soviet Union, and China."[30] Anami quickly telephoned General Umezu at the War Ministry. He stopped the communiqué minutes before it would be broadcast. Apparently, both Anami and Umezu had no knowledge of it.

"I did not believe that the War Minister would lend himself to any attempt at a coup d'état," said Togo, "but I did fear that mutiny among his officers might compel him to resign, or that disorder might otherwise develop."[31]

Finally, the cabinet took a vote. Thirteen members voted for acceptance of the Allies' reply, and three voted against it. Those in favor argued that the Japanese people "could decide the ultimate form of government," while those opposed said the emperor's position "should not be dependent on the people."[32] Faced with a continuing deadlock, Suzuki adjourned the meeting. He warned the Cabinet, however, that if the impasse remained, he would have to ask "the Emperor for one final decision."[33]

Meanwhile, five junior officers from the War Ministry were planning a coup d'état set for 10:00 a.m., August 14. They included Lieutenant Colonels Masahiko Takeshita, Anami's brother-in-law; Masao Inaba and Jiro Shiizaki; Major Kenji Hatanaka; and Colonel Okikatsu Arao. Their plan included imprisoning Suzuki, Yonai, Togo, and Kido, proclaiming marital law, seizing the Imperial Palace, and persuading Hirohito to continue the war. They hoped to get Anami to lead them, and with his help, to persuade Generals Umezu, Shizuichi Tanaka, commander of the Eastern District Army, and Takeshi Mori, commander of the First Imperial Guards Division to join the conspiracy.

At 8:00 p.m., August 13, the five conspirators met with Anami at his one-story wooden house in Tokyo. They informed him of the plan and asked him to lead the coup. Anami did not want to "antagonize the group" by saying no. He promised to use his influence "first thing in the morning" with Umezu, who he knew was already resolved to support the emperor's decision to end the war.[34]

Early the next morning, the conspirators met with Anami at army headquarters. While they waited in his office, Anami and Arao met with Umezu alone in his office. "It is doomed to failure," said Umezu. "But even more important, it calls for the use of soldiers inside the sacred ground of the Imperial Palace. That would be a sacrilege."[35] Turning to Anami, he quietly pointed out that the duty of a loyal soldier was to obey an imperial decision, and he urged him "to control his unruly staff."[36] Back at his office, Anami told the conspirators that the coup d'état would have to be abandoned: "The Chief of Staff disapproves of it."[37] After an initial uproar of protest, Anami's personality prevailed, and the conspirators left in silence.

The Second Imperial Conference

As dawn broke over Tokyo on August 14, a lone B-29 released tens of thousands of leaflets over the sleeping city. These leaflets gave the verbatim text, in Japanese, of the government's note of acceptance of August 10 and of the Allies' reply of August 11. The text had been drafted in Washington by the Office of War Information, translated into Japanese and radio-photoed to Saipan.

At 8:30 a.m. Kido and Suzuki met with Hirohito in the imperial library. "It is my concern," said Kido, "that when the troops read this leaflet, they will become enraged, making a military coup inevitable and the execution of our planned policy very difficult."[38] Under the circumstances, Suzuki asked the emperor to take the unprecedented step of calling an imperial conference on his own authority.[39] This would bypass the need to obtain the signatures of Umezu and Toyoda, the two chiefs of staff. Hirohito agreed, and he summoned the Cabinet, the Supreme Council, and the president of the Privy Council for a 10:30 a.m. Imperial conference. In case of a deadlock, Hirohito would command the government to accept the Allies' reply.[40]

At 10:30 a.m., August 14, twenty-five men assembled for the first fully attended Imperial conference with the emperor since the historic one on December 1, 1941, during which the decision was made to go to war with the United States. Those in attendance included Suzuki and the fifteen Cabinet members; Umezu and Toyoda, the two Supreme Council members who were not also Cabinet members Baron Kiichiro Hiranuma, president of the Privy Council; General Sumihisa Ikeda, chief of the Cabinet planning board; Naoyasu Murase, director of Legislative Bureau; Kingo Machimura, super-intendent-general of the Tokyo Metropolitan Police; General Masao Yoshizumi and Admiral Zenchiro Hoshina, directors of the army and navy military affairs bureaus; and Sakomizu, chief cabinet secretary.

At 10:55 a.m. Hirohito entered the room accompanied by his chief military aide, General Shigeru Hasunuma. Everyone stood, and bowed deeply. Hirohito, dressed in a plain army uniform, sat down in a straight-backed, wooden chair at the same small table he had used for the August 9 imperial conference. Behind him was a gold screen. The twenty-five men sat in rows of chairs facing the emperor. In the front row were six members of the Supreme Council, and to the emperor's right sat General Hasunuma.

After apologizing to the emperor for the continued deadlock, Suzuki asked the three principal dissenters, Umezu, Toyoda, and Anami, to state their case to the emperor. Responding nervously, they argued that the Allies' reply would "endanger the national polity" and that "there was no alternative to carrying on the struggle even at the cost of a hundred million lives."[41] When General Anami looked at the emperor, his eyes clouded with tears; he choked and was unable to continue. Bowing to the emperor, "he suddenly sat down."[42]

When no one else spoke, Hirohito issued a command. "The American answer seems to me acceptable," he said. "I have decided, without suggestions from anyone, to order the conclusion of the war as I cannot endure the thought of having to kill tens, even hundreds of thousands of my subjects, and moreover to have to be called the disturber of world peace."[43] Wearing snow-white gloves, Hirohito paused and "put his hand to his eyes to brush away the tears." At that point, everyone began crying and two ministers collapsed, sobbing uncontrollably on the floor.

"We who were present fully realized the extent of his determination," said Yonai, "and could not hold back the tears that welled up."[44]

"I had the conviction," said Sakomizu, "that the Emperor was with the people, really near them, for always."[45]

Hirohito asked that all members of the government cooperate together. "The military and naval forces especially will be shocked," he said, "so I will go anyplace the ministers want and explain the situation to the soldiers personally."[46]

He also volunteered to speak to the nation over the radio. He then asked the government to draft the Imperial Rescript announcement to stop the war, and rose and left the room. "It was an inexpressibly solemn and moving scene," said Togo later, "as we retired down the long corridor, while returning in our cars, each of us in his thoughts wept again."[47]

Immediate Results of the Imperial Decision

At 1:00 p.m. the Cabinet formally met to sanction Hirohito's decision to accept the Allies' note, and Sakomizu drafted the imperial edict to end the war. "I remembered his very words," said Sakomizu, "the Emperor's words to this day, just like a dream."[48] As the meeting ended, Anami apologized to Togo for speaking "so zealously at the Imperial Conference." Togo said later: "I felt that he was overly polite, but at any rate we all parted with smiles, saying to each other that it was good that it was over."[49]

After the Cabinet meeting Anami and Yonai informed the army and navy of the imperial decision to surrender. As a precaution, Anami wrote a short statement that the army would act "in accordance with the Imperial desire," and he persuaded five of the highest-ranking officers, including Umezu, to sign it.[50] "I took every possible measure to forestall untoward incidents," said Yonai, "but the thing that made it possible to avoid serious trouble of any kind was the power of the Emperor rather than anything that I or the army were able to do."[51]

Meanwhile, Suzuki telephoned Vice Minister Shunichi Matsumoto at the Foreign Office to inform him that the surrender was official. He immediately sent a cablegram through Switzerland and Sweden to the four Allied Powers announcing Japan's acceptance of the Byrnes note.

At 4:00 p.m., August 14, Byrnes received the Japanese surrender by way of Berne, Switzerland. He immediately informed Truman that the Japanese had accepted the Allies' terms of surrender and then teletyped the information to London, Moscow, and Chungking.[52]

Early that evening, Truman's Cabinet, Cordell Hull (former secretary of state), Admiral Leahy, and news correspondents assembled at the White House. A large crowd gathered outside; Truman announced that he had received a reply from the Japanese concerning the Allies' surrender note of August 11. "I deem this reply," said Truman, "a full acceptance of the Potsdam Declaration which specifies the unconditional surrender of Japan."[53] At that instant, the correspondents, shouting congratulations, rushed out the door to report the news to the nation. Truman then went out to the fountain on the North Lawn and made a "V" sign in the manner of Churchill. A great cheer went up. "No nation with the military power of the United States of America had been so generous to its enemies," said Truman later. "Maybe the teachings of the Sermon on the Mount could be put into effect."[54]

At 11:30 p.m., Tokyo time, Hirohito met Hiroshi Shimomura, director of the Information Bureau, at the imperial household ministry. Followed by Chamberlain Sukemasa Irie, Hirohito and Shimomura hurried to the imperial administration room on the second floor, where they were met by a crew of radio Tokyo technicians. Hirohito then recorded the Imperial Rescript that would announce the ending of the war. Radio Tokyo would broadcast it throughout Japan at noon August 15. As a precaution in the event of a coup, Chamberlain Yoshikiro Tokugawa locked the recordings in a safe concealed under a stack of papers in a room in the household ministry used only infrequently by a lady-in-waiting to the empress.[55]

In the early morning hours of August 15, War Minister Anami decided to commit hara-kiri, suicide by the samurai sword, at his home in Tokyo. He spent his last two hours in the company of Colonels Masahiko Takeshita and Masataka Ida. Anami showed them two scrolls. One was a poem: "Having received great favors from his Majesty, the Emperor, there is nothing more for me to say in the hour of my death." The other was a three-line acknowledgment of Anami's responsibility as war minister: "Believing firmly that our sacred land will never perish, I, with my death, humbly apologize to the Emperor for the great crime."[56]

While Takeshita and Ida waited by the garden, Anami went to his corridor porch facing the Imperial Palace. He laid out a straw mat, sat cross-legged, and thrust the dagger deep into his abdomen, then slashed twice, to the right and straight-up, disemboweling himself.[57] He took the dagger out with his right hand, searched with his left for the jugular vein, and plunged it into his throat. When he was unconscious, Takeshita came in, picked up the dagger and "drove it all the way into the nape of his neck." He then draped Anami's coat, heavy with medals, over the dying man.[58]

The Failed Coup d'État

Led by Major Kenji Hatanaka and Colonel Masataka Ida, several staff officers of the Bureau of Military Administration decided to carry out a coup. Their plan included enlisting staff officers from the Imperial Guards Division, seizing the Imperial Palace, destroying the emperor's broadcast recording of the Imperial Rescript, and placing the emperor under protective custody. "It was their dastardly plot," said Kido later, "to prosecute the war under the name of the Emperor and the imperial standard."[59]

At 11:30 p.m., August 14, the conspirators called upon General Takeshi Mori, commander of the Imperial Guard Division, at his office just inside the palace grounds. While Ida waited in the hall, Hatanaka pleaded with Mori for more than an hour to help them "nullify the Emperor's decision for peace" which had been "forced upon him by his unpatriotic advisers."[60] When Mori refused, Hatanaka "shot him to death," and another conspirator beheaded Colonel Michinori Shiraishi, Mori's chief of staff.[61] Staggering out of the office, Hatanaka, weapon in hand, said to Ida, "I did it because there was no time left. I'm sorry."[62]

With help from Majors Hidemasa Roga and Sadakichi Ishihara, the two Imperial guard staff officers who were most deeply committed to the plot, Hatanaka forged an order for the Imperial Guard Division to occupy all of the palace gates and disarm the palace police. One company took over the NHK (Japan Broadcasting Corporation) building to control what was broadcast. More than a thousand soldiers cordoned off the palace grounds. They shut the great iron gates, cut telephone lines, and placed machine guns at strategic points.[63] This cut off all communication with the outside. None of the key regimental and battalion commanders or the Imperial Guards themselves realized that a coup was in progress.

After learning that a chamberlain had hidden the emperor's phonograph record at the imperial household ministry, Hatanaka sent out a search party to find it and to look for the imperial seal so that he could forge imperial orders. In addition, he ordered them to imprison Kido, the "well-known symbol of evil advice to the Emperor."[64]

As soon as the soldiers arrived at the imperial household ministry, Chamberlain Yasuhide Toda woke up Kido on the fourth floor to inform him "that part of the Imperial Guard Division had apparently risen in revolt."[65] Quickly dressing, Kido secured confidential documents, tore them up, and "threw them away into the toilet."[66] Chamberlain Yoshihiro Tokugawa led Kido down a dark staircase to a storage room in the basement. He hid there with Household Minister Sotaro Ishinatari. "Our fight with the militarists," said Kido later, "actually continued longer than our fight with the United States."[67]

Almost immediately, Chamberlains Toda and Tokugawa left the ministry and went to Hirohito's residence a short distance away. Once inside, they reported the events to the chamberlain on duty and to the court ladies. After taking the precaution of closing the iron shutters of the residence, they agreed not to awaken the emperor.[68]

Despite an exhaustive search of the imperial household ministry, the soldiers could not find the Rescript recording, the imperial seal, or Kido. Their search was in vain.[69]

Meanwhile, General Shizuichi Tanaka, commander of the Eastern District Army who had authority over all troops in the Tokyo area, had arrived at the Imperial Guard Division's headquarters near the northwest corner of the palace. He ordered the regimental commanders to disband their troops. Whether these staff officers had been deceived by the forged orders or were willing accomplices to the coup was unclear, but they obeyed Tanaka.[70] "If it had not been for Tanaka," said Kaze, "the prospects of a peaceful termination of hostilities would have been ruined."[71]

Late in the morning on August 15, Hatanaka and Colonel Jiro Shiizaki, the two conspirators who remained steadfast to the end, stood on the spacious plaza in front of the Imperial Palace, passing out leaflets calling on the people to reject the surrender. When nobody seemed interested, Hatanaka put a bullet through his forehead with the same pistol he had used to assassinate General Mori, and Shiizaki thrust a dagger into his stomach and then shot himself.[72] In Hatanaka's pocket was a poem: "I have nothing to regret now that the dark clouds have disappeared from the reign of the Emperor."[73]

Meanwhile, in Yokohama, forty soldiers, led by Captain Takeo Sasaki, commandeered several cars and drove to Tokyo intent on assassinating all members of the Cabinet peace faction. Their first target was Suzuki, whom they called an "arch-traitor." When they discovered he was not at his Cabinet office, they machine-gunned it and set fire to the empty building. Alerted by the fire, Sakomizu telephoned Suzuki just five minutes before the assassins arrived at his home; he "escaped by a hair's breadth."[74] After setting fire to Suzuki's house, the soldiers drove to Baron Hiranuma's house and surrounded it, but Hiranuma escaped through an unguarded side gate. The frustrated soldiers set fire to his house and, "their spleen vented," headed home to Yokohama.[75]

Other incidents occurred on August 15. Throughout Tokyo, posters were put up urging the people to kill Suzuki, Sakomizu, Yonai, Togo, and Hiranuma. This forced them to become more cautious, to keep on the move or to stay in hiding. "For one month I lived with two policemen at all times," said Sakomizu, "and at the recommendation of the police I changed my sleeping place every night."[76] At the same time, at Atsugi Airfield, twenty-five miles southwest of Tokyo, the Divine Wind Squadrons (kamikaze) broke all regulations and flew over Tokyo "ominously low," dropping hundreds of leaflets that read, "We will continue the war," and "The Imperial Rescript is a forgery."[77]

Hirohito's Speech

At noon, August 15, the Japanese people crowded around radios in offices, factories, and homes, or stood in front of public loudspeakers to hear the emperor speak for the first time on radio. Most presumed that he would declare war on the Soviet Union or outline preparations for an enemy invasion.[78] Few considered the idea that he would announce Japan's surrender.

A well-known radio announcer, Nobukata Wada, came on the air. "A broadcast of the highest importance is about to begin," he said. "All listeners will please rise." Seventy million Japanese came to attention. The radio played "Kimigayo," the national anthem. "His Majesty," said Wada, "will now read his Imperial Rescript to the people of Japan." In awe, the entire nation listened, for the first time, to Emperor Hirohito.[79]

Hirohito's tremulous voice came over the air. "In view of world conditions," he announced, "we have instructed the Japanese Government to accept the Joint Declaration of the United States, Great Britain, the Soviet Union, and China." Japan, he continued, declared war against the United States and Britain to "maintain the stability of East Asia" and not to "infringe on the sovereignty of other nations or carry out acts of aggression on their soil." The enemy, he said, had employed "its outrageous bomb and slaughtered untold numbers of innocent people." We must "face the long road ahead," he concluded, as one united nation "in full confidence in the indestructibility of our Divine land."[80]

After the emperor's voice faded away, the radio remained silent for a moment and then "Kimigayo" again came on the air. When the radio went dead, the people were in a state of shock. The emperor's words came "as a bolt from the blue," and many wept from a mixture of "vast relief and deep despair."[81]

"As I heard the words," said Togo, "I imagined all the nation listening, profoundly moved, as were we all."[82]

Throughout the day, the nation mourned and the Japanese experienced a mixture of emotions—shock, grief, confusion, and relief that the tragic war had come to an end. Thousands gathered in the front yard of the Imperial Palace, kneeling or bowing in silent respect of the emperor's will.[83] Some wandered the streets aimlessly, while others prayed at Buddhist shrines and Shinto temples. Still others stood "gazing numbly at each other for several minutes before speaking."[84]

Many soldiers committed hara-kiri, more than 1,000 officers, in some estimates.[85] Signaling their opposition to surrender, many committed suicide at the Niju-bashi Bridge forming the approach to the main entrance of the palace compound.[86] In Tokyo, at the Yoyogi Parade Ground, ten young men registered their protest by disembowelment.[87] In a message addressed to the "spirits of the Special Attack Squads," Admiral Tahijiro Onishi, organizer of the kamikaze units, wrote that his death was an effort "to make atonement to the souls of my former subordinates and their bereaved families."[88]

At the Oita field on Kyushu, Vice Admiral Matome Ugaki, commander of the navy's Fifth Air Fleet, addressed his two-man crews standing beside their eleven fighter-bombers. Ugaki asked, "Are you so willing to die for me?" All twenty-two men responded by raising their hands in salute. At 7:24 p.m., August 15, the squadron took off and Ugaki ordered an attack position. Ugaki radioed base: "I am going to make an attack on Okinawa." That was the last anyone heard of Ugaki's suicide squadron."[89]

At 2:00 p.m., August 15, Suzuki assembled his Cabinet for the last time. "The Premier proposed our resignation en bloc," said Togo, "on the grounds that it was regrettable that the emperor had twice been troubled to make decisions at the crisis of surrender, and that it was proper that men younger and more capable of carrying out the rebuilding of our country should replace us."[90] All agreed, and

Suzuki submitted their resignations to the emperor later that afternoon.

On August 18 Hirohito commanded Prince Higashikuni to form a new Cabinet. This was the first time in Japan's history that a member of the imperial family had been commanded to head the government. Hirohito knew that military extremists would not assassinate a member of the royal family. In making his selection, Hirohito did not consult a conference of the senior statesmen (Jushin), as was customary, "but personally took the decision."[91] He instructed the new prime minister to "respect the Constitution fully and strive hard to cope with the situation by enforcing discipline in the army and maintaining law and order throughout the country."[92]

Prince Higashikuni immediately formed a new cabinet. He picked General Shimomura, chief of staff in North China, as war minister, Admiral Yonai remained navy minister, and Mamoru Shigemitsu became foreign minister. The new prime minister selected the foreign-style Akasaka Detached Palace, still left standing in the burned-out area, for the Cabinet officers.

The Surrender

General Douglas MacArthur, the supreme commander of the Allied Powers, asked Japan to send delegates to Manila in the Philippines to discuss the surrender. Because of the humiliating aspect of the mission, General Umezu refused to participate. He sent his deputy, General Torashiro Kawabe, who persuaded fifteen reluctant officers and diplomats to accompany him to Manila. Early in the morning of August 19 in Tokyo Kawabe's delegation boarded two Mitsubishi bombers. These had been painted white with large green crosses on the sides of their fuselages. When they arrived at Nichols Field, thousands of "catcalling soldiers and civilians pressed in on them clicking cameras like machine guns fired at strange animals."[93]

Kawabe's delegation cooperated with MacArthur on all matters. They revealed the remaining secrets of all army and navy units, ammunition dumps, coastal guns, and mine-fields.[94] But they made an earnest protest against MacArthur's landing at Japan's Atsugi Air-field on August 26. It was a training base for kamikaze pilots, many of whom had refused to surrender. In addition, in the Kanto plain of Tokyo alone, they said, twenty-two Japanese divisions, 300,000 well-trained soldiers, remained with scores of well-armed troops scattered throughout the country. They argued that MacArthur should wait until the U.S. army had secured the island.[95]

Returning to Japan on August 21, Kawabe's delegation brought back a copy of the Instrument of Surrender and Directive No. 1. The first was written in accordance with the Potsdam Declaration and required the signatures of the emperor and representatives of the government and military headquarters. But Directive No. 1 was stern. It contained detailed orders for the unconditional surrender of all Japanese forces, the "complete cessation of operation of munition works; rapid disarmament of troops; evacuation of military establish-ments and cessation of flying.[96]

Shortly after dawn on August 28, forty-five U.S. C-47 transports swept in from the south, circled the Atsugi Airfield, thirty miles southwest of Tokyo, and landed, one after another, in clocklike pre-cision in under thirty minutes. Understandably nervous, Colonel Charles Tench, the leader of the U.S. advance party, was the first to step onto the tarmac at Atsugi. His fleet of forty-five C-47s carried supplies and 146 U.S. soldiers. This was the vanguard of a contingent of nearly a half million U.S. soldiers who would land during the next month.[97]

Tench's immediate task was to secure Atsugi and prepare for MacArthur's arrival two days later. In this initial occupation, every-thing went without a hitch.

The following day, a huge armada of Allied warships anchored in Tokyo Bay, including 258 battleships, cruisers, destroyers, and other vessels of the U.S. Pacific Fleet and a sampling of ships from other Allied countries.[98] All of their guns were directed at the Japanese shore.

Throughout the morning of August 30, U.S. planes landed at Atsugi Airfield at the rate of a plane a minute, "bringing men, equip-ment, supplies, and hundreds of newsmen."[99] At 2:00 p.m.,

MacArthur arrived in his private transport plane, *Bataan*, and, wearing dark sunglasses and smoking a long-stemmed corncob pipe, he stepped out. General Robert Eichelberger strode forward to greet him. In a quiet voice, MacArthur said: "Bob, from Melbourne to Tokyo is a long way, but this seems to be the end of the road."[100]

At dawn on September 2, the eleven-man Japanese delegation, headed by Foreign Minister Mamoru Shigemitsu and Chief of Staff Umezu gathered at the official residence of the prime minister. After bowing toward the Imperial Palace, the delegation set out for Yokohama. From Yokohama Pier, they boarded a U.S. destroyer and for an hour threaded their way through the Allied warships that filled Tokyo Bay, before arriving at the U.S.S. *Missouri*. They clambered up the gangway and made their way to the upper deck, where the surrender ceremony was to take place. From the crowd of sailors lining up the way, they heard the excited murmur, "Japs!"[101]

As thousands of U.S. sailors, soldiers, and newsmen watched, the Japanese delegation stood in front of a battered, felt-covered mess table on which the surrender documents had been placed. "We waited a few minutes, standing in the public gaze like penitent schoolboys awaiting a dreaded schoolmaster," said Tosahikazu Kaze, a member of the delegation.[102]

The sixty-five-year-old MacArthur took his place behind the mess table facing the Japanese. "We are gathered here," he said, his hands were shaking visibly, "to conclude a solemn agreement whereby peace may be restored." As Supreme Commander of the Allied Powers, he continued, "it is my firm intention to discharge my responsibilities with justice and tolerance, while taking all necessary dispositions to insure that the terms of the surrender are fully, promptly and faithfully complied with."[103]

After Shigemitsu and Umezu signed the surrender document for Japan, General MacArthur asked General Sir Arthur Percival, the British commander who surrendered Singapore to the Japanese, and General Jonathan Wainwright, who surrendered Corregidor, to stand beside him while he signed the document. The Japanese had recently released both men from confinement as prisoners of war. While Percival showed no sign of having suffered from the experience, said one observer, Wainwright appeared "pale and worn" and "seemed dazzled and bewildered, like a man who had just emerged into the light after long confinement in darkness."[104]

MacArthur used five pens to sign the surrender document. As he finished with them, he handed one to Wainwright and one to Percival. Fleet Admiral Chester W. Nimitz signed for the United States, followed by representatives of the other Allied nations in turn. MacArthur concluded: "Let us pray that peace be now restored to the world and that God will preserve it always."[105] The surrender proceedings were over in twenty minutes.

8.

Recapitulation and Analysis

Prevent an Invasion

President Truman argued that the atomic bombs dropped on Hiroshima and Nagasaki forced Japan to surrender and thus prevented an invasion of the home islands and saved American lives. He usually cited the cost of an invasion of the home islands as 500,000 Americans dead and wounded. This number fluctuated; sometimes he lowered it to 200,000 and at other times raised it to 1,000,000. "I wasn't worried about being crucified," said Truman later. "It was a question of saving hundreds of thousands of American lives."[1]

U.S. military planners set the casualty figure considerably lower than Truman's. On June 15, 1945, the Joint War Plans Committee, a high-level advisory group to the Joint Chiefs of Staff, reported that the United States would suffer 40,000 dead and 150,000 wounded soldiers in the invasions of Kyushu, set for November 1, 1945, and Honshu, set for March 1945.[2] In the first thirty days of the invasion of Kyushu, General Marshall told Truman on June 18, 1945, casualties would not exceed 31,000 killed and wounded. Admiral King placed the casualty rate between 31,000 and 41,000 for the invasion of Kyushu.

The loss of Japanese lives and the morality of dropping the atomic bombs apparently did not enter into Truman's decision. Throughout the war, U.S. war propaganda had dehumanized the Japanese, referring to them as "wicked beasts." In his diary, Truman's references to "savages, ruthless, merciless, and fanatic" mirrored these stereotypes. In addition, by 1945, the American tolerance for killing civilians had been raised in the Allied bombings of German and Japanese cities, and the firestorms created by a combination of napalm and bombs in Hamburg in July 1943, Dresden in February 1945, and Tokyo in March 1945, which killed hundreds of thousands of civilians.

Until his death in 1972, Truman held firm to his original reasons for ordering the dropping of the atomic bombs. He kept repeating that the bombs forced Japan to surrender, prevented an invasion of the home islands, and saved American lives. "I never lost any sleep over my decision," said Truman.[3] He had no sympathy with anyone who expressed second thoughts. When Robert Oppenheimer admitted to having "known sin" for helping to build the bomb, Truman referred to him as one of those "crybaby scientists" who thought they had "blood on their hands."[4]

Many Americans accepted Truman's explanations as fact. They found them more acceptable than less noble reasons, such as hatred and revenge. Nevertheless, physicist Leo Szilard said: "If the Germans had dropped atomic bombs on cities instead of us, we would have defined the dropping of atomic bombs on cities as a war crime, and we would have sentenced the Germans who were guilty of this crime to death at Nuremberg and hanged them."[5]

Stimson, Byrnes, and Marshall were as adamant as Truman on the need to drop the atomic bombs. "There is no question in my mind," said Byrnes, "that only havoc wrought by our new weapon caused the war lords of Japan to surrender when they did."[6]

"My chief purpose was to end the war in victory with the least possible cost in the lives of the men in the armies which I helped to raise," said Stimson. "I believe that no man holding in his hands a weapon of such possibilities for accomplishing this purpose and saving those lives, could have failed to use it and afterwards looked his countrymen in the face."[7] The Japanese, said Marshall, could only be "slugged into submission," and "we slugged them."[8]

Was the Invasion Necessary

By mid-summer 1945 Admirals King and Leahy, air force general Curtis LeMay, army air force general Henry Arnold, and General Douglas MacArthur agreed that an invasion of Japan was not necessary. "It always appeared to us," said General Arnold, "atomic bomb or no atomic bomb, the Japanese were already on the verge of collapse."[9]

"The use of this barbarous weapon at Hiroshima and Nagasaki was of no material assistance in our war against Japan," said Admiral Leahy. "The Japanese were already defeated and ready to surrender because of the effective sea blockade and the successful bombing with conventional weapons."[10]

In the last 157 days of the war, said General LeMay, "the B-29s literally wrecked Japan" and "brought about the collapse of Japan before the date set for our land invasion."[11]

Many Japanese leaders, such as Kido, Suzuki, and Konoye, agreed that America's conventional air attacks and naval actions were crucial in Japan's decision to end the war. "I felt the biggest threat was the action of the American navy coming across the Pacific," said Toyoda. "That is not to overlook the effect of the United States air force, but even that was made effective only through the cooperation of the American Naval Task Force.[12]

To Rear Admiral Toshitane Takata, "The superfortresses were the greatest single factor in forcing Japanese surrender."[13]

By the end of July, Japan's military situation was hopeless. The U.S. air force and navy had clamped a total naval blockade around its home islands, destroyed its navy and merchant marine, and controlled its air space. Japan lived by trade, and without it, it "must surrender or starve."[14]

"It seems clear," said the U.S. Strategic Bombing Survey, "that air supremacy and its later exploitation over Japan proper was the major factor which determined the timing of Japan's surrender and obviated any need for invasion." Without the use of the atomic bombs, the Soviet entry into the war, or an invasion of the home islands, the survey concluded that Japan would probably have surrendered prior to November 1, 1945, and no later than December 31, 1945.[15]

By dropping the atomic bombs, the United States only hastened the surrender of an already defeated enemy. Long before the dropping of the bombs, Japan's leaders had decided to surrender and were taking preliminary steps to that end, as U.S. leaders knew from naval intelligence interception of Japan's top-secret codes. "Our decision to seek a way out of this war," said Kido, "was made in early June before any atomic bomb had been dropped and Russia had not entered the war. It was already our decision."[16]

The Decision

As secretary of war, Henry Stimson had been closely involved in the discussions on the use of the bomb. In 1947, at the urging of government officials concerned about the growing number of people questioning the use of the bomb, Stimson wrote an article for *Harper's Magazine* titled "The Decision to Use the Atomic Bomb." He argued that the decision to drop the atomic bomb on Hiroshima was made only after careful consideration by Truman and his advisers of all of the courses of action open to them to end the war at the lowest possible cost.

Nevertheless, the question arose as to whether there was anything like a decision to use the bombs, or whether Truman and his advisers were carried along by events.

According to one interpretation, Truman ordered the dropping of the atomic bombs to justify the cost and resources used to build them. The bombs cost $2 billion, and required the work of scores of top scientists, tens of thousands of workers, and numerous industrial firms. After all this time and expenditure, could Truman not have used them? Congressmen would have asked, said General Groves, "Why did you spend all this money and all this effort and then when you got it, why didn't you use it?"[17] To be sure, congressional committees had long been grumbling about the "huge secret appropriations" going into the Manhattan Project, and they warned that "the results had better be worth the $2 billion investment."[18]

Byrnes told Szilard, "How would you get Congress to appropriate money for atomic energy research if you do not show results for the money which has been spent already?"[19]

And upon hearing of the successful explosion over Hiroshima, Truman seemed relieved: "We have spent 2 billion dollars on the greatest scientific gamble in history—and won."[20]

The dropping of the second bomb seemed to have its own momentum. Truman's July 24 strike order commanded the use of the "bombs" as they were ready, and the technicians on Tinian Island worked feverishly to ready the second bomb in response to that order. Admiral William R. Purnell, the navy's representative on the Manhattan Project, and General Groves hoped the second bomb coming on August 9, so soon after the first, would keep the Japanese "off balance." Still, the combination of the atomic bombing on Hiroshima on August 6 and the Soviet entry into the war on August 8, a one-two punch, was the "shock effect" some of Truman's advisers had advocated. In addition, the second bombing came too soon on the heels of the first to allow the Japanese enough time to reach a decision.

Widespread hatred of and revenge against the Japanese for the bombing of Pearl Harbor may have generated the momentum for dropping the atomic bombs. Japan's Pearl Harbor attack united Americans in a "flaming rage" against it. To many Americans, including Truman, it justified almost any act against it in retaliation. Expressing his feeling for "retribution," Truman said in a private letter written shortly after the bombing of Nagasaki, that nobody was more "disturbed" by the use of the atomic bombs than he, "but I was greatly disturbed over the unwarranted attack by the Japanese on Pearl Harbor." He concluded: "The only language they seem to understand is the one that we have been using to bombard them. When you have to deal with a beast, you have to treat him as a beast."[21]

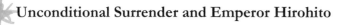

Unconditional Surrender and Emperor Hirohito

To the Japanese, a proud people with a tradition of loyalty, bravery, self-sacrifice, and honor in combat, surrender on any terms was humiliating. But by April 1945 Japan's leaders realized that the war was lost. Their main stumbling block was the United States' insistence on unconditional surrender. They specifically, needed to know whether the United States would allow Hirohito to remain on the throne. They feared that America would depose him, try him as a war criminal, or even execute him.

As long as the United States insisted on unconditional surrender, Japan's leaders rejected opening up direct negotiations with it. But by the spring and summer of 1945, with the U.S. air attacks and naval blockade of the home islands, Japan had much to gain by direct negotiations with the United States. It would have encouraged those forces in the U.S. and Britain, therefore urging Truman to modify the demand for unconditional surrender and allow the Japanese to retain Hirohito.

Instead, Suzuki and Togo sent peace signals through Sweden, Switzerland, and Portugal. When this failed, the Supreme Council decided in mid-May 1945 to turn to the Soviets for help in mediating an end to the war. Yet all indications from the Soviet Union showed it moving toward belligerency. On April 5, 1945, it announced non-renewal of the Neutrality Pact with Japan and began shifting troops and armaments from Europe to the Manchurian border. In intelligence circles, too, there was fairly "wide knowledge of the fact" that the Soviets had made a deal with the United States at Yalta to enter the war after the defeat of Germany. But Japan's intelligence services did not pick this up, and Japan's leaders did not suspect it. This illustrated Japan's poor judgment and lack of astuteness in foreign affairs.

Truman knew that the Japanese were trying to persuade the Soviets to mediate an end to the war. U.S. cryptographers had broken the Japanese codes and naval intelligence had intercepted messages between Foreign Minister Togo and Ambassador Sato in Moscow. Although Truman had read the intercepted messages, he refused to open up direct negotiations with the Japanese.

On May 8, 1945, shortly after Germany's surrender, Truman issued a press statement modifying the terms of unconditional surrender. After calling for Japan's military and naval forces to lay down their arms unconditionally, he said the United States would neither destroy nor enslave the Japanese people. However, the State Department wanted him to add a clear statement on the retention of Hirohito, which Truman refused. Acting Secretary of State Grew considered Truman's refusal to retain the emperor a missed opportunity for peace. A statement on the retention of Hirohito, said Grew, would have strengthened the peace forces in Japan and hastened surrender.

Domestic political concerns may offer an explanation for Truman's failure to include a statement on the retention of Hirohito in his May 8 statement. Resentment against the emperor in the United States ran deep. "Hirohito must go!" was a favorite war slogan, and a 1945 public opinion poll showed that only 3 percent of Americans favored his retention, while one-third advocated his execution.[22]

On May 28 Grew gave Truman the first draft of the Potsdam Declaration, drawn up by the State Department. Paragraph twelve allowed the possibility of the retention of Hirohito. It read: "The Allies would withdraw from Japan as soon as a government representative of the people of Japan was established," and "this may include a constitutional monarchy under the present dynasty." Truman said he agreed with it, but he asked Grew to discuss it first with Secretary of War Stimson, Secretary of the Navy Forrestal, and the Joint Chiefs of Staff. At the Pentagon the next day, they told Grew that the timing was not right because the Japanese were still fighting on Okinawa and would view it as "a confession of weakness." This was not the real reason, however. In his diary that night, Stimson wrote that the real reason that would "govern the whole situation" was "S-1." Thus, Truman had misled Grew: He was not ready to retain Hirohito.

On June 18 the release of the Combined Chiefs of Staff's intelligence report strengthened Grew's argument. It said that the Japanese would find foreign custody of the emperor and terms of unconditional surrender "most revolting." Apparently, Stimson agreed. Although he revised paragraph twelve of Grew's Potsdam Declaration, it conformed to the original version. It read: "The Allied occupying forces would be withdrawn from Japan as soon as the Japanese established a peacefully inclined responsible government of a character representative of the Japanese people," which "may include a constitutional monarchy under the present dynasty if the peace-loving nations can be convinced of the genuine determination of such a government to follow policies of peace."

Before Truman left for Potsdam on July 2, Stimson gave him a copy of the revised Potsdam Declaration. Truman turned it over to Byrnes, the new secretary of state. In turn, Byrnes read it to Cordell Hull, former secretary of state under Roosevelt, who did not like paragraph twelve. It sounded like "appeasement," said Hull. He argued that the emperor should be stripped of "all extraordinary privileges" and placed on the same level as everybody else. How much influence Hull's opinion had on Byrnes was unclear, but Byrnes was not yet ready to revise Stimson's version of paragraph twelve.

A July 8 Allied intelligence report strengthened the earlier June 18 Combined Chiefs of Staff's report on the importance of the emperor to the Japanese people. If the Allies allowed Japan to retain Hirohito, said the report, the Japanese might agree to withdraw from the Asiatic continent and the southern Pacific, and begin partial disarmament of their military forces.

On July 18, in contradiction of the two military reports on the importance of the emperor to Japan's surrender, the Joint Chiefs of Staff informed Truman that they wanted paragraph twelve of Stimson's proposed Potsdam Declaration not to include any definite references to the future structure of Japanese politics. More specifically, they wanted the last sentence of paragraph twelve to read: "Subject to suitable guarantees against further acts of aggression the Japanese people will be free to choose their own form of government."

The Joint Chiefs of Staff decision to disregard their own intelligence reports, and not to include the retention of the emperor in the

Potsdam Declaration, came two days after the successful atomic bomb test at New Mexico. Apparently, this influenced their decision.

Unknown to the Joint Chiefs of Staff, on July 17, the day after the successful test, Truman and Byrnes had already deleted paragraph twelve's reference to "a constitutional monarchy under the present dynasty." It now read in part: "The occupying forces of the Allies shall be withdrawn from Japan as soon as there has been established in accordance with the freely expressed will of the Japanese people a peacefully inclined and responsible government."

Truman and Byrnes's version left out Stimson's more definite commitment on the retention of the emperor. Did the successful atomic bomb test on July 16 influence their decision? To be sure, they had read the naval intelligence reports stating that Japan's leaders would not surrender unless they could retain Emperor Hirohito. Watering down paragraph twelve suggests that Truman and Byrnes were not in a hurry for Japan to surrender.

The United States and the Soviet Union

In 1965, historian Gar Alperowitz published *Atomic Diplomacy: Hiroshima and Potsdam*, in which he argued that Truman dropped the atomic bombs on Japan to impress the Soviet Union with America's firepower and to act as a warning not to expand into Western Europe. Alperowitz's book directly challenged the generally accepted version that Truman had dropped the atomic bombs solely to prevent an invasion, save American lives, and end the war with Japan.

Perhaps Truman's decision to drop the bombs was an attempt both to impress the Soviets with America's fire power and to end the war before the Soviets entered and seized the Far Eastern territories that Roosevelt had promised them at the February 1945 Yalta Conference.

At Yalta, Roosevelt had promised Stalin a considerable amount of Far Eastern territory for entering the war two or three months after Germany's defeat. The territory included the Kunile Islands, South Sakhalin and adjacent islands, access to the Manchurian port city of Dairen in northeast China, and a naval base at nearby Port Arthur. The Soviets would have access to these ports by crossing

Manchuria on a railroad line owned jointly by the Soviet Union and China. At Roosevelt's insistence, Stalin agreed to support a non-communist Chinese government friendly to the United States.

Roosevelt and his advisers considered Soviet entry crucial to defeating Japan's Kwantung Army in Manchuria, which contained, they said, the best Japanese troops and military equipment. But they greatly overestimated its strength. Partly, they began to take too seriously their own war propaganda, which stated that Japan's goal was to conquer the world, including the Western hemisphere. That Japan did not have the industrial capacity to conquer the Western Hemisphere contradicted America's war propaganda, and U.S. leaders would not readily admit it. They insisted that Japan was holding back its resources, and that the Kwantung Army was part of this hidden strength. On paper, it had twenty-four divisions, but in fact, they were undermanned and ill-equipped. When the Red Army invaded Manchuria, it defeated the Kwantung Army in about six days.

U.S. leaders took their own war propaganda too seriously and made policy from it rather than the reality of power-politics. By encouraging the Soviets to enter the war against Japan, an already defeated enemy, Roosevelt and his advisers were acting against America's national self-interests. The Soviet Union had already expanded deep into Eastern Europe, and by 1945 it had upset the balance of power in Europe. By acquiring more land in East Asia, the they would become the strongest power in Eurasia. Traditionally, America's main enemy in Europe and Asia was the strongest power.

When Truman took over in April 1945 he followed Roosevelt's policy of encouraging Soviet entry into the war against Japan. In fact, one of his immediate purposes for going to Potsdam was to get the Soviet Union into the war. General Marshall argued that Soviet entry would hasten the Japanese surrender either immediately or shortly after the United States invaded the home islands. But Admirals King and Leahy and General MacArthur discounted the importance of Soviet entry.

Despite word of the successful atomic bomb test at Alamogordo on July 16, Truman's attitude on Soviet entry into the war remained unchanged. At lunch the next day, Stalin informed Truman that the Soviet Union would enter the war on August 15. In his diary that night, Truman wrote, "Fini Japs when that comes about," and he wrote Bess, "I've gotten what I came for."

On July 21, with the successful results of the atomic bomb test confirmed from New Mexico, Truman's attitude toward Soviet entry changed considerably. Noticing this changed attitude, Churchill said that Truman "no longer felt that we needed Stalin's aid to conquer Japan." Stalin, too, may have sensed Truman's change on the issue of Soviet entry. On July 23, for the first time, Stalin publicly announced his intention to enter the war against Japan. We began to hope, said Byrnes, that a Japanese surrender would occur before the Soviets entered the war. Did Truman's changed attitude on Soviet entry into the war influence his decision to drop the atomic bombs?

The Drop-Order and *Mokusatsu*

On July 24 the U.S. and British Combined chiefs of Staff met with Truman and Churchill at the Little White House. At this meeting, two days before he released the Potsdam Declaration on July 26, Truman gave the formal order to drop the atomic bomb on Japan no sooner than August 2. Of course, if Japan had surrendered before August 2, he could have countermanded the order. Apparently, he did not place much faith in Japan's acceptance of the Potsdam Declaration.

For two days, Japan's Supreme Council had debated how best to respond to the Potsdam Declaration. The unsettled status of the emperor needed clarification. All agreed that the government should not make any decision until it received the Soviet response to the Konoye mission. The Japanese continued foolishly to hope for Soviet mediation despite evidence that the Soviets were amassing large troop concentrations on the Manchurian border. Meanwhile, they decided to give the press a text of the Potsdam Declaration but with no accompanying comment.

When asked about the Potsdam Declaration at a press conference on July 28, Suzuki made his unfortunate *Mokusatsu* statement, which had several different meanings: to ignore, to treat with silent contempt, to take no notice of, or to give no comment at this time. War Minister Anami told the Information Board, which cleared all news, that it meant "reject by ignoring." Sakomizu later said that "no comment" would have more accurately expressed Suzuki's true meaning.

Despite Suzuki's *Mokusatsu* statement, Truman knew that the Japanese were still trying to surrender. On July 28, the day of Suzuki's press conference, Stalin informed Truman that he had received a message from Japan requesting that the Soviet Union mediate an end to the war and saying that the emperor desired to "avoid more bloodshed." When Stalin said he would give "a negative reply," Truman thanked him. Three days later, rejecting a "wait and see" attitude, Truman finalized the order to drop the atomic bomb.

On August 2, four days before the dropping of the bomb on Hiroshima, William Donovan, head of the Office of Strategic Services, informed Truman that Japanese diplomats in Switzerland explained that Suzuki's *Mokusatsu* statement was meant to mollify the military, and that Japan's "real response" would follow in a week.[23]

The Donovan report, combined with the navy's intelligence intercepts and Stalin's announcement of Japan's peace efforts, meant that the Japanese needed more time to clarify the Potsdam Declaration and to get all factions to agree to surrender terms. At this point, Truman could have countermanded the drop-order of the atomic bomb, called for a cease-fire, and opened up direct negotiations with the Japanese. This would have forestalled Soviet entry and saved lives.

Japanese Surrender

On August 8 the Soviet Union declared war on Japan, and its armies invaded Manchuria. The Red Army defeated the Kwantung Army in about six days and pushed to within 100 miles where it linked up with Mao Tse-tung's Communist Army.

To Japan's military leaders, the Soviet entry into the war was probably a greater blow than the dropping of the atomic bombs on Hiroshima and Nagasaki. They were not prepared for war with the Red Army; neither was the Kwantung Army capable of any effective resistance to it. In addition, the Soviet declaration of war stunned the civilian leadership, which had pinned its hopes on Soviet mediation of the war. Instead, the Soviet Union had joined the coalition of powers arrayed against them.

Between August 6 and 9, as Japan was hit by the triple blows of Hiroshima, Soviet entry, and Nagasaki, the Supreme Council was deadlocked over conditions of surrender. Suzuki, Togo, and Yonai advocated acceptance of the Potsdam Declaration on the condition that Hirohito remain on the throne. Anami, Umezu, and Toyoda wanted three additional conditions: 1) voluntary withdrawal of Japanese overseas forces; 2) no allied occupation of the home islands; and 3) allowing Japan to conduct its own war crimes trials.

Unless the Supreme Council could reach unanimous agreement, the government would remain deadlocked, and the war would continue. To prevent this, Suzuki, Togo, and Cabinet Secretary Sakomizu worked out a plan with Hirohito to break the deadlock. First, Hirohito called an imperial conference with the Supreme Council. Then, after both sides presented their case, Suzuki, to the dismay of Anami, Umezu, and Toyoda, turned to the emperor to make the decision. Wanting to end the war quickly, Hirohito sided with Suzuki, Togo, and Yonai.

The next day Truman and his Cabinet learned that Japan would accept the Potsdam Declaration on the condition that it did not "compromise any demand which prejudices the prerogatives of His Majesty as a sovereign ruler." Advocating acceptance, Stimson and Leahy argued that Hirohito's help was crucial to get the scattered Japanese armies to surrender and to prevent a score of bloody Iwo Jimas and Okinawas. But Byrnes said that acceptance would leave the United States open to criticism of retreating from the "severity of the Potsdam Declaration." He added: "It was not the time for the Japanese to present conditions."

Forrestal suggested that the United States draft a reply that would "indicate willingness to accept yet define the terms of surrender," and Truman asked Byrnes to draft a reply that would convey such an understanding.

For both countries, the problem had to do with "saving face," meaning honor. Despite the importance of keeping the emperor, the Japanese needed to save face by tacking on to the Potsdam Declaration a conditional surrender term. But to some Americans, acceptance of Japan's conditional surrender term would mean a loss of face for the United States. While the leaders of both countries argued over saving face, the war continued, and thousands lost their lives.

To resolve the dilemma, Byrnes and Benjamin Cohen, a State Department lawyer, were to tell the Japanese how they could keep their emperor and on what terms. They changed the Japanese condition from "the understanding that said declaration does not compromise any demand which prejudices the prerogatives of His Majesty as a sovereign ruler" to "the Japanese Emperor's authority and that of his government of rule the state would be subject to the authority of a Supreme Commander of the Allied Power." The change acknowledged that the emperor would continue to rule, but it did not guarantee him ultimate authority.

Despite prolonged discussion and debate on August 12 and 13, Japan's leaders could not reach an agreement on acceptance of the Allies' reply. As usual, the Supreme Council divided three to three: Suzuki, Togo, and Yonai for acceptance, while Umezu, Anami, and Toyoda were against it. In the Cabinet, thirteen members voted for acceptance of the Allies' reply while three voted against it. The emperor would have to decide the issue.

On August 14 the Hirohito convened another imperial conference, this time with both the Supreme Council and the Cabinet. Umezu, Toyoda, and Anami were against acceptance of the Allies' condition because it placed the emperor subordinate to the Allies' Supreme commander. But Anami, usually the most outspoken, had lost his zest for the debate. When he looked at the emperor, his eyes clouded with tears, and he was unable to continue. Hirohito then issued an imperial order to accept the Allies' reply.

For the most part, Hirohito's direct intervention ended Japanese resistance to surrender. The military's code would not allow it to disobey an imperial order. Most important, Anami, the only Army general who probably could have obtained widespread military support for a coup, would not go against the emperor. Without Anami's support, the attempted coup by a small group of junior officers never had a chance.

The Postwar Situation

In 1943, with Stalin's enthusiastic support, Roosevelt and Churchill called for the unconditional surrender of Germany and Japan. This was a policy of hatred and revenge and took no notice of postwar balance-of-power realities.

At the beginning of World War II, the three great industrial powers of Germany, the Soviet Union, and Japan dominated Europe and Asia. Because the Allies offered no conditions of surrender, unconditional surrender undermined the peace forces in both Germany and Japan and prolonged the war until 1945. By that time, the Allies had destroyed the cities and economies of both countries, and the balance of power had collapsed in Europe and Asia. The Soviet Union filled the void by expanding into Eastern Europe and East Asia.

Instead of following a policy of revenge, the United States and Britain should have adopted a surrender policy that better fit postwar realities. If they had stipulated terms of conditional surrender, the peace forces in Germany and Japan would have been in stronger positions to overthrow the more militaristic factions and negotiate surrender while their industries were still strong. This would have better enabled them to hold down the rising power of the Soviet Union and keep the balance of power in Europe and Asia intact.

Immediately after the war, the United States continued to follow a policy of further weakening Japan. U.S. occupation forces either dynamited or dismantled most of Japan's remaining industries. But since East Asia depended on Japan's industries, U.S. policy only further weakened that area and increased the power vacuum. The United States hoped a rising China, under Chiang Kai-shek, would fill it, but the Chinese Communists had grown in strength during the war with Japan, and America's attempt to prevent civil war between Chiang and the Communists failed. Despite U.S. aid, Chiang lost that war, and in 1949 he withdrew his remaining troops to the island of Taiwan.

When Mao's Communist armies won the civil war in China, America switched from a policy of building up China's strength as a barrier against Japan to adopting a policy of rebuilding Japan to counterbalance the Soviet Union and Communist China. Halting the destruction of Japan's industries, U.S. leaders gave it more than $12 billion in aid to rebuild them and even urged it to rearm.

MacArthur further strengthened Japan with a series of progressive reforms. He split up large estates into smaller farms, broke up large corporations, promoted labor unions, levied progressive taxes, and implemented universal education. He drafted a new constitution that strengthened democracy, gave women equal rights, and protected free speech. His policies had reduced the concentration of wealth and raised consumer buying power. Along with this, progressive taxation and wage increases kept income more equally divided among the people. These policies helped raise and sustain consumer purchasing power and created a large home market for the products of Japan's factories and farms.

Unconditional surrender was a policy of revenge, and it hurt America's national self-interest. It prolonged the war in both Europe and East Asia, and it helped to expand Soviet power in those areas. With the onset of the Cold War between the United States and the Soviet Union, America's leaders switched from a policy of destroying Japan's industry to one of rebuilding it. U.S. policy toward Germany followed a similar pattern.

If the United States had given Japan conditional surrender terms, including retention of the emperor, at the war's outset, Japan would probably have surrendered sometime in the spring or early summer of 1945, if not sooner. This would have saved countless lives, avoided the horrible destruction of many of Japan's cities, and prevented Soviet expansion in East Asia. Most important, it would have avoided the need to plan for an invasion or to drop the atomic bombs. As it was, the dropping of the bombs only hastened the surrender of an already defeated enemy.

Selected Bibliography

Documents, Manuscripts, Records, and Reports

Arnold, Henry H. Papers. Library of Congress, Washington, D.C.

Elsey, George M. Papers, Harry S. Truman Library, Independence Missouri

Kido, Marquis, Koichi. *Family Documents.* K 27-3-60, National Diet Library, Tokyo.

Leahy, William D. Papers. Library of Congress, Washington, D.C.

LeMay, Curtis Papers. Library of Congress, Washington, D.C.

Manhattan Engineer District Records. Microfilm 1108, Record Group 77, National Archives, Washington, D.C.

National Institute Defense Studies, Archives of the War Office. *Records of Army Supreme Headquarters; National Policy Decisions; and Highest War Guidance Meetings.* Parliamentary Museum, Tokyo.

Report of the British Mission to Japan. *The Effects of the Atomic Bombs at Hiroshima and Nagasaki.* London: His Majesty's Stationery Office, 1946.

Spaatz, Carl E. Papers. Library of Congress, Washington, D.C.

Stimson, Henry L. Papers. Sterling Memorial Library, Yale University, New Haven, Connecticut.

Truman, Harry S. Papers. Harry S. Truman Library, Independence, Missouri.

U.S. Air Force. U.S. Strategic Bombing Survey. *The Effects of the Atomic Bombings of Hiroshima and Nagasaki.* Washington, D.C.: U.S. Government Printing Office, June 19, 1946.

——. *The Interrogations of Japanese Leaders.* Microfilm 1654, Record Group 243. National Archives, Washington, D.C.

——. *Japan's Struggle to End the War.* Washington, D.C.: U.S. Government Printing Office, 1946.

——. *The Pacific War.* Washington, D.C.: U.S. Government Printing Office, July 1946.

——. *The Prosecution of War Criminals.* Record Group 331. National Archives, Washington, D.C.

U.S. Department of Army. Combined Chiefs of Staff Records. Record Group 218, Modern Military Records. National Archives, Washington, D.C.

——. Joint Chiefs of Staff Records. Record Group 218, Modern Military Records. National Archives, Washington, D.C.

U.S. Department of Defense. *The Entry of the Soviet Union into the War Against Japan: Military Plans, 1941–1945.* Washington, D.C.: Department, 1955.

U.S. Navy. Naval Intelligence Reports, Russo-Japanese Relations. Record Group 457. National Archives, Washington, D.C.

U.S. Department of State. Decimal File, Record Group 59, National Archives, Washington, D.C.

——. *Foreign Relations of the United States. Potsdam*, 1945, vol.1, Washington, D.C.: U.S. Government Printing Office, 1960.

—-. *Foreign Relations of the United States. Potsdam* 1945, vol. 2, Washington, D.C.: U.S. Government Printing Office, 1960.

——. *Foreign Relations of the United States. The British Commonwealth and the Far East, 1945,* vol. 6. Washington, D.C.: U.S. Government Printing Office, 1969.

Memoirs, Diaries, Biographies, Special Studies, Official Histories, and Articles

Acheson, Dean. *Present at the Creation: My Years in the State Department.* New York: W.W. Norton and company, 1969.

Alperowitz, Gar. *Atomic Diplomacy: Hiroshima and Potsdam.* New York: Simon and Schuster, 1965.

——. "More on Atomic Diplomacy." *Bulletin of the Atomic Scientists*, vol. 41, December 1985, pp. 35–39.

Arnold, H. H. *Global Mission.* New York: Harper and Brothers Publishers, 1949.

Attlee, Clement R. *As It Happened.* New York: Viking Press, 1954.

Bailey, Charles W., and Knebel, Fletcher. "Hiroshima: The Decision that Changed the World." *Look*, vol. 24 (12), June 7, 1960, pp. 70–82.

Bailyn, Bernard and Fleming, Donald, eds. *The Intellectual Migration: Europe and America 1930–1960.* Cambridge, Mass.: Harvard University Press, 1969.

Bagby, Wesley M. *The Eagle-Dragon Alliance: America's Relations with China in World War II.* Newark: University of Delaware Press, 1992.

Baker, Paul R., ed. *The Atomic Bomb: The Great Decision.* New York: Holt, Rinehart and Winston, 1968.

Baldwin, Hanson W. *The Price of Power.* New York: Harper and Brothers Publishers, 1947.

Behr, Edward. *Hirohito: Behind the Myth*. New York: Villard Books, 1989.

Bergamini, David. *Japan's Imperial Conspiracy*, vol. 2. New York: William Morrow and Company, 1971.

Bernstein, Barton J. "A Postwar Myth: 500,000 U.S. Lives Saved." *Bulletin of the Atomic Scientists*, Vol. 42, June/July 1986, pp. 38–40.

———. "The Dropping of the A-Bomb," *The Center Magazine*, March/April, 1983, pp. 14–21.

———. "Roosevelt, Truman, and the Atomic Bomb: A Reinterpretation." *Political Science Quarterly*, vol. 90 (1), Spring, 1975, pp. 63–71.

Bess, Michael. "Leo Szilard: Scientist, Activist, Visionary." *Bulletin of the Atomic Scientists,* vol. 41, December 1985, pp. 11–18.

Blackett, P.M.4S. *Fear, War, and the Bomb*. New York: Whittlesey House, 1948.

Bohlen, Charles E. *Witness to History 1929–1969*. New York: W. W. Norton and Company, 1973.

Browne, Courtney. *Togo: The Last Banzai*. New York: Holt, Rinehart, and Winston, 1967.

Bullock, Alan. *Ernest Bevin: Foreign Secretary 1945–1951*. New York: W. W. Norton and Company, 1983.

Bundy, McGeorge, and Stimson, Henry L. *On Active Service in Peace and War*. New York: Harper and Brothers Publishers, 1948.

Bundy, H. H. "Remembered Words" *The Atlantic*, March 1957, pp. 56–57.

Butow, Robert J. C. *Japan's Decision to Surrender*. Stanford: Stanford University Press, 1954.

Byrnes, James F. *All in One Lifetime*. New York: Harper and Brothers Publishers, 1958.

———. *Speaking Frankly*. New York: Harper and Brothers Publishers, 1947.

Churchill, Winston S. *Triumph and Tragedy*. Boston: Houghton Mifflin Company, 1953.

Clay, Lucius D. *Decision in Germany*. Garden City, N.Y.: Doubleday and Company, 1950.

Coffey, Thomas M. *Imperial Tragedy: Japan in World War II*. New York: World Publishing Company, 1970.

Compton, Arthur H. *Atomic Quest: A Personal Narrative*. New York: Oxford University Press, 1956.

Compton, Karl T. "If the Atomic Bomb Had Not Been Used," *Atlantic Monthly*, December 1946, pp. 82–86.

Craven, W. F., and Cate, J. L., eds. *The Army Air Forces in World War II: The Pacific-Matterhorn to Wagasaki, June 1944 to August 1945*, vol. 5. Chicago: University of Chicago Press, 1953.

Davies, John P. *Dragon by the Tail*. New York: W. W. Norton and Company, 1972.

Deane, John R. *The Strange Alliance*. New York: Viking Press, 1947.

Eden, Anthony. *The Reckoning*. Boston: Houghton Mifflin Company, 1965.

Ehrman, John. *Grand Strategy: October 1944–August 1945*, vol. 6. London: Her Majesty's Stationery Office, 1956.

Eisenhower, Dwight D. *Crusade in Europe*. New York: Doubleday and Company, 1948.

Emmerson, John K. *The Japanese Thread: A Life in the U.S. Foreign Service*. New York: Holt, Rinehart, and Winston, 1978.

Feis, Herbert. *The Atomic Bomb and the End of World War II*. Princeton, N.J.: Princeton University Press, 1966.

Ferrell, Robert H. ed. *Truman in the White House: The Diary of Eben A. Ayers*. Columbia, M.: University of Missouri Press, 1991.

———. *Dear Bess: The Letters from Harry to Bess Truman 1910–1959*. New York: W. W. Norton and Company, 1983.

———. *Off the Record: The Private Papers of Harry S. Truman*. New York: Harper and Row Publishers, 1980.

Finn, Richard B. *Winners in Peace*. Berkeley, California: University of California Press, 1992.

Freed, Fred, and Giovannitti, Len. *The Decision to Drop the Bomb*. New York: Coward-McCann, 1965.

Forrestal, James. *The Forrestal Diaries*, ed. Walter Millis. New York: Viking Press, 1951.

Goodchild, Peter. *J Robert Oppenheimer: Shatterer of Worlds*. New York: Houghton Mifflin Company, 1980.

Grew, Joseph C. *Turbulent Era: A Diplomatic Record of Forty Years 1904–1945*, vol. 21, ed. Walter Johnson. Boston: Houghton Mifflin Company, 1952.

Groves, Leslie R. *Now It Can Be Told: The Story of the Manhattan Project*. New York: Da Capo Press, 1975.

Hachiya, Michihiko. *Hiroshima Diary*, ed. Warner Wells, Chapel Hill, N.C.: University of North Carolina Press, 1955.

Harriman, Averell W., and Abel, Elie. *Special Envoy to Churchill and Stalin 1941–1946*. New York: Random House, 1975.

Herbert, Richard. *Japan Surrenders*. Washington, D.C.: National Archives and Records Administration, 1989.

Herken, Gregg. *The Winning Weapon: The Atomic Bomb in the Cold War 1945–1950*. New York: Vintage Books, 1982.

Hillman, William. *Mr. President: The First Publication from the Personal Diaries, Private Letters, Papers, and Revealing Interviews of Harry S. Truman.* New York: Farrar, Straus, and Young, 1952.

Hull, Cordell. *The Memoirs of Cordell Hull*, vol. 2. New York: MacMillan Company. 1948.

Iriye, Akira. *Power and Culture: The Japanese-American War, 1941–1945.* Cambridge, Mass.: Harvard University Press, 1981.

———. *Across the Pacific: An Inner History of American-East Asian Relations.* New York: Harcourt Press, 1969.

Isaacson, Walter. "Why Did We Drop the Bomb?" *Time*, August 19, 1985.

Kase, Toshikazu. *Journey to the Missouri*, ed. David Nelson Rowe. New Haven, CT: Yale University Press, 1950.

Kato, Masuo. *The Lost War: A Japanese Reporter's Inside Story.* New York: Alfred A. Knopf, 1946.

Kido, Marquis, Koichi. *The Diary of Marquis Kido, 1931–45.* Frederick, MD: University Publications of America, 1984.

King, Ernest J., and Whitehill, Walter. *Fleet Admiral King: A Naval Record.* New York: W. W. Norton, 1952.

Kolko, Gabriel. *The Politics of War: The World and United States Foreign Policy, 1943–1945.* New York: Random House, 1968.

Kurzman, Dan. *Day of the Bomb: Countdown to Hiroshima.* New York: McGraw-Hill Book Company, 1986.

Large, Stephen S. *Emperor Hirohito and Showa Japan: A Political Biography.* New York: Chapman Hall, 1992.

Lawrence, William L. *Man and Atoms: The Discovery, the Uses, and the Future of Atomic Energy.* New York: Simon and Schuster, 1959.

Leahy, William D. *I Was There.* New York: Whittlesey House, 1950.

———. *Diaries*, 1945. Microfilm No. 4, William D. Leahy Papers, Library of Congress, Washington, D.C.

Leckie, Robert. *Delivered from Evil: The Saga of World War II.* New York: Harper and Row Publishers, 1987.

Lifton, Robert Jay. *Death in Life: Survivors of Hiroshima.* New York: Random House, Inc., 1967.

Lilienthal, David E. *The Journals of David E. Lilienthal: The Atomic Energy Years 1945–1950*, vol. 2. New York: Harper and Row, 1964.

MacArthur, Douglas. *Reminiscences: General of the Army.* New York: McGraw-Hill Book Company, 1964.

Matsumoto, Michihiro. *The Unspoken Way, Haragei: Silence in Japanese Business and Society.* Tokyo: Kodansha International, 1988.

McCloy, John J. *The Challenge to American Foreign Policy.* Cambridge, Mass.: Harvard University Press, 1953.

McCullough, David. *Truman.* New York: Simon and Schuster, 1992.

Messer, Robert L. "New Evidence on Truman's Decision." *Bulletin of the Atomic Scientists*, vol. 41, August 1985.

Moran, Charles. *Churchill: The Struggle for Survival, 1940–1965, Taken from the Diaries of Lord Moran.* Boston: Houghton Mifflin, 1966.

Morgan, Henry G. *Planning the Defeat of Japan: A Study of Total War Strategy.* Washington, D.C.: Modern Military Records, National Archives.

Morrison, Samuel E. "Why Japan Surrendered." *The Atlantic*, October 1960, pp. 41–47.

Mosley, Leonard. *Marshall: Hero for Our Times.* New York: Hearst Books, 1982.

——. *Hirohito: Emperor of Japan.* Englewood Cliffs, N.J.: Prentice-Hall, 1966.

Murphy, Robert. *Diplomat Among Warriors.* Garden City, N.Y.: Doubleday and Company, 1964.

Nimitz, Chester, and Potter, E. B. *Sea Power: A Naval History.* Englewood Cliffs, N.J.: Prentice-Hall, 1960.

Oka, Yoshitake. *Konoe Fumimaro: A Political Biography.* Trans. Shumpei Okamoto and Patricia Murry. Tokyo: University of Tokyo Press, 1972.

O'Neal, Michael. *President Truman and the Atomic Bomb: Opposing Viewpoints.* San Diego: Greenhaven Press, 1990.

Osada, Arata. *Children of the A-Bomb: The Testament of the Boys and Girls of Hiroshima.* Trans. Jean Dan and Ruth Sieben Morgan. New York: G. P. Putnam Sons, 1959.

Pacific War Research Society. *The Day Man Lost: Hiroshima August 6, 1945.* Tokyo: Kodansha International, 1981.

Peierls, Rudolf. "Reflections of a British Participant." *Bulletin of the Atomic Scientists*, vol. 41, August 1985, pp. 27–29.

Pogue, Forrest C. *George C. Marshall: Statesman.* New York: Viking Penguin, 1987.

Quigley, Martin S. *Peace Without Hiroshima.* New York: Madison Books, 1991.

Rhodes, Richard. *The Making of the Atomic Bomb.* New York: Simon and Schuster, 1986.

Sherwin, Martin J. *A World Destroyed: Hiroshima and the Origins of the Arms Race.* New York: Vintage Books, 1987.

——. "How Well They Meant." *Bulletin of the Atomic Scientists*, vol. 41, August 1985.

——. *A World Destroyed: The Atomic Bomb and the Grand Alliance*. New York: Alfred A. Knopf, 1975.

——. "Old Issues in New Editions." *Bulletin of the Atomic Scientists,* vol. 41, December 1945.

Sherwood, Robert E. *Roosevelt and Hopkins: An Intimate History*. New York: Harper and Brothers Publishers, 1950.

Shigemitsu, Mamoru. *Japan and Her Destiny: My Struggle for Peace*. ed. FSG. Piggott, trans. Oswald White. New York: E. P. Dutton and Company, 1958.

Shigenori, Togo. *The Cause of Japan*. New York: Simon and Schuster, 1956.

Shiroyama, Saburo. *War Criminal: The Life and Death of Hirota Koki*, trans. John Bester. Tokyo: Kodansha International Ltd., 1978.

Shohno, Naomi. *The Legacy of Hiroshima: It's Past Our Future*. Tokyo: Kosei Publishing Company, 1982.

Smith, Alice K. "The Elusive Dr. Szilard." *Harper's Magazine*, vol. 221, July 1960.

Stimson, Henry L. "The Decision to Use the Atomic Bomb." *Harper's Magazine*, vol. 194, no. 1161, February, 1947.

Spector, Ronald H. *Eagle Against the Sun*. New York: Free Press, 1985.

Stimson, Henry L. "The Decision to Use the Atomic Bomb." *Harper's Magazine*, vol. 194 (1161), February 1947.

Stoler, Mark A. *George C. Marshall: Soldier-Statesman of the American Century*. Boston: Twayne Publishers, 1989.

Sutherland, John P. "The Story General Marshall Told Me." *U.S. News and World Report*, November 2, 1959, pp. 50–56.

Szilard, Leo. "We Turned the Switch." *The Nation*, vol. 161, December 22, 1945, pp. 718–719.

Takemi, Taro. "Remembrances of the War and the Bomb." *Jama*, vol. 250, (5), August 5, 1983, pp. 42–46.

Thorne, Christopher. *The Issue of War: States, Societies, and the Far Eastern Conflict of 1941–1945*. New York: Oxford University Press, 1985.

——. *Allies of a Kind: The United States, Britain, and the War Against Japan, 1941–1945*. New York: Oxford University Press, 1978.

Toland, John. *The Rising Sun: The Decline and Fall of the Japanese Empire 1936–1945,* vol. 2. New York: Random House, 1970.

Truman, Harry. *Letters Home by Harry Truman*, ed. Monte M. Poen. New York: G. P. Putnam's Sons, 1984.

——. *Public Papers of the Presidents of the United States,* vol. 1, 1945. Washington D.C.: United States Government Printing Office, 1961.

——. *Mr. Citizen*. New York: Random House, 1960.

———. *Memoirs: Year of Decisions,* vol. 1. Garden City, N.Y.: Doubleday and Company, 1955.

Unsigned article. "Was A-Bomb on Japan a Mistake?" *U.S. News and World Report,* August 15, 1960, p. 15.

Wheeler, Keith. *The Fall of Japan.* Alexandria, VA: Time-Life Books, 1983.

Wyden, Peter. *Day One: Before Hiroshima and After,* New York: Simon and Schuster, 1984.

Yoshida, Shigeru. *The Yoshida Memoirs: The Story of Japan in Crisis.* Trans. Kenichi Yoshida. Boston: Houghton Mifflin Company, 1962.

Notes

Introduction – Japan's Desperate Military Situation, April to July 1945

1. U.S. Strategic Bombing Survey (USSBS), *The Interrogations of Japanese Leaders Teijiro Toyoda*, November 13, 1945, microfilm 1654, Record Group 243, National Archives, Washington, D.C.

2. Ibid., *Interrogations*, Yonai Mitsumasa, November 17, 1945, Microfilm 1654, Record group 243, National Archives, Washington, D.C.

3. Ibid., *Interrogations*, Toyoda.

4. Ibid., *Interrogations*, Prince Toshihiko Higashikuni, November 14, 1945, Microfilm 1654, Record Group 243, National Archives, Washington, D.C.

5. Curtis E. LeMay, *Air Power*, November 19, 1945, Box 41, Folder: LeMay's Speeches, Curtis E. LeMay Papers, Library of Congress, p. 5.

6. Robert Leckie, *Delivered from Evil: The Saga of World War II* (New York: Harper and Row, 1987), p. 863.

7. Ibid., p. 865.

8. Baron J. Bernstein, "A Postwar Myth: 500,000 U.S. Lives Lost." *Bulletin of the Atomic Scientists*, 42, (June/July 1986): pp. 38–40.

9. USSBS, *The Pacific War* (Washington, D.C.: U.S. Government Printing Office, July 1946), p. 10.

10. Mamoru Shigemitsu, *Japan and Her Destiny: My Struggle for Peace*, ed. FSG. Piggott, trans. Oswald White (New York: E. P. Dutton and Co. 1958), p. 340.

11. *Impact*, vol. 3, September/October 1945, Box 95, Folder: Commentary on Air War, Carl E. Spaatz Papers, Library of Congress, p. 103.

12. Pacific War Research Society, *The Day Man Lost: Hiroshima, August 6, 1945* (Tokyo: Rodansha International, 1981), p. 115.

13. Marquis Koichi Kido, *Family Documents*, K27-3-60, National Diet Library, Tokyo.

14. Leckie, *Delivered*, p. 878.

15. Shigemitsu, *Japan*, p. 354.

16. Leckie, *Delivered*, p. 889.

17. Harry S. Truman, *Decision*, Motion Picture Archives, Harry S. Truman Library, Independence, Missouri.

18. Leckie, *Delivered*, p. 418.

19. Truman, *Decision*.

20. Keith Wheeler, *The Fall of Japan* (Alexandria: Time-Life, Books, 1983), p. 63.

21. USSBS, *Interrogations*, Admiral Sadatoshi Tomioka, November 15, 1945, Microfilm 1654, Record Group 243, National Archives, Library of Congress, Washington, D.C.

22. *Impact*, vol. 3, September/October 1945, p. 103.

23. Pacific War Research Society, *The Day Man Lost*, p. 99.

24. LeMay, *Air Power*, p. 11.

25. Henry L. Stimson, *Diary*, June 6, 1945, Henry L. Stimson Papers, Sterling Memorial Library, Yale University, New Haven, Connecticut.

26. LeMay, *Air Power*, p. 11.

27. *Impact,* vol. 3, September/October 1945, p. 79.

28. *Brief*, undated, Box 41, Folder: Inside Japan, LeMay Papers, p. 5, Library of Congress, Washington, D.C.

29. USSBS, *Interrogations*, Genki Abe, October 10, 1945, Microfilm 1654, Record Group 243, National Archives, Washington, D.C.
30. Ibid., *Interrogations*, Higashikuni.
31. *Impact*, vol. 3, September/October 1945, p. 85.
32. USSBS, *Interrogations*, Higashi-Kuni.
33. Masuo Kato, *The Lost War: A Japanese Reporter's Inside Story* (New York: Alfred A. Knopf, 1946), p. 204.
34. Pacific War Research Society, *The Day Man Lost*, p. 101.
35. *Impact*, vol. 3, September/October 1945, p. 79.
36. War Journal, undated, Box 41, Folder: Ninth Bombardment Group. LeMay Papers, p. 3.
37. Kato, *The Lost War*, p. 210.
38. *Impact*, vol. 3, September/October 1945, p. 103.
39. Kido, *Family Documents*, K27-3-60, National Diet Library, Tokyo.
40. *Mission Accomplished*, May 1946, box 95, Folder: Commentary on Air War, LeMay Papers, p. 49.
41. Kato, *The Lost War*, pp. 214–15.
42. USSBS, *Pacific War*, pp. 16–17.
43. *Brief*, undated, Box 41, p. 3.
44. *Impact*, vol. 3, September/October 1945, p. 102.
45. Ibid., p. 79.
46. *War Journal*, undated, Box 41, p. 6.
47. *Impact*, vol. 3, September/October 1945, p. 80.
48. *Brief*, undated, Box 41, pp. 3–4.
49. LeMay, *Air Power*, p. 11.
50. *Brief*, undated, Box 41, pp. 3–4.
51. Ibid.
52. *War Journal*, undated, Box 41, p. 5.
53. *Brief*, undated, Box 41, Folder: Inside Japan, LeMay Papers, p. 4.
54. *Impact*, vol. 3, September/October 1945, p. 82.
55. Toshikazu Kase, *Journey to the* Missouri, ed. David Nelson Rowe (New Haven, Conn.: Yale University Press, 1950), p. 206.
56. Kato, *The Lost War*, pp. 197–98.
57. Kase, *Journey*, p. 206.
58. John Ehrman, *Grand Strategy: October 1944–August 1945*, vol. 6 (London: Her Majesty's Stationery Office, 1956), pp. 279–80.
59. Kido, *Family Documents*.
60. *Impact,* vol. 3, September/October 1945, p. 103.
61. Ibid
62. *Mission Accomplished*, p. 39.
63. Ibid.
64. Ibid., p. 40.
65. USSBS, *Japan's Struggle to End the War* (Washington, D.C.: U.S. Government Printing Office, 1946), p. 12.
66. LeMay, *Air Power*, p. 4.
67. *Impact*, vol. 3, September/October 1945, p. 543.
68. Ibid., p. 49.
69. Ibid., p. 50.
70. *War Journal*, undated, Box 41, p. 9.
71. *Impact,* vol. 3, September/October 1945, p. 50.
72. Wheeler, *Fall of Japan*, p. 65.
73. USSBS, *Japan's Struggle*, p. 11.
74. *Impact*, vol. 3, September/October 1945, p. 43.
75. Ernest J. King and Walter Whitehill, *Fleet Admiral King: A Naval Record* (New York: W. W. Norton, 1952), p. 603.

76. USSBS, *Interrogations*, Toyoda.
77. *Mission Accomplished*, p. 38.
78. USSBS, *The Pacific War*, p. 14.
79. Kido, *Family Documents*.
80. Kato, *The Lost War*, p. 14.
81. William D. Leahy, *Diaries*, January 1, 1945, Microfilm No. 4, William D. Leahy Papers, Library of Congress, Washington, D.C.
82. USSBS, *Japan's Struggle*, p. 13.
83. Ibid., *Pacific War*, p. 27.
84. *Impact*, vol. 3, September/October 1945, p. 103.
85. USSBS, *Interrogations*, Toyoda.
86. Ibid., *Interrogations*, General Kawabe Ija, November 26, 1945, Microfilm 1654, Record Group 243, National Archives, Washington, D.C.
87. Kato, *The Lost War*, p. 13.
88. Kase, *Journey*, p. 197.
89. Ibid., pp. 186–97.
90. Kato, *The Lost War*, p. 10.
91. Pacific War Research Society, *The Day Man Lost*, p. 207.
92. Ibid., p. 67.
93. *Pacific Intelligence Report*, Editorial summary, May 21, 1945, SRH-075, Folder: 400-12, Record Group 457, National Archives, Washington, D.C.
94. Kido, *Family Documents*.
95. *Mission Accomplished*, p. 71.
96. USSBS, *Interrogations*, Higashikuni.
97. Ibid., *Interrogations*, Dr. Kwai, November 19, 1945, M1654, Record Group 243, National Archives.
98. Ibid., *Pacific War*, p. 12.
99. Shigemitsu, *Japan and Her Destiny*, pp. 353–54.
100. Ibid., p. 354.
101. Pacific War Research Society, *The Day Man Lost*, p. 206.
102. USSBS, *Pacific War*, p. 10.
103. Ibid., *Japan's Struggle*, p. 12.
104. Wheeler, *Fall of Japan*, p. 69.

Chapter 1 – Japan's Peace Moves: Tojo and Koiso Cabinets

1. Robert Leckie, *Delivered From Evil: The Saga of World War II* (New York: Harper and Row Publishers, 1987), p. 306.
2. U.S. Strategic Bombing Survey (USSBS), *Japan's Struggle to End the War* (Washington, D.C.: U.S. Government Printing Office, 1946), p. 3.
3. Ibid., *The Effects of the Atomic Bombings of Hiroshima and Nagasaki* (Washington, D.C.: U.S. Government Printing Office, 1946), p. 27.
4. Ibid., *Interrogations*, Prince Fumimaro Konoye, November 9, 1945, Microfilm 1658, Record Group 243, National Archives, Washington, D.C.
5. Ibid., *Interrogations*, Marquis Koichi Kido, November 10, 1945, Microfilm 1658, Record Group 243, National Archives, Washington, D.C.
6. *Mission Accomplished*, May 1946, Box 95, Folder: Commentary on Air War, Curtis E. LeMay Papers, Library of Congress, Washington, D.C., p. 48.
7. USSBS, *Interrogations*, Prince Higashikuni, November 14, 1945, Microfilm 1654, Record Group 243, National Archives, Washington, D.C.
8. Ibid., *Interrogations*, Konoye.
9. Ibid., *Japan's Struggle*, p. 5.
10. Ibid.
11. Ibid., p. 2.

12. Dan Kurzman, *Day of the Bomb: Countdown to Hiroshima* (New York: McGraw-Hill Book Company, 1986), p. 81.
13. *Nippon Times*, April 9, 1946.
14. USSBS, *Japan's Struggle*, p. 22.
15. Shigeru Yoshida, *The Yoshida Memoirs: The Story of Japan in Crisis*, trans. Kenichi Yoshida (Boston: Houghton Mifflin Company, 1962), p. 26.
16. Ibid.
17. Pacific War Research Society, *The Day Man Lost: Hiroshima August 6, 1945* (Tokyo: Kodansha International, 1981), p. 90.
18. Yoshitake Oka, *Konoe Fumimaro: A Political Biography*, trans. Shumpei Okamoto and Patricia Murray (Tokyo: University of Tokyo Press, 1972), p. 174.
19. Marquis Koichi Kido, *Family Documents*, K27-3-60, National Diet Library, Tokyo.
20. USSBS, *Interrogations*, Kido.
21. Kido, *Family Documents*.
22. Marquis Koichi Kido, *The Diary of Marquis Kido* (Frederick, Md.: University Publications of America, 1984), p. 420.
23. Kido, *Family Documents*.
24. Kido, *Diary*, p. 423.
25. Kido, *Family Documents*.
26. Kido, *Diary*, p. 427.
27. Kido, *Family Documents*.
28. Kido, *Diary*, p. 428.
29. USSBS, *Interrogations*, Kido.
30. Ibid., *The Pacific War* (Washington, D.C.: U.S. Government Printing Office, 1946) p. 26.
31. Masuo Kato, *The Lost War: A Japanese Reporter's Inside Story* (New York, Alfred A. Knopf, 1946), p. 133.
32. Robert J. C. Butow, *Japan's Decision to Surrender* (Stanford: Stanford University Press, 1954), p. 62.
33. USSBS, *Japan's Struggle*, p. 6.
34. *Mission Accomplished*, p. 36.
35. USSBS, *Interrogations*, Konoye.
36. Michihiro Matsumoto, *The Unspoken Way, Haragei: Silence in Japanese Business and Society* (Tokyo: Kodansha International, 1988), p. 26.
37. *Pacific Intelligence Report*, Naotake Sato to Shigenori Togo, July 2, 1945, Microfilm 1654, folder: 400-18, Record Group 457, National Archives, Washington, D.C., p. 7.
38. Kurzman, *Day of the Bomb*, p. 271.
39. Kato, *The Lost War*, p. 131.
40. Shigenori Togo, *The Cause of Japan* (New York: Simon and Schuster, 1956), p. 271.
41. John Toland, *The Rising Sun: The Decline and Fall of the Japanese Empire 1936–1945*, vol. 1 (New York: Random House, 1970), p. 189.
42. Kurzman, *Day of the Bomb*, p. 73.
43. Ibid., p. 234.
44. Toshikazu Kase, *Journey to the* Missouri, ed. David Nelson Rowe (New Haven, Conn.: Yale University Press, 1950), pp. 143–144.
45. *Pacific Intelligence Report*, Editorial Summary, May 21, 1945, SRH-075, folder: 400-12, Record Group 457, National Archives, Washington, D.C., p. 15.
46. Pacific War Research Society, *The Day Man Lost*, pp. 136–137.
47. Mamoru Shigemitsu, *Japan and Her Destiny: My Struggle for Peace*, ed. FSG. Piggott, trans. Oswald White (New York: E. P. Dutton and Co., 1958) p. 339.
48. U.S. embassy in Sweden to Edward R. Stettinius, April 7, 1945, *Foreign Relations of the United States* (hereafter as FRUS), vol. 6, Library of Congress, Washington, D.C. p. 477.
49. Stettinius to Johnson, April 19, 1945, *FRUS*, vol. 6, p. 478
50. U.S. embassy in Portugal to Stettinius, May 7, 1945, *FRUS*, vol. 6, p. 482.
51. Johnson to Stettinius, May 11, 1945, *FRUS*, vol. 6, p. 479.
52. *Pacific Intelligence Report*, Summary, p. 13.
53. William J. Donovan to James F. Byrnes, July 16, 1945, *FRUS*, vol. 6, p. 490.

54. Charles W. Bailey and Fletcher Knebel, "Hiroshima: The Decision that Changed the World," *Look*, vol. 24 (12), June 7, 1960, p. 26.
55. Kase, *Journey*, p. 227.
56. James F. Byrnes, *All in One Lifetime* (New York: Harper and Brothers Publisher, 1958), p. 307.
57. *Pacific Intelligence Report*, Summary, April 23, 1945, SRH-071, Folder: 400-8, Record Group 457, National Archives, p. 2.
58. Ibid., p. 3
59. Ibid., p. 8.
60. *Pacific Intelligence Report*, Summary, July 2, 1945, SRH-079, Folder 400-18, Record Group 457, National Archives, p. 11.
61. Ibid., April 23, 1945, SRH-071, Folder: 400-8, Record Group 457, National Archives, p. 11.
62. Ibid., pp. 11–12.
63. Ibid., p. 12.
64. Ibid., p. 15.
65. Togo, *Cause of Japan*, p. 285.
66. *Nippon Times*, April 9, 1946.
67. *Pacific Intelligence Report*, Summary, June 18, 1945, SRH-078, Folder: 400-16, Record Group 457, National Archives, p. 5.
68. Kase, *Journey*, p. 169.
69. Ibid., p. 153.
70. *Pacific Intelligence Report*, Summary, June 18, 1945, SRH-078, Folder: 400-16, Record Group 457, National Archives, p. 6.
71. Ibid., p. 12.
72. Ibid., July 14, 1945, SRH-084, Folder 400-21, Record Group 457, National Archives, p. 1.
73. Kase, *Journey*, pp. 170–171.
74. *Pacific Intelligence Report*, Summary, June 18, 1945, SRH-078, Folder: 400-16, Record group 457, National Archives, p. 2.
75. Ibid., July 2, 1945, SRH-079, Folder; 400-18, Record Group 457, National Archives, p. 10.
76. Ibid., June 18, 1945, SRH-078, Folder: 400-16, Record Group 457, National Archives, p. 1.
77. Kase, *Journey*, pp. 165–166.
78. *Pacific Intelligence Report*, Summary, June 18, 1945, SRH-078, Folder: 400-16, Record Group 457, National Archives, p. 1.
79. Ibid., p. 2.
80. Ibid., p. 1.
81. Pacific War Research Society, *The Day Man Lost*, p. 158.
82. USSBS, *Japan's Struggle*, p. 11.
83. Togo, *Cause of Japan*, p. 291.
84. *Mission Accomplished*, p. 36.
85. Kato, *The Lost War*, p. 17.
86. USSBS, *Interrogations*, Konoye.
87. Keith Wheeler, *Fall of Japan* (Alexandria: Time-Life Books, 1983), p. 63.
88. USSBS, *Interrogations*, Admiral Yonai Mitsumasa, November 17, 1945, Microfilm 1654, Record Group 243, National Archives, Washington, D.C.
89. Kase, *Journey*, p. 150.
90. Edward Behr, *Hirohito: Behind the Myth* (New York: Villard Books, 1989), pp. 292–293.
91. *Pacific Intelligence Report*, Summary, July 13–20, 1945, SRH-085, Folder: 400-22, Record Group 457, National Archives.
92. USSBS, *Interrogations*, Hisatsume Sakomizu, December 11, 1946, Microfilm 1654, Record Group 243, National Archives.
93. Butow, *Japan's Decision*, p. 112.
94. Kido, *Family Documents*.
95. Kido, *Diary*, pp. 434–35.
96. Kido, *Family Documents*.
97. Ibid.
98. Ibid.
99. Shigemitsu, *Japan and Her Destiny*, p. 356.
100. Togo, *Cause of Japan*, p. 296.
101. Togo, *Cause of Japan*, p. 296.
102. Kase, *Journey*, pp. 184–85.

103. Ibid., p. 187.
104. *Pacific Intelligence Report*, Summary, July 21, 1945, SRH-085, Folder: 400-22, Record Group 457, National Archives, p. 1.
105. Togo, *Cause of Japan*, p. 296.
106. Kido, *Family Documents*.
107. USSBS, *Interrogations*, Admiral Teijiro Toyoda, November 13, 1945, Microfilm 1654, Record Group 243, National Archives.
108. Butow, *Japan's Decision*, p. 120.
109. Togo, *Cause of Japan*, p. 298.
110. Kase, *Journey*, pp. 185–86.
111. *Mission Accomplished*, p. 37.
112. USSBS, *Interrogations*, Sakomizu.
113. Ibid.
114. Butow, *Japan's Decision*, p. 121.
115. Ibid.
116. *Pacific Intelligence Report*, Summary, July 14, 1945, SRH-084, Folder: 400-21, Record Group 457, National Archives, pp. 1–2.
117. Kase, *Journey*, p. 187.
118. *Pacific Intelligence Report*, Summary, July 14, 1945, SRH-084, Folder: 400-21, Record Group 457, National Archives, p. 2.
119. Ibid.
120. Ibid.
121. *Pacific Intelligence Report*, Summary, July 13–20, 1945, SRH-085, Folder: 400-22, Record Group 457, National Archives, p. 1.
122. Butow, *Japan's Decision*, pp. 122–123.
123. Kase, *Journey*, p. 188.
124. USSBS, *Japan's Struggle*, p. 8.
125. James F. Byrnes, *Speaking Frankly* (New York: Harper and Brothers, 1947), p. 211.
126. Kase, *Journey*, pp. 188–89.
127. Kido, *Family Documents*.
128. Togo, *Cause of Japan*, pp. 301–302.
129. Kido, *Diary*, p. 440.
130. Oka, *Konoe Fumimaro*, p. 174.
131. Kido, *Family Documents*.
132. Ibid.
133. USSBS, *Japan's Struggle*, p. 13.
134. *Nippon Times*, April 9, 1946.
135. *Pacific Intelligence Report*, Summary, July 13–20, 1945, SRH-085, Folder: 400-22, Record Group 457, National Archives, p. 2.
136. Ibid.
137. Ibid., p. 3.
138. Ibid.
139. Ibid.
140. *Pacific Intelligence Report*, Togo to Sato, July 14, 1945, Record Group 457, National Archives, p. 8.
141. Togo to Sato, July 11, 1945, *FRUS*, vol. 1 (Potsdam), p. 875.
142. Bailey and Knebel, "Hiroshima," p. 26.
143. *Pacific Intelligence Report*, Sato to Togo, July 12, 1945, SRH-085, Folder: 400-22, Record Group 457, National Archives, p. 6.
144. Sato to Togo, July 12, 1945, *FRUS*, vol. 1 (Potsdam), p. 877.
145. *Pacific Intelligence Report*, Sato to Togo, July 12, 1945, SRH-085, Folder: 400-22, Record Group 457, National Archives, p. 6.
146. Ibid., p. 11.
147. Ibid., Summary, July 21, 1945, SRH-085, Folder: 400-22, Record Group 457, National Archives, p. 12.
148. Togo to Sato, July 12, 1945, *FRUS*, p. 876.
149. *Pacific Intelligence Report*, Sato to Togo, July 13, 1945, SRH-085, Folder: 400-22, Record Group 457, National Archives, p. 7.
150. Ibid., p. 8.
151. Togo, *Cause of Japan*, p. 306.

152. *Pacific Intelligence Report*, Sato to Togo, July 13, 1945, SRH-085, Folder: 400-22, Record Group 457, National Archives, p. 9.
153. Ibid., p. 1.
154. *Pacific Intelligence Report*, Summary, July 13–20, 1945, SRH-085, Folder: 400-22, Record Group 457, National Archives, p. 12.
155. James Forrestal, *The Forrestal Diaries*, ed. Walter Millis (New York: Viking Press, 1951), pp. 74–75.

Chapter 2 – Truman and the A-Bombs

1. Dan Kurzman, *Day of the Bomb: Countdown to Hiroshima* (New York: McGraw-Hill Book Company, 1986), p. 210.
2. Margaret Truman, *Harry S. Truman* (New York: William Morrow and Company, 1973), pp. 238–39.
3. Harry S. Truman, *Memoirs: Year of Decisions*, vol. 1 (Garden City, NY: Doubleday and Company, 1955), pp. 10–11.
4. Harry S. Truman, *Decision*, Motion Picture Archives, Harry S. Truman Library, Independence, MO.
5. Truman, *Memoirs*, pp. 10–11.
6. Truman, *Decision*.
7. Henry L. Stimson, *Diary*, April 13, 1945, Henry L. Stimson Papers, Sterling Memorial Library, Yale University, New Haven, CT.
8. Ibid.
9. McGeorge Bundy and Henry L. Stimson, *On Active Service in Peace and War* (New York: Harper and Brothers, 1948), p. 636.
10. Ibid.
11. Ibid.
12. Margaret Truman, *Harry S. Truman*, p. 239.
13. Stimson, *Diary*, April 25, 1945.
14. R. Gordon Arneson, "Notes," May 17, 1945, *Manhattan Engineer District Records* (hereafter cited as *MED*), Microfilm 1108, Record Group 77, National Archives, Washington, D.C.
15. Charles W. Bailey and Fletcher Knebel, "Hiroshima: The Decision that Changed the World," Look, vol. 24, 12, June 7, 1960, p. 26.
16. Margaret Truman, *Harry S. Truman*, p. 239.
17. Henry L. Stimson, "The Decision to Use the Atomic Bomb," *Harper's Magazine*, vol. 194, 1161, February 1947.
18. Arneson, "Notes," May 17, 1945, *MED*.
19. James F. Byrnes, *All in One Lifetime* (New York: Harper and Brothers, 1958), p. 283.
20. Stimson, *Diary*, May 31, 1945.
21. J. Barton Bernstein, "The Dropping of the A-Bomb," The *Center Magazine*, March/April, 1983.
22. Byrnes, *Lifetime*, pp. 283–84.
23. Kurzman, *Day of the Bomb*, p. 13.
24. Michael Bess, "Leo Szilard: Scientist, Activist, Visionary," *Bulletin of the Atomic Scientists*, December 1985, p. 11.
25. Leo Szilard, "We Turned the Switch," *The Nation*, vol. 161, December 22, 1945, p. 718.
26. Bess, "Szilard," p. 11.
27. Alice Kimball Smith, "The Elusive Dr. Szilard," *Harper's Magazine*, vol. 221, July 1960, p. 79.
28. Ibid., p. 80.
29. Albert Einstein to Franklin D. Roosevelt, March 25, 1945, Box 345, Folder: General File, Harry S. Truman Papers, Harry S. Truman Library, Independence, MO.
30. Byrnes, *Lifetime*, p. 284.
31. Bess, "Szilard," p. 13.
32. Bernard Bailyn and Donald Fleming, *The Intellectual Migration: Europe and America, 1930–1960* (Cambridge, Mass: Harvard University Press, 1969), p. 124.
33. Leo Szilard, *U.S. News and World Report*, August 15, 1960, p. 69.
34. Ibid.
35. Bailyn and Fleming, *The Intellectual Migration*, pp. 124–25.
36. Ibid., p. 126.
37. Byrnes, *Lifetime*, pp. 284–85.
38. Bess, "Szilard," p. 13.
39. Szilard, *U.S. News and World Report*, p. 69.
40. Bailyn and Fleming, *The Intellectual Migration*, pp. 126–27.

41. Szilard, *U.S. News and World Report*, p. 69.
42. Bailyn and Fleming, *The Intellectual Migration*, p. 127.
43. Ibid., p. 128.
44. Ibid., pp. 127–28.
45. Bess, "Szilard," p. 12.
46. Bailyn and Fleming, *The Intellectual Migration*, p. 128.
47. Byrnes, *Lifetime*, p. 285.
48. Bailyn and Fleming, *The Intellectual Migration*, p. 128.
49. Arthur H. Compton, *Atomic Quest: A Personal Narrative* (New York: Oxford University Press, 1956), p. 220.
50. Ibid., p. 221.
51. "Notes," May 31, 1945, Box 26, Folder: Interim Committee, Harry S. Truman Papers, p. 10.
52. Ibid., p. 13.
53. R. Gordon Arneson to George Harrison, June 25, 1945, *MED*.
54. Ibid.
55. "Notes," May 31, 1945, p. 11.
56. Ibid., p. 12.
57. Bailey and Knebel, "Hiroshima," p. 26.
58. Rudolf Peierls, "Reflections of a British Participant," *Bulletin of the Atomic Scientists*, vol. 41, August 1985, pp. 28–29.
59. Stimson, "The Decision to Use the Atomic Bomb," pp. 100–101.
60. Byrnes, *Lifetime*, p. 285.
61. Bailey and Knebel, "Hiroshima," p. 26.
62. Arneson to Harrison, June 25, *MED*.
63. "Notes," May 31, 1945, pp. 14–15.
64. Stimson, "The Decision to Use the Atomic Bomb," p. 100.
65. Bailey and Knebel, "Hiroshima," p. 26.
66. Byrnes, *Lifetime*, p. 286.
67. Truman, *Memoirs*, p. 419.
68. Stimson, "The Decision to Use the Atomic Bomb," p. 101.
69. Martin J. Sherwin, A World Destroyed: *The Atomic Bomb and the Grand Alliance* (New York: vintage Books, 1977), p. 323.
70. Arthur H. Compton to Henry L. Stimson, June 12, 1945, *MED*.
71. Ibid.
72. Ibid.
73. Ibid.
74. Ibid.
75. Ibid.
76. Compton, *Atomic Quest*, p. 236.
77. Compton to Stimson, June 12, 1945, *MED*.
78. Compton, *Atomic Quest*, p. 240.
79. J. Robert Oppenheimer, "Recommendations on the Immediate Use of Nuclear Weapons," June 16, 1945, *MED*.
80. Fred Freed and Len Giovannitti, *The Decision to Drop the Bomb* (New York: Coward-McCann, 1965), p. 328.
81. Truman, *Decision*.
82. Arneson to Harrison, June 25, 1945, *MED*.
83. Harrison to Stimson, June 26, 1945, *MED*.
84. "Notes," June 21, 1945.
85. "Notes," June 21, 1945, *MED*.
86. J. Martin Sherwin, "How Well They Meant," *Bulletin of Atomic Scientists*, vol. 41, August 1985, p. 13.
87. Freed and Giovannitti, *The Decision*, p. 328.
88. Ibid., pp. 323–24.
89. Ibid., p. 327.
90. Leslie R. Groves, *Now It Can Be Told: The Story of the Manhattan Project* (New York: Da Capo Press, 1975), p. 266.
91. John P. Sutherland, "The Story General Marshall Told Me," *U.S. News and World Report*, November 2, 1959, p. 52.
92. Sherwin, "How Well They Meant," p. 14.

93. Szilard, *U.S. News and World Report*, p. 69.
94. Truman, *Decision*.
95. Gar Alperovitz, "More on Atomic Diplomacy," vol. 41, December 1985, p. 36.
96. Szilard, *U.S. News and World Report*, p. 69.
97. Ralph Bard, Memo, June 27, 1945, *MED*.
98. Szilard, *U.S. News and World Report*, p. 69.
99. Bailyn and Fleming, *The Intellectual Migration*, p. 130.
100. Leo Szilard, "A Petition to the President of the United States," July 17, 1945, Box 26, Folder: Interim Committee, Truman Papers, Harry S. Truman Library, Independence, MO.
101. Ibid.
102. Leo Szilard, cover letter to petition, July 4, 1945, *MED*.
103. Ibid.
104. Bailyn and Fleming, *The Intellectual Migration*, p. 130.
105. G. C. Thompson to John Lansdale, July 11, 1945, *MED*.
106. Bailyn and Fleming, *The Intellectual Migration*, p. 132.
107. Gordon Arneson, Memorandum, May 24, 1946, *MED*.
108. K. D. Nichols to Leslie Groves, Memorandum, July 25, 1945, *MED*.
109. Ibid.
110. Kurzman, *Day of the Bomb*, p. 325.
111. Truman, *Decision*.

Chapter 3 – Ending the War: The American Point of View

1. Akira Iriye, *Power and Culture: The Japanese-American War, 1941–1945* (Cambridge, Mass.: Harvard University Press, 1981), p. 244.
2. *The Entry of the Soviet Union into the War Against Japan: Military Plans 1941–1945* (Washington, D.C.: U.S. Department of Defense, 1955), Modern Military Records, National Archives, Washington, D.C.
3. Joseph C. Grew, *Turbulent Era: A Diplomatic Record of Forty Years 1904–1945*, ed. Walter Johnson, vol. 2 (Boston: Houghton Mifflin Company, 1952), p. 1422.
4. John K. Emmerson, *The Japanese Thread: A Life in the U.S. Foreign Service* (New York: Holt, Rinehart, and Winston, 1978), p. 231.
5. Ibid., p. 232.
6. Harry S. Truman, *Public Papers of the Presidents of the United States*, vol. 1, 1945 (Washington, D. C.: United States Government Printing Office, 1961), p. 98.
7. Harry S. Truman, *Memoirs: Year of Decisions*, vol. 1 (Garden City, NY: Doubleday and Company, 1955), p. 207.
8. Pacific War Research Society, *The Day Man Lost: Hiroshima August 6, 1945* (Tokyo: Kodansha International, 1981), pp. 186–87.
9. *Entry of the Soviet Union*, Modern Military Records, pp. 72–74.
10. Ibid.
11. Ibid., p. 72.
12. Grew, *Turbulent Era*, p. 1433.
13. Truman, *Memoirs*, pp. 416–17.
14. Grew, *Turbulent Era*, p. 1423.
15. John Paton Davies, *Dragon by the Tail* (New York: W. W. Norton and Company, 1972), p. 400.
16. Grew, *Turbulent Era*, pp. 1423–24.
17. Ibid., p. 1424.
18. Henry L. Stimson, *Diary*, May 29, 1945, Henry L. Stimson Papers, Sterling Memorial Library, Yale University, New Haven, CT.
19. William D. Leahy, *Diaries*, June 18, 1945, Microfilm No. 4, Library of Congress, Washington, D.C.
20. James Forrestal, *The Forrestal Diaries*, ed. Walter Millis (New York: Viking Press, 1951), pp. 68–69.
21. Leonard Mosley, *Marshall: Hero for Our Times* (New York: Hearst Books, 1982) p. 340.
22. Grew, *Turbulent Era*, p. 1435.
23. Ibid., pp. 1435–36.
24. Ibid., p. 1437.
25. Truman, *Memoirs*, p. 417.
26. Grew, *Turbulent Era*, p. 1425.
27. U.S. Department of Defense, *Entry of the Society Union*, p. 87.

28. Ernest J. King and Walter Whitehill, *Fleet Admiral King: A Naval Record* (New York: W. W. Norton, 1952), p. 606.
29. Forrestal, *Diaries*, p. 70.
30. Truman, *Memoirs*, p. 416.
31. J. Barton Bernstein, "Roosevelt, Truman, and the Atomic Bomb: A Reinterpretation," *Political Science Quarterly*, vol. 90 (1), Spring 1975, p. 43.
32. Douglas MacArthur, *Reminiscences: General of the Army* (New York: McGraw-Hill Book Company, 1964), p. 261.
33. Ibid.
34. Forrest Pogue, *George C. Marshall: Statesman* (New York: Viking Penguin, 1987), p. 18.
35. A. J. McFarland, "Campaign Against Japan" Memorandum, June 18, 1945, *Foreign Relations of the United States* (hereafter as FRUS), vol. 1, Library of Congress, Washington, D.C., p. 905.
36. King and Whitehill, *Admiral King*, p. 605.
37. Harry S. Truman, *Decision*, Motion Picture Archives, Harry S. Truman Library, Independence, MO.
38. King and Whitehill, *Admiral King*, p. 605.
39. Henry L. Stimson, "The Decision to Use the Atomic Bomb," *Harper's Magazine*, vol. 194 (1161), February 1947, p. 102.
40. Henry H. Arnold, *Global Mission* (New York: Harper and Brothers Publishers, 1949), p. 566.
41. U.S. Department of Defense, *Entry of the Soviet Union*, p. 78.
42. McFarland, "*Campaign Against Japan*" Memorandum, p. 909.
43. Forrestal, *Diaries*, p. 70.
44. Truman, *Decision*.
45. Leahy, Diaries, June 18, 1945, Microfilm No. 4.
46. McFarland, "Campaign Against Japan" Memorandum, p. 908.
47. Ibid., p. 909.
48. William D. Leahy, *I Was There* (New York: Whittlesey House, 1950), p. 384.
49. Ibid., p. 384.
50. John J. McCloy, *The Challenge to American Foreign Policy* (Cambridge, Mass.: Harvard University Press, 1953), p. 42.
51. Ibid.
52. Ibid.
53. Stimson, *Diary*, June 18, 1945.
54. Christopher Thorne, *The Issue of War: States, Societies, and the Far Eastern Conflict of 1941–1945* (New York: Oxford University Press, 1985), p. 527.
55. Margaret Truman, *Harry S. Truman* (New York: William Morrow and company, 1973), p. 261.
56. Christopher Thorne, *Allies of a Kind: The United States, Britain, and the War Against Japan, 1941–1945.* (New York: Oxford University Press, 1978) p. 526.
57. Ibid.
58. John P. Sutherland, "The Story General Marshall Told Me," *U.S. News and World Report*, November 2, 1959, p. 52.
59. William D. Leahy to Truman, January 23, 1945, Box 19, Folder: Memorandum to the President 1945, Record Group 218, National Archives, Washington, D.C.
60. U.S. Department of Defense, *Entry of the Soviet Union*, p. 60.
61. Thorne, *Allies of a Kind*, p. 531.
62. Elie Abel and Averell W. Harriman, *Special Envoy to Churchill and Stalin 1941–1946* (New York: Random house, 1975), p. 489.
63. Thorne, *Allies of a Kind*, pp. 528–29.
64. Truman, *Memoirs*, pp. 314–15.
65. Ibid., pp. 264–65.
66. Mamoru Shigemitsu, *Japan and Her Destiny: My Struggle for Peace*, ed. FSG. Piggott, trans. Oswald White (New York: E.P. Dutton and Company, 1958), p. 354.
67. Stimson, "The Decision to Use the Atomic Bomb," p. 104.
68. Stimson to Truman, "Proposed Program for Japan," July 2, 1945, *FRUS*, (Potsdam), vol. 1, pp. 890–91.
69. Ibid., p. 892.
70. Stimson to Truman, "Draft Proclamation by the Heads of State," undated, *FRUS* (Potsdam), vol. 1, p. 899.
71. Ibid.
72. Stimson to Truman, "Proposed Program for Japan," July 2, 1945, *FRUS* p. 891.

73. Ibid., p. 892.
74. Stimson, "The Decision to Use the Atomic Bomb," p. 104.
75. Stimson, *Diary*, July 2, 1945.
76. Gabriel Kolko, *The Politics of War: The World and United States Foreign Policy, 1943–1945* (New York: Random House, 1968), p. 554.
77. Charles E. Bohlen, *Witness to History 1929–1969* (New York: W. W. Norton and Company, 1973), p. 225.
78. Grew, *Turbulent Era*, p. 225
79. Forrestal, *Diaries*, p. 74.
80. John Ehrman, *Grand Strategy, October 1944–August 1945*, vol. 6 (London: Her Majesty's Stationery Office, 1956), p. 298.
81. Stimson, *Diary*, July 4, 1945.

Chapter 4 – The Potsdam Conference

1. Charles E. Bohlen, *Witness to History 1929–1969* (New York: W. W. Norton and Company, 1973), p. 229
2. Monte M. Poen, ed., *Letters Home by Harry Truman* (New York: G. P. Putnam's Sons, 1984) pp. 190–91.
3. Harry S. Truman, *Memoirs: Year of Decisions*, vol. 1 (Garden City, NY: Doubleday and Company, 1955), p. 335.
4. James F. Byrnes, *All in One Lifetime* (New York: Harper and Brothers, 1958), 289.
5. Robert Murphy, *Diplomat Among Warriors* (Garden City, NY: Doubleday and Company, 1964) p. 269.
6. Bohlen, *Witness to History*, p. 226.
7. David McCullough, *Truman* (New York: Simon and Schuster, 1992), p. 409.
8. Truman, *Memoirs*, pp. 336–37.
9. Robert H. Ferrell, ed., *Off the Record: The Private Papers of Harry S. Truman* (New York: Harper and Row Publishers, 1980), p. 50.
10. McCullough, *Truman*, p. 411.
11. Harry S. Truman-Winston S. Churchill Meeting, July 16, 1945, *FRUS*, vol. 2, *Foreign Relations of the United States* (hereafter as FRUS), vol. 2, Library of Congress, Washington, D.C., p. 35.
12. Ferrell, *Off the Record*, p. 51.
13. Charles Moran, *Churchill: The Struggle for Survival 1940–1965* (Boston: Houghton-Mifflin, 1966) p. 293.
14. Harry S. Truman to Bess Truman, July 20, 1945, Box 9, Folder: Letters to Bess, Harry S. Truman Library, Independence, MO.
15. James F. Byrnes, *Speaking Frankly* (New York: Harper and Brothers Publishers, 1947), p. 68.
16. William D. Leahy, *I Was There* (New York: Whittlesey House, 1950) p. 396.
17. George Harrison to Henry L. Stimson, July 16, 1945, *FRUS*, vol. 2, p. 1360.
18. Truman, *Memoirs*, p. 415.
19. Poen, *Letters Home*, p. 192.
20. Harry S. Truman to James L. Cate, December 31, 1952, Box 112, Folder: Atomic Bomb, Harry S. Truman Papers, Harry S. Truman Library, Independence, MO.
21. Henry L. Stimson, "The Decision to Use the Atomic Bomb," *Harper's Magazine*, vol. 194 (1161), February 1947, p. 105.
22. Henry H. Arnold, *Global Mission*, (book manuscript) Box 239, Folder: Chapter 31, Henry H. Arnold Papers, Library of Congress, Washington, D.C., p. 99.
23. Dwight D. Eisenhower, *Crusade in Europe* (Garden City, NY: Doubleday and Company, 1948), p. 443.
24. Leonard Mosley, *Marshall: Hero for Our Times* (New York: Hearst Books, 1982), p. 338.
25. Henry H. Arnold, *Global Mission* (New York: Harper and Brothers Publisher, 1949), p. 585.
26. Harry S. Truman, *Diary*, July 17, 1945, Box 230, Folder: Potsdam Conference, Truman Papers. Harry S. Truman Library, Independence, MO.
27. Bohlen, *Witness to History*, p. 230.
28. Truman, *Diary*, July 17, 1945.
29. McCullough, *Truman*, p. 417.
30. Truman, *Memoirs*, p. 342.
31. Poen, *Letters Home*, p. 196.

32. Bohlen, *Witness to History*, p. 228.
33. Truman, *Diary*, July 17, 1945.
34. Truman, *Memoirs*, p. 411.
35. Leahy, *I Was There*, p. 397.
36. Truman, *Diary*, July 17, 1945.
37. Robert H. Ferrell, ed., *Dear Bess: The Letters from Harry to Bess Truman 1910–1959* (New York: W. W. Norton and Company, 1983), p. 519.
38. Truman, *Memoirs*, p. 411.
39. Ferrell, *Off the Record*, p. 53.
40. Winston S. Churchill, *Triumph and Tragedy* (Boston: Houghton Mifflin Company, 1953), pp. 637–38.
41. Henry L. Stimson, Diary, July 17, 1945, Stimson Papers, Sterling Memorial Library, Yale University, New Haven, CT.
42. Churchill, *Triumph and Tragedy*, p. 638.
43. Moran, *Churchill*, p. 302.
44. Gar Alperovitz, "More on Atomic Diplomacy," *Bulletin of the Atomic Scientists*, vol. 41, December 1985, p. 36.
45. Churchill, *Triumph and Tragedy*, p. 641.
46. John Ehrman, *Grand Strategy October 1944–August 1945*, vol. 6 (London: Her Majesty's Stationery Office, 1956), p. 302.
47. Harrison to Stimson, July 17, 1945, *FRUS*, pp. 1360–61.
48. Leslie R. Groves to Stimson, July 18, 1945, *FRUS*, p. 1362.
49. Frank W. Craven and James L. Cate, *The Army Air Forces in World War II, The Pacific: Matterhorn to Nagasaki June 1944 to August 1945* (Chicago: University of Chicago Press, 1953), p. 712.
50. Churchill, *Triumph and Tragedy*, p. 640.
51. Ibid.
52. Ibid., pp. 641–42.
53. Ehrman, *Grand Strategy*, p. 303.
54. Ibid.
55. Bohlen, *Witness to History*, p. 236.
56. Byrnes, *Lifetime*, p. 290.
57. Byrnes, *Speaking Frankly*, p. 205.
58. Truman, *Diary*, July 18, 1945.
59. Stimson, "The Decision to Use the Atomic Bomb," p. 102.
60. Churchill, *Triumph and Tragedy*, p. 641.
61. John R. Deane, *The Strange Alliance* (New York: Viking Press, 1947), p. 267.
62. Stimson, *Diary*, June 6, 1945.
63. U.S. Strategic Bombing Survey, *The Pacific War* (Washington, D.C.: U.S. Government Printing Office, July, 1946), p. 29.
64. Ernest J. King and Walter Whitehill, *Fleet Admiral King: A Naval Record* (New York: W. W. Norton, 1952), p. 621.
65. Leahy, *I Was There*, p. 441.
66. Curtis E. LeMay, *Air Power*, November 19, 1945, Box 41, Folder: LeMay Speeches, Library of Congress, Washington, D.C., p. 12.
67. Douglas MacArthur, *Reminiscences: General of the Army* (New York: McGraw-Hill Book Company, 1964), p. 260.
68. Charles W. Bailey and Fletcher Knebel, "Hiroshima: The Decision that Changed the World," *Look*, vol. 24 (12), June 7, 1960.
69. Gar Alperovitz, "More on Atomic Diplomacy," *Bulletin of the Atomic Scientists*, vol. 41, December 1985, p. 36.
70. U.S. Strategic Bombing Survey, *Japan's Struggle to End the War* (Washington, D.C.: U.S. Government Printing Office, 1946), p. 13.
71. John P. Sutherland, "The Story General Marshall Told Me," *U.S. News and World Report*, November 2, 1959, p. 53.
72. Ferrell, *Off the Record*, p. 47.
73. Gabriel Kolko, *The Politics of War: The World and United States Foreign Policy, 1943–1945* (New York: Random House, 1968), p. 559.
74. Stimson, *Diary*, July 21, 1945.
75. Leo Szilard, *U.S. News and World Report*, August 15, 1960, p. 69.

76. Walter Isaacson, "Why Did We Drop the Bomb?" *Time*, August 19, 1985, p. 72.
77. Robert Murphy, *Diplomat Among Warriors* (Garden City, NY: Doubleday and Company, 1964), p. 273.
78. Stimson, *Diary*, July 22, 1945.
79. Ferrell, *Dear Bess*, p. 522.
80. McGeorge Bundy and Henry L. Stimson, *On Active Service in Peace and War* (New York: Harper and Brothers Publishers, 1948), p. 637.
81. Churchill, *Triumph and Tragedy*, p. 640.
82. Szilard, *U.S. News and World Report*, p. 69.
83. Eisenhower, *Crusade in Europe*, p. 442.
84. Stimson, *Diary*, July 23, 1945.
85. Arnold, *Global Mission* (book manuscript), Chapter 31, p. 100.
86. Stimson, "Conference with Stalin," July 25, 1945, Stimson Papers, New Haven, CT.
87. William D. Leahy, *Diaries*, January 1, 1945, Microfilm No. 4, Library of Congress, Washington, D.C.
88. Arthur H. Compton, *Atomic Quest: A Personal Narrative* (New York: Oxford University Press, 1956), p. 245.
89. Sutherland, "The Story General Marshall Told Me," p. 53.
90. David E. Lilienthal, *The Journals of David E. Lilienthal: The Atomic Energy Years 1945–1950*, vol. 2 (New York: Harper and Row, 1964), pp. 198–99.
91. Harry S. Truman, *Decision*, Motion Picture Archives, Harry S. Truman Library.
92. Truman, *Memoirs*, p. 419.
93. Bundy and Stimson, *On Active Service*, p. 629.
94. Isaacson, "Why Did We Drop the Bomb?" p. 72.
95. Churchill, *Triumph and Tragedy*, p. 639.
96. Fred Freed and Len Giovannitti, *The Decision to Drop the Bomb* (New York: Coward-McCann, 1965), pp. 320–21.
97. Barton J. Bernstein, "A Postwar Myth: 500,000 U.S. Lives Saved," *Bulletin of Atomic Scientists*, vol. 42, June/July 1986, p. 40.
98. Leslie R. Groves, *Now It Can Be Told: The Story of the Manhattan Project* (New York: Da Capo Press, 1975), p. 266.
99. Barton J. Bernstein, "Roosevelt, Truman, and the Atomic bomb: A Reinterpretation," *Political Science Quarterly*, vol. 90, (1), Spring, 1975, pp. 59–60.
100. Leahy, *I Was There*, p. 441.
101. Ibid., pp. 384–85.
102. Ibid., p. 441.
103. Thomas T. Handy to Carl Spaatz, July 25, 1945, Box 112, Folder: Atomic Bomb, Truman Papers.
104. James L. Cate to Truman, December 31, 1952, Box 1122, Folder: Atomic Bomb, Truman Papers.
105. Cate to Truman, December 31, 1952, Box 112, Folder: Atomic Bomb, Truman Papers.
106. King and Whitehill, *Fleet Admiral King*, p. 616.
107. Leahy, *I Was There*, p. 415.
108. Ibid.
109. Truman, *Memoirs*, p. 383.
110. Arnold, *Global Mission* (book manuscript), Chapter 31, pp. 101–102.
111. Truman, *Memoirs*, p. 383.
112. Ibid.
113. Ibid., p. 416.
114. Truman, *Decision*.
115. Bohlen, *Witness to History*, p. 237.
116. Byrnes, *Lifetime*, pp. 300–301.
117. Bohlen, *Witness to History*, p. 237.
118. Anthony Eden, *The Reckoning* (Boston: Houghton Mifflin Company, 1965) p. 635.
119. G. K. Zhukov, *The Memoirs of Marshal Zhukov* (New York: Delacorte Press, 1969), pp 674–75.
120. Shigenori Togo to Naotake Sato, July 19, 1945, *FRUS*, p. 1249.
121. *Pacific Intelligence Report*, Sato to Togo, July 18, 1945, SRH-086, Folder: 400-23, Record Group 457, National Archives, Washington, D.C., p. 2.
122. Ibid., Summary, July 19-25, 1945, SRH-086, Folder: 400-23, Record Group 457, National Archives, p. 1.

123. Ibid., Sato to Togo, July 19, 1945, SRH-086, Folder: 400-23, Record Group 457, National Archives, p. 1.
124. Sato to Togo, July 20, 1945, *FRUS*, p. 1257.
125. *Pacific Intelligence Report*, Sato to Togo, July 20, 1945, SRH-086, Folder: 400-23, Record Group 457, National Archives, p. 5.
126. Ibid., Togo to Sato, July 21, 1945, SRH-088, Folder: 400-26, Record Group 457, National Archives, p. 1.
127. Togo to Sato, July 21, 1945, *FRUS*, p. 1258.
128. Byrnes, *Lifetime*, p. 308.
129. *Pacific Intelligence Report*, Togo to Sato, July 25, 1945, SRH-088, Folder: 400-26, Record Group 457, National Archives, p. 7.
130. Togo to Sato, July 25, 1945, *FRUS*, p. 1261.
131. *Pacific Intelligence Report*, Sato to Togo, July 25, 1945, SRH-086, Folder: 400-23, Record Group 457, National Archives, p. 6.
132. Sato to Togo, July 25, 1945, *FRUS*, p. 1263.
133. *Pacific Intelligence Report*, Summary, July 18–25, 1945, SRH-088, Folder: 400-26, Record Group 457, National Archives, p. 1.
134. Ibid.
135. Szilard, *U.S. News and World Report*, p. 71.
136. Arnold, *Global Mission*, p. 591.
137. Churchill, *Triumph and Tragedy*, p. 634.
138. Byrnes, *Lifetime*, p. 296.
139. Moran, *Churchill*, p. 306.
140. Ibid., p. 297.
141. Eden, *Reckoning*, p. 636.
142. Arnold, *Global Mission* (book manuscript) Chapter 31, p. 97.
143. Bohlen, *Witness to History*, pp. 239–240.
144. Poen, *Letters Home*, p. 195.
145. Zhukov, *Memoirs*, p. 676.
146. Murphy, *Diplomat Among Warriors*, pp. 276–76.
147. Stimson to Truman, July 1, 1945, "Proposed Program for Japan, *FRUS*, p. 891.
148. Cordell Hull, *The Memoirs of Cordell Hull*, vol. 2 (New York: MacMillan Company, 1948), pp. 1593–94.
149. Ibid.
150. Truman, *Decision*.
151. A. J. McFarland, "Meeting of the Combined Chiefs of Staff," July 16, 1945, *FRUS*, pp. 36–37.
152. Ibid.
153. Ibid.
154. Ibid.
155. Churchill, *Triumph and Tragedy*, p. 642.
156. Ibid.
157. Moran, *Churchill*, p. 294.
158. James Forrestal, *The Forrestal Diaries*, ed. Walter Millis (New York: Viking Press, 1951), p. 80.
159. Hull, *Memoirs*, p. 1594.
160. Ibid.
161. Stimson to Truman, July 2, 1945, "Proposed Program for Japan," *FRUS*, p. 891.
162. Leahy to Truman, Memorandum, July 18, 1945, *FRUS*, pp. 1268–69.
163. Leahy to Truman, Memorandum, July 18, 1945, Box 19, Folder: Memo to President 1945, Record Group 218, National Archives, Washington, D.C.
164. Ibid.
165. Ibid.
166. Stimson to Truman, July 20, 1945, Naval Aide File, Box 1, Folder: Berlin Conference, Truman Papers.
167. Shigenori Togo, *The Cause of Japan* (New York: Simon and Schuster, 1956), pp. 310–11.
168. Stimson, *Diary*, July 24, 1945.
169. Stimson to Truman, Memorandum, July 20, 1945, *FRUS*, p. 1272.
170. Stimson, *Diary*, August 10, 1945.
171. Harry S. Truman, Winston Churchill, and Chiang Kai-shek, "Proclamation Calling for the Surrender of Japan," July 26, 1945, *FRUS*, p. 1476.

172. Truman, *Decision.*
173. Brynes, *Lifetime*, p. 296.
174. Joseph C. Grew, *Turbulent Era: A Diplomatic Record of Forty Years 1904–1945*, ed. Walter Johnson, vol. 2 (Boston: Houghton Mifflin Company, 1952), p. 1426.
175. Groves, *Now It Can Be Told*, p. 304.
176. Pacific War Research Society, *The Day Man Lost: Hiroshima August 6, 1945* (Tokyo: Kodansha International, 1981), p. 211.
177. Ibid., p.215.
178. U.S. Strategic Bombing Survey (USSBS), *Interrogation*, Hisatsume Sakomizu., July 1, 1946, folder: Japan Surrenders, Microfilm 1654, Record Group 243, National Archives, Washington, D.C.
179. USSBS, *Interrogation*, Hisatsume Sakomizu, December 11, 1946, Microfilm 1654, Record Group 243, National Archives.
180. Togo, *Cause of Japan*, p. 312.
181. Ibid.
182. Toshikazu Kase, *Journey to the* Missouri, ed. David Welson Rowe (New Haven, CT.: Yale University Press, 1950), p. 210.
183. Togo, *Cause of Japan*, p. 312.
184. USSBS, *Interrogation*, Hisatsume Sakomizu, December 11, 1946, Microfilm 1654, Record Group 243, National Archives.
185. Kase, *Journey to the* Missouri, pp. 210–11.
186. Dan Kurzman, *Day of the Bomb: Countdown to Hiroshima* (New York: McGraw-Hill Book Company, 1986), pp. 400–401.
187. Togo, *Cause of War*, p. 313.
188. Kantaro Suzuki, "Press Conference Statement," July 28, 1945, FRUS, p. 1293.
189. Thomas M. Coffey, *Imperial Tragedy: Japan in World War II, The First Days and the Last* (New York: World Publishing Company, 1970), p. 267.
190. Ibid.
191. Kolko, *The Politics of War*, p. 566.
192. John K. Emmerson, *The Japanese Thread: A Life in the U.S. Foreign Service* (New York: Holt, Rinehart, and Winston, 1978), p. 237.
193. Kurzman, *Day of the Bomb*, p. 403.
194. Kogo, *Cause of War*, p. 314.
195. *New York Times*, July 30, 1945.
196. Leahy, *I Was There*, p. 420.
197. Llewellyn E. Thompson, "Tenth Plenary Meeting," July 28, 1945, *FRUS*, p. 460.
198. Ibid.
199. Byrnes, *Lifetime*, pp. 297–98.
200. Leahy, *Diaries*, July 28, 1945.
201. Leahy, *I Was There*, p. 424.
202. Ibid.
203. Togo to Sato, July 28, 1945, *FRUS*, pp. 1291–93.
204. *Pacific Intelligence Report*, Summary, July 28–August 6, SRH-088, Folder: 400-26, Record Group 457, National Archives, p. 4.
205. Ibid., Sato to Togo, July 30, 1945, SRH-088, Folder: 400-26, Record Group 457, National Archives, Washington, D.C., p. 4.
206. Truman, *Decision.*
207. Stimson, "The Decision to Use the Atomic Bomb," p. 105.
208. Byrnes, *Speaking Frankly*, p. 263.
209. Grew, *Turbulent Era*, pp. 1427–28.
210. Stimson to Truman, July 30, 1945, Box 112, Folder: Japan Surrenders, Elsey Papers, Harry S. Truman Library, Independence, MO.
211. Truman to Stimson, July 31, 1945, Box 112, Folder: Japan Surrenders, Elsey Papers.
212. Truman, *Decision.*
213. *Pacific Intelligence Report*, Togo to Sato, August 2, 1945, SRH-088, Folder: 400-26, Record Group 457, National Archives, p. 10.
214. Ibid., Sato to Togo, August 3, 1945, SRH-088, Folder: 400-26, Record Group 457, National Archives, p. 10.
215. Ibid., Summary, SRH-088, Folder: 400-26, Record Group 457, National Archives, p. 16.
216. Alperovitz, "More on Atomic Diplomacy," p. 39.

Chapter 5 – The Atomic Bombings

1. Leslie R. Groves, *Now It Can Be Told: The Story of the Manhattan Project* (New York: Da Capo Press, 1975), p. 306.
2. Charles W. Bailey and Fletcher Knebel, "Hiroshima, The Decision that Changed the World," *Look*, vol. 24 (12), June 7, 1960, p. 27.
3. Groves, *Now It Can Be Told*, p. 306.
4. Bailey and Knebel, "Hiroshima," p. 27.
5. Groves, *Now It Can Be Told*, p. 258.
6. Ibid.
7. Dan Kurzman, *Day of the Bomb: Countdown to Hiroshima* (New York: McGraw-Hill Book Company, 1986), p. 4.
8. Harry S. Truman, *Decision*, Motion Picture Archives, Harry S. Truman Library.
9. Groves, *Now It Can Be Told*, pp. 284–85.
10. Frank W. Craven and James L. Cate, *The Army Air Forces in World War II, The Pacific: Matterhorn to Magasaki June 1944 to August 1945* (Chicago: University of Chicago Press, 1953), pp. 707–708.
11. Groves, *Now It Can Be told*, pp. 274–75.
12. Kurzman, *Day of the Bomb*, p. 394.
13. Henry L. Stimson, "The Decision to Use the Atomic Bomb," *Harper's Magazine*, vol. 194 (1161), February 1947, p. 105.
14. Groves, *Now It Can Be Told*, p. 273.
15. Stimson, "The Decision to Use the Atomic Bomb," p. 105.
16. Truman, *Decision*.
17. U.S. Strategic Bombing Survey (USSBS), *The Effects of the Atomic Bombings of Hiroshima and Nagasaki* (Washington, D.C.: U.S. Government Printing Office, 1946), p. 6.
18. Pacific War Research Society, *The Day Man Lost: Hiroshima August 6, 1945* (Tokyo: Kodansha International, 1981), p. 97.
19. USSBS, *The Effects of the Atomic Bombings*, pp. 23–24.
20. Groves, *Now It Can Be Told*, p. 315.
21. Peter Wyden, *Day One: Before Hiroshima and After* (New York: Simon and Schuster, 1984), p. 240.
22. Kurzman, *Day of the Bomb*, p. 410.
23. Craven and Cate, *The Army Air Forces in World War II*, p. 716.
24. Ibid., p. 717.
25. U.S. Strategic Bombing Survey, *The Pacific War* (Washington, D.C.: U.S. Government Printing Office, 1946), p. 23.
26. Ibid., p. 22.
27. USSBS, *The Effects of the Atomic Bombings*, p. 17.
28. Ibid., p. 3.
29. Ibid., p. 23.
30. Michihiko Hachiya, *Hiroshima Diary*, ed. Warner Wells (Chapel Hill, NC: The University of North Carolina Press, 1955), pp. 54–55.
31. Arata Osada, *Children of the A-Bomb: The Testament of the Boys and Girls of Hiroshima*, trans. Jean Dan and Ruth Sieben-Morgan (New York: G. P. Putnam's Sons, 1959) pp. 115–16.
32. USSBS, *The Effects of the Atomic Bombings*, p. 16.
33. Ibid., *The Pacific War*, p. 22.
34. William D. Leahy, *I Was There* (New York: Whittlesey House, 1950), p. 441.
35. Groves, *Now It Can Be Told*, p. 319.
36. USSBS, *The Effects of the Atomic Bombings*, p. 16.
37. Report of the British Mission to Japan, *The Effects of the Atomic Bombs at Hiroshima and Nagasaki* (London: His Majesty's Stationery Office, 1946), p. 18.
38. John Toland, *The Rising Sun: The Decline and Fall of the Japanese Empire 1936–1945*, vol. 2 (New York: Random House, 1970), p. 977.
39. Harry S. Truman, *Memoirs: Year of Decisions*, vol. 1 (Garden City, NY: Doubleday and Company, 1955), p. 421.
40. James F. Byrnes, *All in One Lifetime* (New York: Harper and Brothers, 1958), p. 304.
41. Truman, *Memoirs*, p. 421.
42. *New York Times*, August 7, 1945.
43. Truman, *Decision*.

44. Groves, *Now It Can Be Told*, p. 324.
45. Ibid.
46. Ibid.
47. Harry S. Truman, August 6, 1945, "Statement by the President of the United States," *Foreign Relations of the United States* (hereafter as FRUS), vol. 2, p. 1376.
48. Groves, *Now It Can Be Told*, p. 331.
49. Truman, *Decision*.
50. Leahy, *I Was There*, p. 441.
51. Richard B. Russell to Truman, August 7, 1945, Box 112, Folder: Japan Surrenders, George M. Elsey Papers, Harry S. Truman Library, Independence, MO.
52. Truman to Russell, August 9, 1945, Box 197, Folder: Japan Surrenders, Truman Papers, Harry S. Truman Library, Independence, MO.
53. Wyden, *Day One*, p. 297.
54. Truman, August 6, 1945, "Statement by the President of the United States," *FRUS*, p. 1377.
55. Kurzman, *Day of the Bomb*, p. 418.
56. Toland, *The Rising Sun*, p. 982.
57. Kurzman, *Day of the Bomb*, p. 419.
58. *Pacific Intelligence Report*, "The Soviet Declaration of War," August 8, 1945, Folder: 400-29, Record Group 457, National Archives, Washington, D.C., p. 4.
59. USSBS, *The Prosecution of War Criminals*, M1683, Record Group 331, National Archives, Washington, D.C.
60. Truman, *Memoirs*, p. 425.
61. Ibid.
62. *Pacific Intelligence Report*, Summary, August 29, 1945, Folder: 400-29, Record Group 457, National Archives, p. 3.
63. Keith Wheeler, *The Fall of Japan* (Alexandria, VA: Time-Life Books, 1983), p. 156.
64. Truman to James L. Cate, December 31, 1952, Box 112, Folder: The Atomic Bomb, Truman Papers.
65. Toshikazu Kase, *Journey to the* Missouri, ed. David Nelson Rowe (New Haven, CT: Yale University Press, 1950), p. 226.
66. Ibid., p. 224.
67. Shigenori Togo, *The Case of Japan* (New York: Simon and Schuster, 1956), p. 316.
68. Fred Freed and Len Giovannitti, *The Decision to Drop the Bomb* (New York: Coward-McCann, 1965), p. 333.
69. Toland, *The Rising Sun*, pp. 998–99.
70. USSBS, *Japan's Struggle to End the War* (Washington, D.C.: U.S. Government Printing Office, 1946), p. 8.
71. Groves, *Now It Can Be Told*, p. 342.
72. Ibid., p. 344.
73. Toland, *The Rising Sun*, p. 991.
74. USSBS, *The Effects of the Atomic Bombings*, p. 10.
75. Craven and Cate, *The Army Air Forces in World War II*, p. 720.
76. Toland, *The Rising Sun*, p. 996.
77. USSBS, *The Effects of the Atomic Bombings*, p. 11.
78. Ibid., p. 4.
79. Ibid., p. 12–13.
80. USSBS, *Interrogations*, Tatsuichiro Akizuki, November 8, 1945, Microfilm 1654, Record Group 243, National Archives, Washington, D.C.
81. Ibid., *The Effects of the Atomic Bombings*, p. 4.
82. Groves, *Now It Can Be Told*, p. 346.

Chapter 6 – The First Imperial Decision

1. U.S. Strategic Bombing Survey (USSBS), *Interrogations*, Hisatsume Sakomizu, December 11, 1946, Microfilm 1654, Record Group 243, National Archives, Washington, D.C.
2. USSBS, *Japan's Struggle to End the War* (Washington, D.C.: U.S. Government Printing Office, 1946), p. 13.
3. Marquis Koichi Kido, *Family Documents*, K 27-3-60, National Diet Library, Tokyo.

4. Thomas M. Coffey, *Imperial Tragedy: Japan in World War II: The First Days and the Last* (New York: World Publishing Company, 1970), p. 331.
5. Shigenori Togo, *The Cause of Japan* (New York: Simon and Schuster, 1956), pp. 317–18.
6. Masuo Kato, *The Lost War: A Japanese Reporter's Inside Story* (New York: Alfred A. Knopf, 1946), p. 235.
7. Togo, *Cause of Japan*, pp. 317–18.
8. Coffey, *Imperial Tragedy*, p. 334.
9. Kido, *Family Documents*.
10. Toshikazu Kase, *Journey to the* Missouri, ed. David Nelson Rowe (New Haven, CT: Yale University Press, 1950), p. 232.
11. Ibid., p. 231.
12. Togo, *Cause of Japan*, p. 319.
13. USSBS, Hisatsume Sakomizu, June 1, 1946, Box 112, Folder: Japan Surrenders, George M. Elsey Papers, Harry S. Truman Library, Independence, MO.
14. Ibid., *Interrogations*, Hisatsume Sakomizu, December 11, 1946, Microfilm 1654, Record Group 243, National Archives, Washington, D.C.
15. Keith Wheeler, *The Fall of Japan* (Alexandria, VA: Time-Life Books, 1983), p. 153.
16. Robert Butow, *Japan's Decision to Surrender* (Stanford: Stanford University Press, 1954), p. 167.
17. Ibid.
18. Dan Kurzman, *Day of the Bomb: Countdown to Hiroshima* (New York: McGraw-Hill Book Company, 1986), p. 421.
19. Mamoru Shigemitsu, *Japan and Her Destiny: My Struggle for Peace*, ed. FSG Piggott, trans. Oswald White (New York: E. P. Dutton and Company, 1958), p. 360.
20. Marquis Koichi Kido, *The Diary of Marquis Kido, 1931–45* (Frederick, MD.: University Publications of America, 1984), p. 444.
21. Togo, *Cause of Japan*, p. 319.
22. Kido, *Family Documents*.
23. John Toland, *The Rising Sun: The Decline and Fall of the Japanese Empire 1936–1945*, vol. 2 (New York: Random House, 1970), p. 1003.
24. Coffey, *Imperial Tragedy*, p. 347.
25. Kase, *Journey*, pp. 237–38.
26. USSBS, Interrogations, Hisatsume Sakomizu, June 1, 1946, Box 112, Folder: Japan Surrenders, George M. Elsey Papers, Harry S. Truman, Library, Independence, MO.
27. Togo, *Cause of Japan*, p. 320.
28. Kase, *Journey*, pp. 233–34.
29. Kato, *The Lost War*, p. 236.
30. Butow, *Japan's Decision*, p. 170.
31. Coffey, *Imperial Tragedy*, p. 351.
32. Wheeler, *Fall of Japan*, p. 154.
33. Coffey, *Imperial Tragedy*, pp. 351–52.
34. Butow, *Japan's Decision*, pp. 173–74.
35. Coffey, *Imperial Tragedy*, pp. 352–53.
36. USSBS, *Interrogations*, Hisatsume Sakomizu, December 11, 1946, Microfilm 1654, Record Group 243, National Archives, Washington, D.C.
37. Kase, *Journey*, pp. 234–35.
38. Coffey, *Imperial Tragedy*, p. 353.
39. USSBS, *Interrogations*, Sakomizu, December 11, 1946, Microfilm 1654, Record Group 243, National Archives.
40. Toland, *The Rising Sun*, p. 1005.
41. USSBS, *Interrogations*, Hisatsume Sakomizu, June 1, 1946, Box 112, Folder: Japan Surrenders, George M. Elsey Papers, Harry S. Truman Library, Independence, MO.
42. Toland, *The Rising Sun*, p. 1006
43. Kido, *Family Documents*.
44. USSBS, *Interrogations*, Hisatsume Sakomizu, December 11, 1946, Microfilm 1654, Record Group 243, National Archives, Washington, D.C.
45. Coffey, *Imperial Tragedy*, p. 359.
46. Shigemitsu, *Japan and Her Destiny*, p. 361.
47. Kase, *Journey*, p. 238.
48. Coffey, *Imperial Tragedy*, pp. 359–60.

49. Kase, *Journey*, p. 239.
50. *Pacific Intelligence Report*, Summary, August 29, 1945, Folder: 400-29, Record Group 457, National Archives, Washington, D.C.
51. Coffey, *Imperial Tragedy*, pp. 363–64.
52. Wheeler, *Fall of Japan*, p. 155.
53. Toland, *The Rising Sun*, p. 1008.
54. Butow, *Japan's Decision*, p. 182.
55. Coffey, *Imperial Tragedy*, p. 375.
56. Wheeler, *Fall of Japan*, p. 155.
57. Kase, *Journey*, p. 241.
58. Harry S. Truman, *Memoirs: Year of Decisions*, vol. 1 (Garden City, NY: Doubleday and Company, 1955), p. 427.
59. Ibid., p. 428.
60. Henry L. Stimson, *Diary*, August 10, 1945, Henry L. Stimson Papers, Sterling Memorial Library, Yale University, New Haven, CT.
61. William D. Leahy, *I Was There* (New York: Whittlesey House, 1950), p. 434.
62. James F. Byrnes, *All in One Lifetime* (New York: Harper and Brothers, 1958), p. 305.
63. James Forrestal, *The Forrestal Diaries*, ed. Walter Millis (New York: Viking Press, 1951) p. 83.
64. Stimson, *Diary*, August 10, 1945.
65. Truman, *Memoirs*, p. 428.
66. Stimson, *Diary*, August 10, 1945.
67. Forrestal, *Diaries*, p. 83.
68. Stimson, *Diary*, August 10, 1945.
69. John K. Emmerson, *The Japanese Thread: a Life in the U.S. Foreign Service* (New York: Holt, Rinehart, and Winston, 1978) pp. 238–39.
70. Truman, *Memoirs*, p. 429.
71. Stimson, *Diary,* August 10, 1945.
72. Robert H. Ferrell, ed. *Off the Record: The Private Papers of Harry S. Truman* (New York: Harper and Row Publishers, 1980), p. 61.
73. Averell W. Harriman to Byrnes, August 11, 1945, *Foreign Relations of the United States* (hereafter as FRUS), vol. 6, Library of Congress, Washington, D.C., p. 629.
74. Byrnes, *Lifetime*, p. 305.
75. Truman, *Memoirs*, p. 431.
76. Abel Elie and Averell W. Harriman, *Special Envoy to Churchill and Stalin 1941–1946* (New York: Random House, 1975), p. 499.
77. Truman, *Memoirs*, p. 432.
78. John R. Deane, *The Strange Alliance* (New York: Viking Press, 1947), pp. 278–79.
79. Truman, *Memoirs*, p. 432.
80. Harriman to Byrnes, August 11, 1945, *FRUS*, p. 631.
81. James F. Byrnes, *Speaking Frankly* (New York: Harper and Brothers Publishers, 1947), p. 210.
82. Leahy, *I Was There*, p. 435.
83. Chester W. Nimitz and E. B. Potter, *Sea Power: A Naval History* (Englewood Cliffs, NJ: Prentice-Hall, 1960), p. 834.
84. Douglas MacArthur, *Reminiscences: General of the Army* (New York: McGraw-Hill Book Company, 1964), pp. 264–65.

Chapter 7 – The Second Imperial Decision and Its Aftermath

1. Thomas M. Coffey, *Imperial Tragedy: Japan in World War II, The First Days and the Last* (New York: World Publishing Company, 1970), pp. 395–97.
2. John Toland, *The Rising Sun: The Decline and Fall of the Japanese Empire 1936–1945*, vol. 2 (New York: Random House, 1970), pp. 1016–17.
3. Keith Wheeler, *The Fall of Japan* (Alexandria, VA.: Time-Life Books, 1983), p. 158.
4. Masuo Kato, *The Lost War: A Japanese Reporter's Inside Story* (New York: Alfred A. Knopf, 1946), p. 238.
5. Mamoru Shigemitsu, *Japan and Her Destiny: My Struggle for Peace*, ed. FSG. Piggott, trans. Oswald White (New York: E. P. Dutton and Company, 1958), p. 362.
6. Coffey, *Imperial Tragedy*, p. 400.
7. Shigenori Togo, *The Cause of Japan* (New York: Simon and Schuster, 1956), p. 325.

8. Robert Butow, *Japan's Decision to Surrender* (Stanford: Stanford University Press, 1954), p. 194.
9. Toland, *The Rising Sun*, p. 1018.
10. Togo, *Cause of Japan*, p. 328.
11. Ibid., p. 326.
12. Ibid., p. 327.
13. Wheeler, *Fall of Japan*, p. 158.
14. Toshikazu Kase, *Journey to the* Missouri (New Haven, CT: Yale University Press, 1950), pp. 244–45.
15. Wheeler, *Fall of Japan*, p. 158.
16. Butow, *Japan's Decision*, p. 195.
17. Togo, *Cause of Japan*, p. 327.
18. Butow, *Japan's Decision*, p. 195.
19. Togo, *Cause of Japan*, p. 328.
20. Kase, *Journey*, p. 244.
21. Marquis Koichi Kido, *Family Documents*, K 27-3-60, National Diet Library, Tokyo.
22. Wheeler, *Fall of Japan*, p. 158.
23. U.S. Strategic Bombing Survey (USSBS*), Interrogations*, Teijiro Toyoda, November 13, 1945, Microfilm 1654, Record Group 243, National Archives, Washington, D.C.
24. Coffey, *Imperial Tragedy*, p. 417.
25. Togo, *Cause of Japan*, pp. 328–29
26. Kase, *Journey*, p. 245.
27. Ibid., pp. 246–47.
28. USSBS, *Interrogations*, Hisatsume Sakomizu, December 11, 1946, Microfilm 1654, Record Group 243, National Archives, Washington, D.C.
29. Togo, *Cause of Japan*, p. 329.
30. Toland, *The Rising Sun*, p. 1022.
31. Togo, *Cause of Japan*, p. 331.
32. USSBS, *Interrogations*, Hisatsume Sakomizu, June 1, 1946, Box 112, Folder: Japan Surrenders, George M. Elsey Papers, Harry S. Truman Library, Independence, MO.
33. Wheeler, *Fall of Japan*, p. 159.
34. Toland, *The Rising Sun*, pp. 1024–25.
35. Coffey, *Imperial Tragedy*, p. 435.
36. Shigemitsu, *Japan and Her Destiny*, pp. 364–65.
37. Coffey, *Imperial Tragedy*, p. 435.
38. Ibid., p. 437.
39. USSBS, *Interrogations*, Hisatsume Sakomizu, December 11, 1946, Microfilm 1654, Record Group 243, National Archives, Washington, D.C.
40. Kase, *Journey*, pp. 251–52.
41. Togo, *Cause of Japan*, p. 334.
42. Coffey, *Imperial Tragedy*, p. 442.
43. USSBS, *Interrogations*, Toyoda, November 13, 1945.
44. *Pacific Intelligence Report*, Mitsumasa Yonai, August 14, 1945, Folder: 400-29, Record Group 457, National Archives, Washington, D.C., p. 23.
45. USSBS, *Interrogations*, Sakomizu, December 11, 1946.
46. Ibid.
47. Togo, *Cause of Japan*, p. 334.
48. USSBS, *Interrogations*, Sakomizu, December 11, 1946.
49. Togo, *Cause of Japan*, p. 335.
50. Coffey, *Imperial Tragedy*, p. 455.
51. USSBS, *Interrogations*, Mitsumasa Yonai, November 17, 1945, Microfilm 1654, Record Group 243, National Archives, Washington, D.C.
52. Harry S. Truman, *Memoirs: Year of Decisions*, vol. 1 (Garden City, NY: Doubleday and Company, 1955), pp. 435–36.
53. William D. Leahy, *I Was There* (New York: Whittlesey House, 1950), p. 437.
54. Truman, *Memoirs*, pp. 435–36.
55. Wheeler, *Fall of Japan*, p. 161.
56. Coffey, *Imperial Tragedy*, pp. 491–92.
57. *Pacific Intelligence Report*, Summary, August 15, 1945, Folder: 400-29, Record Group 457, pp. 28–29.
58. Toland, *The Rising Sun*, p. 1049.
59. Kido, *Family Documents*.

60. Kase, *Journey*, p. 258.
61. Kido, *Family Documents*.
62. Wheeler, *Fall of Japan*, p. 163.
63. Ibid.
64. Coffey, *Imperial Tragedy*, pp. 501–502.
65. Kido, *Family Documents*.
66. Marquis Koichi Kido, *The Diary of Marquis Kido, 1931–45* (Frederick, MD: University Publications of America, 1984), pp. 449–50.
67. Kido, *Family Documents*.
68. Butow, *Japan's Decision*, p. 216.
69. Kido, *Family Documents*.
70. Butow, *Japan's Decision*, pp. 217–18
71. Kase, *Journey*, p. 259.
72. Masuo Kato, The *Lost War: A Japanese Reporter's Inside Story* (New York: Alfred A. Knopf, 1946), pp. 243–44.
73. Toland, *The Rising Sun*, p. 1052.
74. USSBS, *Interrogations*, Sakomizu, December 11, 1946.
75. Wheeler, *Fall of Japan*, p. 164.
76. USSBS, *Interrogations*, Sakomizu, December 11, 1946.
77. Ibid.
78. Kato, *The Lost War*, p. 244.
79. Coffey, *Imperial Tragedy*, pp. 518–19.
80. *Pacific Intelligence Report*, Hirohito's Speech, August 15, 1945, Folder: 400-29, Record Group 457, pp. 14–15.
81. Kato, *The Lost War*, p. 244.
82. Togo, *Cause of Japan*, p. 337.
83. Kato, *The Lost War*, p. 245.
84. Coffey, *Imperial Tragedy*, p. 522.
85. Kato, *The Lost War*, p. 245.
86. Shigemitsu, *Japan and Her Destiny*, p. 366.
87. Ibid., pp. 366–367.
88. *Pacific Intelligence Report*, Summary, August 29, 1945, Folder: 400-29, RG 457, pp. 29–30.
89. Wheeler, *Fall of Japan*, p. 167.
90. Togo, *Cause of Japan*, p. 338.
91. United States Strategic Bombing Survey, *Interrogations*, Toshihiko Higashikuni, November 14, 1945, Microfilm 1654, Record Group 243, National Archives, Washington, D.C.
92. Kase, *Journey*, p. 263.
93. Wheeler, *Fall of Japan*, p. 169.
94. Ibid.
95. Douglas MacArthur, *Reminiscences: General of the Army* (New York: McGraw-Hill Book Company, 1964), pp. 269–70.
96. Shigemitsu, *Japan and Her Destiny*, p. 370.
97. Wheeler, *Fall of Japan*, p. 192.
98. Ibid., p. 194.
99. Kato, *The Lost War*, p. 258.
100. MacArthur, *Reminiscences*, p. 270.
101. Kato, *The Lost War*, p. 260.
102. Wheeler, *Fall of Japan*, p. 171.
103. Ibid., pp. 171–72.
104. Kato, *The Lost War*, p. 261.
105. Wheeler, *Fall of Japan*, p. 172.

Chapter 8 – Recapitulation and Analysis

1. Harry S. Truman, *Decision*, Motion Picture Archives, Harry S. Truman Library, Independence, MO.
2. Barton J. Bernstein, "A Postwar Myth: 500,000 U.S. Lives Saved," *Bulletin of the Atomic Scientists*, vol. 42, June/July 1986, pp. 38–40.
3. Ibid., p. 38.

4. Robert L. Messer, "New Evidence on Truman's Decision," *Bulletin of the Atomic Scientists*, vol. 41, August 1985, pp. 50–56.
5. Leo Szilard, *U.S. News and World Report*, August 15, 1960, p. 70.
6. James F. Byrnes, *All in One Lifetime* (New York: Harper and Brothers Publishers, 1958), p. 308.
7. Henry L. Stimson, "The Decision to Use the Atomic Bomb," *Harper's Magazine*, vol. 194, 1161, February 1947.
8. Leonard Mosley, *Marshall: Hero of Our Times* (New York: Hearst Books, 1982), p. 338.
9. Henry H. Arnold, Global Mission (New York: Harper and Brothers Publishers, 1949), p. 598.
10. William D. Leahy, *I Was There* (New York: Whittlesey House, 1950) p. 441.
11. Curtis E. LeMay, *Air Power*, November 19, 1945, box 41, Folder: LeMay Speeches, Curtis E. LeMay Papers, Library of Congress, Washington, D.C., p. 12.
12. U.S. Strategic Bombing Survey (USSBS) *Interrogations*, Teijiro Toyoda, November 13, 1945, Record Group 243, National Archives, Washington, D.C.
13. Curtis E. LeMay, *Air Power*, p. 13.
14. Ernest J. King and Walter Churchill, *Fleet Admiral King: A Naval Record* (New York: W. W. Norton, 1952), p. 623.
15. USSBS, *Japan's Struggle to End the War* (Washington, D.C.: U.S. Government Printing Office, 1946), p. 13.
16. Ibid., *Interrogations*, Marquis Koichi Kido, November 10, 1945, Microfilm 1658, Record Group 243, National Archives, Washington, D.C.
17. Fred Freed and Len Giovannitti, *The Decision to Drop the Bomb* (New York: Coward-McCann, 1965), p. 322.
18. Walter Isaacson, "Why Did We Drop the Bomb?" *Time*, August 19, 1985, p. 72.
19. Bernard Bailyn and Donald Fleming, eds. *The Intellectual Migration: Europe and America 1930–1960* (Cambridge, MA: Harvard University Press, 1969), p. 127.
20. Szilard, *U.S. News and World Report*, p. 71.
21. Barton J. Bernstein, "Roosevelt, Truman, and the Atomic Bomb: A Reinterpretation," *Political Science Quarterly*, vol. 90 (1), Spring 1975, pp. 31–38.
22. Robert L. Messer, "New Evidence on Truman's Decision," *Bulletin of the Atomic Scientists*," vol. 41, August 1985, p. 52.
23. Michael O'Neal, *President Truman and the Atomic Bomb: Opposing Viewpoints* (San Diego: Greenhaven Press, 1990), p. 60.

Index